German-American Socialist Literature, 1865 – 1900

New York University Ottendorfer Series
Neue Folge Band 16

unter Mitarbeit von

Joseph P. Bauke (Columbia), Helmut Brackert (Frankfurt/M.),
Peter Demetz (Yale), Reinhold Grimm (Wisconsin),
Walter Hinderer (Princeton)

herausgegeben von
Volkmar Sander

PETER LANG
Bern und Frankfurt am Main

Carol J. Poore

German-American Socialist Literature 1865 – 1900

PETER LANG
Bern und Frankfurt am Main

CIP-Kurztitelaufnahme der Deutschen Bibliothek

Poore, Carol J.:
[German-American socialist literature eighteen
hundred and sixty-five to nineteen hundred]
German-American socialist literature 1865 – 1900 /
Carol J. Poore. – Bern ; Frankfurt am Main :
Lang, 1982.
   (New York University Ottendorfer series ;
   N. F., Bd. 15)
   ISBN 3-261-04975-8

NE: New York University: New York University . . .

PT
3907
.P6

Printed by fotokop Wilhelm Weihert KG, Darmstadt

ACKNOWLEDGEMENTS

I would like to express my appreciation to the staffs of the following libraries and historical societies for their assistance: Wisconsin State Historical Society, University of Wisconsin Memorial Library and Rare Books Department, St. Louis Public Library, Missouri County Historical Society, Chicago Historical Society, Milwaukee Public Library, Cincinnati Public Library, University of Cincinnati Library, Ohio Historical Society, New York Public Library, New York Public Library at Lincoln Center, New York City Historical Society, Columbia University Library, and Tamiment Institute.

This research was supported by a travel grant from the University of Wisconsin Graduate School, a Wisconsin Alumni Research Foundation Dissertation Fellowship and an American Association of University Women Dissertation Fellowship.

Special thanks are due to Paul Buhle and Mary Jo Buhle for their helpful, detailed criticism of the manuscript. Wolfgang Emmerich, Philip Foner, Pat Herminghouse and Merle Krueger took the time to engage in stimulating discussions or to provide hard-to-find material. Finally, I would like to thank my teacher, Jost Hermand, for his invaluable support at all stages of this project, and his constant willingness to critique and to enter into dialogue with his students. Through his own exemplary work, he encourages us to pose the important questions, so that we may work together towards their solutions.

CONTENTS

I. INTRODUCTION

1. THE CONTEXT OF LABOR HISTORY

> Ausländer, Fremde sind es meist,
> Die unter uns gesät den Geist
> Der Rebellion. Dergleichen Sünder
> Gottlob! sind selten Landeskinder.
>
> Heinrich Heine (quoted in the
> New York Volkszeitung)

In perhaps no other country in the world has the consciousness of radical history and tradition been more thoroughly obliterated than in the United States, and nowhere has this suppression had more significant consequences for the course of the working class movement.[1] In particular, it has been a major trend among historians of immigration to view immigrants as "passive recipients of the dominant values and institutions of American industrial capitalism."[2] The prevailing image of nineteenth century German immigrants which has been fostered by most of the scholarship in this area is no exception. These ethnocentric studies have focused on such prominent features of German-Americana as the model of Carl Schurz, revolutionary turned respectable statesman, the German Lutheran Church, those large numbers of Germans who rabidly supported Bismarck during the Franco-Prussian War, the Milwaukee breweries and opponents of temperance legislation, and of course, "Pennsylvanisch." The list could be continued, but almost without exception both past and present standard histories and handbooks on the German-Americans portray this ethnic group as one which was easily assimilated into the American political system and "way of life" and whose proud contribution to the "melting pot" was the high culture it brought over from the "Land der Dichter und Denker." While a few of the more positivistically oriented historians in this area may, for the sake of completeness, include short sections on German immigrant radicals in their surveys, and while solid research has in fact been accomplished on the more "respectable" group of Forty-Eighters, in general the writing of German-American history is anachronistic, tainted in some cases by volkish tendencies and riddled through and through with cliches. Small wonder, then, that German-American studies has been assessed -- if it was even taken notice of -- as a distasteful field to be avoided, even by those Germanisten seeking ways to make their discipline more relevant to American students and their experiences.[3]

However, when we ask what parts of the German-American heritage have been neglected for the sake of emphasizing its conservative features, and when we step beyond the narrow bounds of one discipline, we find that there is another tradition of German-American history which has been hidden away in widely scattered archives and even destroyed in part. The representatives of this tradition are the socialists and anarchists, who are known only to a small group of scholars and who, in contrast to later immigrant radicals like the Finns or Jews, hardly survive even in the memories of those people whose families participated in their political

9

and cultural activities. It is primarily labor historians who have recognized the crucial political role German immigrants played in introducing the theory of scientific socialism to the United States, helping to organize the American labor movement after the Civil War, and founding this country's first enduring socialist party, the Socialist Labor Party, and these historians have treated German-American radicalism in the context of their surveys of the broader labor movement.

Until recently, these studies of the interrelationship between varieties of socialism and unionism have concentrated on four main areas:[4] 1) the antagonism between the "pure and simple" business unionism of the American Federation of Labor and the "impossibilistic" dual unionism of the Socialist Labor Party under Daniel DeLeon in the 1890's, 2) the post-1901 Socialist Party, 3) individual unions and various farmer-labor parties such as the Greenback-Labor Party and the People's Party, 4) analyses of the ideologies of labor leaders themselves -- such as Samuel Gompers of the American Federation of Labor, DeLeon, or the Austrian-born Victor Berger of the Socialist Party -- as providing clues to the weakness of the socialist movement in America. Methodologically, what these studies have in common is an institutional approach to history which focuses on organizations such as unions and parties (their platforms, alliances, successes, failures, etc.) and their leadership. From the conservative "Wisconsin School" of labor history to even some leftist historians, these scholars have traditionally been preoccupied with chronicling the struggles for power and ideological shifts within labor and socialist leadership. The view of history which is implicit in this method is profoundly undialectical: that political organizations create a certain consciousness in their members rather than themselves, in the form they assume, also being an expression and result of social conflict and rebellion, that movements striving for radical social change are not created by masses of people acting according to their own interests and needs based in daily life but rather by political organizations which dispense enlightenment about "objective interests," in short, that ideology is the main factor in determining political behavior.[5] The history of struggle is reduced to the history of organizations and even of "great men," the "titans of history," the "fathers" of our country or of socialism. History becomes solely the expression of power, and, "as for the use made of the history of the working-class movement . . . , it remains a science of legitimation."[6]

In particular, the institutional approach is characteristic of almost all analyses of the nineteenth century German-American socialists, which focus on the following areas: 1) the First International, the various parties created by the Germans, and the relationship of these organizations to the trade union movement, 2) biographies or chapters about a few important individuals: Joseph Weydemeyer, Wilhelm Weitling, Friedrich Sorge, Johann Most, 3) the Haymarket Affair of 1886, as the most spectacular event involving the German Social-Revolutionaries, 4) the Socialist Party in Milwaukee and its House Representative Victor Berger. While these sources are of varying usefulness for establishing a beginning orientation in this area, there is no full-length study which attempts to utilize fully the available primary materials (mainly newspapers) to give a critical analysis of German-American radicalism founded on a solid sociological investigation of the German-Amercan working class community.[7] Such a broad study, which would go beyond an organizational framework, would necessarily entail painstaking research on class divisions within the immigrant ethnic communities, on immigrant work patterns, on the varying numbers and positions of skilled and unskilled workers within different ethnic groups, on the position of immigrant women in the community and the labor force, on the influence of religion, on the relationship of immigrants to the established political parties -- in short, on almost every aspect of immigrant life.

Fortunately, however, with the revival of progressive scholarship and the opening up of methodological debates within the field of labor history in the 1960's and 1970's, more historians are beginning to relate the history of organizations to their material, social bases and to conceive of labor history in much broader terms, as encompassing the history of the working class as a whole and even of work itself, rather than only of a narrowly defined workers' movement.[8] Historians such as Herbert Gutman and Stanley Aronowitz among others are studying the interaction between working class culture, communities and family life on the one hand and the forms American working class movements have taken, on the other.[9] More specialized sociological and historical investigations are being made of radicalism within particular ethnic communities, and these are overcoming -- to their benefit -- a traditional bias against non-English-language materials.[10] And questions about the role of socialists within trade unionism are finding new answers based on analyses of the rank and file movement.[11] Accordingly, these historians are arriving at new perspectives on what is surely one of the most debated and significant issues in the history of modern industrialized nations. They are situating the failure of a mass socialist working-class movement to emerge in America in the context of the extremely complex class structure and ideology of the United States, as a result of the interplay between economic, social and cultural forces, between material conditions, ideology and experience. In other words, they are rectifying the one-dimensionality of historians who have spent their time "dragging into prominence forces which have triumphed and thrusting into the background those which have been swallowed up."[12] Their view of history does not posit a linear progression of events which necessarily culminates in the status quo of today, rather, it is of history as struggle. Thus, they do not seek a priori to legitimate certain ideologies from the standpoint of present-day political exigencies.[13] On the contrary, they are concerned with uncovering neglected expressions of dissidence, movements which "lost," in all their complexity. Quoting Fernand Braudel, Herbert Gutman reminds us that "victorious events come about as the result of many possibilities," and that "for one possibility which actually is realized, innumerable others have drowned." Usually these others leave "little trace for the historian." "And yet," Braudel adds, "it is necessary to give them their place because the losing movements are forces which have at every moment affected the final outcome."[14] In so doing, these historians are "giving back to the pioneers of the American labor movement the dignity of agents ... rather than the passivity of vectors of impersonal forces."[15] Such an approach to history which attempts "critical reflection on past praxis" thus becomes praxis itself, that is,

a laboratory of experiences, successes, and failures, a field of
theoretical and strategic elaborations, where rigor and critical
examination are indispensable to determine historical reality and
thereby discover its hidden sources of power, and to invent and
thus innovate beginning from a particular historical moment perceived as experience. (16)

Therefore, while the first task in the following chapters will be to provide an in-
formational overview of the political activities and organizations of the German-
American socialists in the last quarter of the nineteenth century, the attempt
will also be made to situate them within the context of the development and particular character of the American working class. Because of the gaps in our historical knowledge of immigrant working-class life, the theses asserted here will
necessarily be tentative and in need of refinement in some respects. However,
it may be that the example of the United States, as discussed here, can illuminate
some aspects of the formation of a working-class socialist movement which are not
so readily apparent in countries where stable, mass socialist parties have long
existed.

2. THE CONTEXT OF GERMAN-AMERICAN STUDIES

If the history of German-American radicalism has remained a marginal area for the most part, the literature produced by German-American socialist writers has been almost totally neglected in areas of scholarship which could logically be expected to make it their concern. To be sure, in the most general sense this is only one of the many manifestations attributable to the pervasive antiradical tendencies in American society which have also influenced literary critics and historians, causing them to neglect some areas and emphasize others. Consequently, it was during the twenties and thirties, when progressive scholars were able to establish themselves in a few enclaves, or under the auspices of the New Deal's Works Progress Administration (WPA), that the greatest attention was given to collecting and preserving workers' literature (almost solely in the form of song collections). However, even these sympathetic recorders of a progressive tradition were concerned almost exclusively with material written in English, often tending to view it apart from its political significance, as a component of folklore worth preserving.[17] After the period of the Second World War, the Cold War and McCarthyism, the capitulation of English Departments to New Criticism spelled a temporary end to research or dissertations dealing with literature from a sociological or historical perspective, or with literature outside the established canon of "masterpieces" which could not measure up to the formal rigors of "intrinsic" analysis. Today, even though the dominance of the Wellek-and-Warren approach can still be felt in most English Departments, in the wake of the New Left, the student movement and the women's movement there has been a resurgence of studies which view literature in a historical, sociological, or psychological context. However, though these studies are of course welcome and long overdue, and in spite of the increased sophistication of their analyses, they share with pre-war progressive criticism a preoccupation with recognized writers and movements and do not focus on working class literature itself. Therefore, with respect to the 19th century, they concentrate on such socially critical writers as Mark Twain, William Dean Howells, Frank Norris or Edward Bellamy, and on genres such as the utopian novel. There have been recently some efforts to collect American labor songs (by far the most comprehensive and informative anthology is Philip Foner's American Labor Songs of the Nineteenth Century (1975), which also includes translations of songs from languages other than English), but the history of American working class literature remains to be written.

If this is the situation with respect to the literature of the English-speaking working class and its political involvement, the problems only become intensified if we turn our attention to working-class literature of other language and ethnic groups. Considering the language barrier and the academic division of labor, there are two groups of scholars who might be expected to stake out "property rights" to this topic: German academics interested in researching the literary activity of emigrants and exiles, and researchers in the United States who are concerned with the area of German-American studies.

The first area, research on German-American literature carried out in Germany, can be briefly summarized and dismissed, as interest in this area was strongest among academicians who supported the Third Reich.[18] After 1933, the German-American group of immigrants, like other groups of Auslandsdeutsche, became an object of preoccupation for volkish writers in Germany who hoped to revive bonds with Germans abroad under the perspective of expanding the nation's boundaries, of Lebensraum, and who thus encouraged what they saw as "struggles towards unification" within these groups. In particular, the way was prepared for an incorporation of German-American literature into "Stammes- und Landschaftsdichtung" by its inclusion in Josef Nadler's Literaturgeschichte der deutschen Stämme und Landschaften (1912ff). Studies originating during the Third Reich which continue and elaborate this perspective include Wilhelm Schneider, Die auslandsdeutsche Dichtung unserer Zeit (1936), Heinz Kloss, Um die Einigung des Deutschamerikanertums. Die Geschichte einer unvollendeten Volksgruppe (1937), which reserves its highest praise for American organizations of Nazi sympathizers,[19] Heinz Kindermann, Rufe über Grenzen. Dichtung und Lebenskampf der Deutschen im Ausland (1938) and Karl K. Klein, "Literaturgeschichte des Deutschtums im Ausland" in: Schrifttum und Geistesleben der deutschen Volksgruppen im Ausland vom Mittelalter bis zur Gegenwart (1939). All of these writers extol the "konservative Haltung" of this literature as a way of preserving so-called "deutsche Eigenart"[20] and avoiding total assimilation. Here even dilettantism -- the perennial criticism made of German-American literature -- is not a problem, for, as Schneider states:

> Selbst wenn die Kunstübung nur unselbständige Nachahmung deutscher Vorbilder ist, hat sie an ihrem Ort noch unschätzbare völkische Lebenswerte, und wir Bevorzugte im Reiche sollten uns vor billigem Spott hüten. Denn dass der auslandsdeutsche Dichter an der Bewahrung der arteignen Kultur und der Erhaltung der deutschen Sprache mitwirkt und die geistigen Bande zwischen dem Mutterland und der Heimat im fremden Volk immer neu knüpft, das ist sein Stolz und seine Sendung. (21)

The foreign ethnic groups remained "unvollendet," the "Thousand-Year Reich" ended twelve years after its founding in 1945, and German literary critics ceased to occupy themselves with German-American literature, dismissing it -- if they mentioned it at all -- as of notoriously bad quality.

A different picture emerges when we turn to the second group of academics who have concerned themselves with this area, those based in the United States. However, like their German counterparts, these researchers have also totally neglected German-American socialist literature. Surveying the secondary literature in this area, we find one pertinent study, William Kamman's dissertation published in 1917 on Socialism in German American Literature, which focuses on Weitling, the Turners and the freethinkers, contains many factual errors, and does not go beyond summaries of content in its analysis. Aside from this monograph, silence prevails for the succeeding fifty years. For example, recent histories of the German-American ethnic group, such as Robert Billigmeier's Americans from Germany (1974) or La Vern Rippley's The German-Americans (1976) content themselves with mentioning in a few sentences that there were German immigrant socialists, but devote no more space to them. And the journal of German-American Studies, published since 1969, has never had a single article on German-American socialists, their politics, literature or culture. At first thought, this seems to be a surprising omission which calls for a somewhat closer examination of the field of German-American studies. What have researchers in this field concentrated their attention on?

As Pat Herminghouse has pointed out in a thought-provoking article on the necessity for a new approach to German-American studies, in the first fifteen years of this century, German-Americans made a concerted effort to preserve their own ethnicity, in the face of diminishing immigration from Germany and increasing immigration of other nationalities.[22] One manifestation of this ethnic consciousness was the Deutsch-Amerikanischer Nationalbund, established in 1901 with this goal of preservation in mind, which soon claimed more than a million and a half members. Another symptomatic phenomenon was the appearance of positivistic, "filiopietistic" (Herminghouse) publications at this time on the German ethnic group, including Georg Bosse's Das deutsche Element in den Vereinigten Staaten (1908) and, most importantly, Albert Faust's two-volume study on The German Element in the United States (1909). Such studies were concerned with detailing the contributions of German immigrants to American society in the areas of high art and culture, education and scholarship, business, commerce and politics, in short, with placing the ethnic group in as favorable a light as possible with respect to the status quo. Faust, for example, emphasizes at the conclusion of his book the following "German traits:" law-abidingness, honesty, industriousness, thriftiness, love of labor, sense of duty, love of home and family, individualism, idealism. That is, these studies are concerned with stressing the frictionless assimilation of the German ethnic group, its quick accomodation, adjustment and positive contributions to the "American way of life," and they pass over less assimilable sectors such as the socialists and anarchists.[23] The emphasis of these historians reflects the public opinion of pre-war America. As John Higham states in his study of nativism, Strangers in the Land,

> During the post-Civil War age of confidence the initial distaste for
> German customs had rapidly worn away. Public opinion had come to
> accept the Germans as one of the most assimilable and reputable of
> immigrant groups. Repeatedly, older Americans praised them as
> law-abiding, speedily assimilated, and strongly patriotic. In 1903 a
> Boston sociologist pronounced the Germans the best ethnic type in the
> city. In 1908 a group of professional people, in rating the traits of
> various immigrant nationalities, ranked the Germans above the
> English and in some respects judged them superior to the native
> whites. These opinions rested on substantial foundations of social
> and economic prestige. By and large the Germans had risen out of
> the working class. They were businessmen, farmers, clerks, and

in a few cases highly skilled workmen. Among workers in the major industries, a German was more likely to own his own home than was a native white. (24)

As is well known, with the beginning of the First World War and the entry of the United States in 1916, these sentiments were rapidly reversed and anti-German hysteria prevailed. "100 Per Cent Americanism," rather than "hyphenated Americanism" was the order of the day. This period saw attempts to obliterate all German political and cultural influence. Aliens were arrested, interned or deported, an act of Congress repealed the charter of the Deutsch-Amerikanischer National-bund, in many places the teaching of German and the sale of German newspapers were banned, and many German societies did not dare to meet.[25] Significantly, anti-German feeling was also connected in public opinion in a twisted way with anti-radicalism directed against the small amount of anti-war propaganda coming from the Industrial Workers of the World (IWW), anarchist groups and the Socialist Party. As Higham states:

> The attack on radicalism was thoroughly interwoven with the anti-German hysteria. The equation between the two was partly an out-growth of the whole anti-radical tradition, with its assumption that militant discontent is a foreign importation, and partly a reflection of the new inclination to see the hand of the Kaiser in any divisive symptom. Any radical critic of the war was customarily designated a "pro-German agitator." Then too the frustrating scarcity of disloyal acts among German groups undoubtedly encouraged the belief that the crafty Hun was actually working through left-wing organizations. (26)

These opinions, coupled with the post-war Red Scare years, made for an even less conducive atmosphere for academics to trace the radical traditions of the German ethnic group. Indeed, it is significant that Kamman's study was published in 1917, the year of the Russian Revolution, and that there are no succeeding attempts to expand or revise his analysis in the period before the Second World War.

The writers in the area of German-American studies after 1945 have continued these trends of emphasizing the most assimilable or conservative sides of the ethnic group, of portraying it as an essentially homogeneous block, and of downplaying conflicts within the group itself or between its less conformist members and the surrounding society.[27] If we survey the contents of the journal of German-American Studies (1969 - present), which, along with yearly conferences held recently,[28] may be taken as representative of the sorts of approaches being taken in this area, we find, along with useful bibliographies and listings of library holdings, a definite trend towards simply collecting material to present without analysis (for example, articles on the German theater in various cities which do little more than enumerate performances). Discussions of writers or single works tend to be applications of unspecified formal criteria or exercises in subjective appreciation which place the highest value on trends towards nostalgia, sentimental sensitivity or that notorious "deutsche Innerlichkeit." This is augmented by the use of this journal as a forum for publication of poetry (along these same escapist lines) by present-day German-American writers. Also, in the last few years, this journal has devoted more and more space to genealogical inquiries and information.

Aside from the inclination to deal with "comfortable" topics in "comfortable" ways, perhaps the tendency which deserves to be emphasized the most here is that of presenting a certain stereotypical image of German immigrants which corresponds to a particular tradition of folkloristic studies.[29] For example, a recent article by Adolf Schroeder on German traditions in Missouri speaks of the "cultural loyalty" within the ethnic group which still manifests itself in church and social gatherings and the "folkloristic evidences of a German tradition"[30] seen in the traditions of wooden shoes and "Alpenkräuter" and the revival of festivals such as "Fastnacht," the Harvest Festival and the "Wurstjäger" Dance. Many more examples of this peculiar understanding of folklore and popular tradition could be cited, but what is most important here is that this particular concept (which claims to be based on careful academic research) has a practical side applicable to most other ethnic groups in the United States, with some variations. Although these academics may not be conscious of it, their concept of ethnicity has much wider ramifications. Throughout the United States, the ethnic experience has been preserved quite selectively, as a means of increasing "local color." In Wisconsin, for example, we find pionier villages ("Little Norway"), pageants ("The Song of Norway" based on the life of Edvard Grieg), and thriving businesses which sell Norwegian clothing and other imports. Similarly, in the town of New Glarus, Wisconsin, the descendants of Swiss immigrants annually present an outdoor pageant of Wilhelm Tell, complete with "Alpenhörner," yodeling and Swiss dances performed by young women dressed in costumes of the cantons. Visitors can stay in a hotel designed like a Swiss chalet, buy Swiss imports and eat Swiss specialties. Or, in New York on the Fourth of July a parade is held featuring ethnic minorities wearing their native costumes and selling native foods along the route. Aside from a certain charm and recreational value, what is most striking here in these manifestations of ethnic folklore is their erasure of all signs of conflict (that is, their integrative effect) and their concomitant utility for purposes of commercialization and tourism. For after all, we find no similar attempts to preserve progressive ethnic experience, not to mention the continuation of socialist festivals, workers' traditions, etc. As Wolfgang Emmerich has stated with regard to the German situation:

> Wesentliche Funktionen des Folklorismus bestehen darin, pseudoge-
> meinschaftliche Vorstellungen zu stabilisieren und Kompensation für
> den grauen Alltag vermittels farbiger Kontrasterlebnisse zu schaffen.
> Gibt es auch keinen Blut- und Bodenfolklorismus mehr, so verdient
> doch der Einsatz "sekundärer, verwalteter Volkswelt" als "stimu-
> lierender Fetisch für Absatzförderung und Weltanschauung," vornehm-
> lich zum Zweck der Hebung des Fremdenverkehrs, alle Aufmerksam-
> keit. (31)

Although the critique given by Emmerich of the historical interrelationship between "Volkskunde" and "Volkstumsideologie" in Germany of course cannot be directly applied to the different historical context of ethnic and folklore studies in
the United States, nevertheless his critique of the connection between the post-
forty-five discipline of "Volkskunde" and its practical manifestations of folklorism
and of the presentation of "Volkskultur" in the schools contains insights which can
indeed be applied to the American situation. If we look at these wider ramifications
(social integration, perpetuation of ethnic stereotypes, upholding of traditional,
conservative "practices and beliefs of the people"[32] in contrast to modern urban
life, and the commercialization of all this with the recent Bicentennial spectacle[33]
as the most glaring example), then areas of specialization such as German-American studies can no longer be dismissed as harmless "Liebhaberwissenschaften."[34]
Rather, they have done their part in promoting a conflict-free, integrative, undialectical view of history, and in justifying and buttressing the existing order of
things. It will be the task for German-American studies in the future to overcome
this "Theoriefeindlichkeit, methodologische Naivität und in deren Folge Dilettan-
tismus."[35] That this is being accomplished in research on immigrant groups in
other academic disciplines such as history and sociology in both the United States
and Germany is a hopeful sign. In this historical context, the effort of this study
to present and analyze the German-American socialist literary and cultural tradition should be viewed as a necessary corrective to previous scholarship in this
area. Therefore, concern with this topic represents a conscious alternative both
to bourgeois literary scholarship which emphasizes "intrinsic" analysis of masterpieces and to the previous image of German-American literature fostered by those
who have an interest in social pacification.

II. A BRIEF HISTORY OF NINETEENTH CENTURY
GERMAN-AMERICAN SOCIALISM

1. INDUSTRIALIZATION AND THE DEVELOPMENT OF THE WORKING CLASS IN PRE-CIVIL-WAR AMERICA

The formation of an indigenous American working class was well under way before the advent of the radical German exiles fleeing the reaction in the aftermath of the 1848 revolution. Industrialization, which had proceeded at first at a slow pace following the Revolutionary War, began to spread more rapidly after the Embargo and Non-Intercourse Acts of the War of 1812 severely restricted the importation of foreign goods and established beyond any doubt the importance of independent, domestic manufactures. In spite of the retarding influence of the southern slave-owners, the United States was making the transition from an agricultural nation of small, independent farmers to an industrial power. A few statistics illustrate this gradual development. Between 1820 and 1860 the population of the United States grew from less than 10,000,000 to 31,000,000. The percentage of people living in towns of 2500 or more inhabitants was 7.2 in 1820, 10.8 in 1840 and 19.8 in 1860. The system of factory manufactures, which was initiated in 1815 with the construction of the first modern textile factory in Waltham, Massachusetts, had expanded by the time of the 1860 census to a total of 140,533 establishments with an output valued at $ 500 or more which employed a total of 1,311,246 workers.[1] The spread of mechanization between 1840 and 1860 meant that production in many branches of manufacture doubled (cotton textiles, stove manufactures, tools and farm machinery), tripled (woolens), or even quadrupled (furniture and upholstery). Iron production — to be expanded enormously by the Civil War -- was being established in New Jersey and Pennsylvania, and the yield of coal mining grew from less than 50,000 tons in 1820 to 14,334,000 tons in 1860.

Concretely, what these figures indicate with respect to the structure of American society is that this period is characterized by the formation of a distinct class of workers -- drawn both from peasant rural and village cultures and from the ranks of skilled artisans, and with correspondingly different work habits, responses to growing industrialization, and cultures.[2] This growing group of wage laborers -- consisting mainly of "native" Americans of English background and the so-called "Old Immigration" from Northern and Western Europe of Irish immigrants fleeing the ravages of the potato famine and German settlers and political emigrés -- was subjected to and entered into conflicts which were to remain fundamental contradictions in American society for generations. Broadly speaking, these may be summarized as the clash between industrialization and agrarian, or even preindustrial societies ordered according to artisanship and craft traditions, the organizational and cultural responses of workers to this, and the nativistic and anti-labor reactions to their efforts.

The transition from an agrarian to a fully industrialized society always entails a corresponding transformation in daily life, in habits of work and leisure. It brings about the creation of a self-disciplined work force adapted to the requirement of sustained factory labor, and instilled (not coerced from outside) with qualities so necessary to developing capitalism such as rationality, thrift, punctuality and industriousness.[3] The United States was, of course, no exception to this general feature of societal development, and already at the time of the Revolutionary War, we can find statements on the crucial importance of the "work ethic." For example, a British manufacturer warned in 1778 that

> It is not enough that a few, or even a great number of people understand manufactures. The spirit of manufacturing must become the general spirit of the nation, and be incorporated, as it were, into their very essence. ... It requires a long time before the personal, and a still longer time, before the national habits are formed.

And President John Adams asserted that "manufactures cannot live, much less thrive, without honor, fidelity, punctuality, and private faith, a sacred respect for property, and the moral obligations of promises and contracts." That this spirit was far from being deeply ingrained into those employed by the "manufactures" was also widely recognized and bemoaned. Thus, in 1768 we find Benjamin Franklin condemning poor relief and complaining about the absence among English workers of regular work habits: "Saint _Monday_ is as duly kept by our working people as _Sunday_; the only difference is that instead of employing their time cheaply at church they are wasting it expensively at the ale house."[4] A different sense of time, of the relationship between work and leisure prevailed. Periods of intense labor were followed by days or even longer periods of rest, and this autonomy based on the rhythms of peasant or artisan life was not given up easily.[5] To cite one random example of the retreat to pre-industrial work habits as a means of resisting the new demands of factory discipline, the following passage from Gutman may be quoted:

> Sometime in the late 1830s merchant capitalists sent a skilled British silk weaver to manage a new mill in Nantucket that would employ the wives and children of local whalers and fishermen. Machinery was installed, and in the first days women and children besieged the mill for work. After a month had passed, they started dropping off in small groups. Soon nearly all had returned "to their shore gazing and to their seats by the sea." The Nantucket mill shut down, its hollow frame an empty monument to the unwillingness of resident women and children to conform to the regularities demanded by rising manufacturers. (6)

Such examples could be multiplied at will for any industrializing country, but what is unique about the American situation is that with each succeeding wave of immigrants from different areas, the process of adjustment from peasant, agrarian life and pre-industrial work habits to a rationalized work process had to be repeated all over again. Shortly before World War I, for example, almost a century after the women of Nantucket left the mill, the International Harvester Corporation began to teach its Polish laborers English by using sentences such as:

> I hear the whistle, I must hurry.
> The starting whistle blows.
> I eat my lunch.
> It is forbidden to eat until then.
> I work until the whistle blows to quit.
> I leave my place nice and clean. (7)

Thus, the history of the formation of the United States working class is not linear, but a series of varied repetitions of a similar process, as each immigrant group is uneasily, and even sometimes violently, integrated into the work force -- from the "old immigration" of Northern and Western Europeans to the "new immigration" beginning in the 1880's of Southern and Eastern Europeans (Slavs, Jews and Italians). The significance of the heterogeneous makeup of this immigrant working class for the character and development of the American labor movement is already apparent before the Civil War and cannot be overemphasized.

As the industrial system became more widespread, it was no longer possible to resist the encroachments of capitalism simply by reverting to pre-industrial habits of work and leisure. Realizing that such total, nostalgic rejection of inevitable transformations in labor would be ineffective in the long run, American workers soon began to organize themselves into small labor parties and craft unions. The first American labor parties (which were also the first in the world) were founded in Philadelphia in 1828 and New York City in 1829 -- the latter, the Workingmen's Party of New York, managing in 1829 to garner 31% of the vote and elect the president of the Carpenters' Union to the State Assembly. In the late 1820's and early 1830's, more than sixty independent workers' parties were formed in towns around the country, and about fifty labor papers were published during the years 1827-1832.[8] The demands of these parties centered around public education, the abolition of monopolies, particularly the banking monopoly, equal taxation, and more democratic participation in government.

After this spate of independent political activity and the era of Jacksonian democracy (1828-1836), labor concentrated primarily on trade union organizing for the rest of the pre-war period. Already as early as 1792, a permanent union had been maintained by shoemakers in Philadelphia, and skilled workers in other cities rapidly followed suit.[9] Periods of depression and crisis spelled the destruction of almost all of these pioneering organizations, but new ones sprang up in their places to advocate higher wages and the shorter, ten-hour day -- the major issues in the antebellum period. By the time of the depression of 1854, more than 200,000 workers belonged to local unions which were "exclusive craft unions composed of skilled mechanics."[10] The disruption caused by the economic crises of 1854 and 1857 led to great declines in membership and even to the destruction of some unions, but they had been able to establish a continuous presence.

Throughout this period, but becoming especially pressing in the 1840's and 1850's, incipient workers' organizations were faced with the problem of competition from immigrant labor. During the decade of 1840-1850, 1,713,251 immigrants arrived in the United States, and in 1850-1860, this increased to a total of 2,598,214. Of these Germans comprised 434,626 in 1841-1850 and 951,667 in 1851-1860. The following table shows the percentage of foreign-born inhabitants of major American cities in 1860:

City	% of Population
New York	47.6
Chicago	49.9
Philadelphia	28.9
Pittsburgh	50.0
St. Louis	59.7

Some unions were able to establish branches for different nationalities and language groups -- a pattern which was to expand and continue far into the twentieth century -- although before 1860 this held true primarily for native Americans and English immigrants, and German skilled workers, since the Irish who made up the other large immigrant group of the period were almost entirely unskilled and were not admitted to the exclusive craft unions.[11] In spite of these attempts at unity, however, many "native" American workers viewed cheap immigrant labor as a threat to their formerly secure way of life and as unfair competition which would undercut the economic gains they had won through organization. Accordingly, substantial numbers took part in the movement knows as "nativism" in the 1840's and 1850's.

Pre-Civil-War nativism was directed primarily against two groups: Catholics (due to the large number of Irish immigrants and the historical, political and religious antagonism between the English and Irish) and foreigners in general, who were perceived as a threat to so-called "American" institutions. Although anti-Catholic feelings directed against the Irish were undoubtedly the strongest current in the nativism of this period, what is particularly relevant here is that a significant measure of anti-foreign sentiment was directed against immigrant workers and foreign (primarily German) radicals. Fearing competition for their jobs, native American workers themselves formed associations advocating the restriction of immigration and a more exclusive process of granting citizenship. The most influential of these was the Order of United Americans, a self-described "benevolent and patriotic society" founded in New York in 1844, which claimed a membership of fifty thousand by 1855 and which only American-born workers were allowed to join. In 1850, the most important of the nativist organizations was formed, a secret party called the Order of the Star-Spangled Banner, which soon became known as the Know-Nothing Party. At the height of its strength in 1855, this party was a serious force to be reckoned with in American politics. It was estimated by Horace Greeley, editor of the New York Tribune, that from 75 to 100 members of Congress were openly or secretly connected with the Order.[12] One of these Representatives to the House, Thomas R. Whitney, in his Defense of the American Policy, As Opposed to the Encroachments of Foreign Influence (1856), expressed quintessentially the Know-Nothings' economic nativism, which played upon already existing prejudices among American skilled workers and mechanics in order to increase support for their party:

> The Mechanics of America have heretofore occupied a position in society which has not been attained by their class in any other nation. In European countries, the word mechanic designated not only a class but a caste in society; and that too, of a low grade . ...
> In the United States the only castes intrinsically recognized are founded upon merit. This is the natural and imperative result of our system of government in its unadulterated form. The American mechanic is morally, socially, and politically on a par with his fellow citizens of every calling, whether rich or poor, and his right to the highest executive office of the nation is as complete, perfect, and undisputed as that of any other living man. ...
> Before the unequal competition of immigrant labor cast its shadow over the industrial interests of our country, every American journeyman mechanic was enabled, by the force of his industry, to maintain a financial position equal to that of his social, moral, and political position. He was sure of employment, at wages adapted to the dignity of his franchise; to the necessities of the present, and the vicissitudes of the future. He could dwell in his own cottage, supply his family with comforts and luxuries, rear his children respectably, find time for his own mental improvement, and lay by a little of his earnings each week for a rainy day. ... But with a superabundant immigration from Europe came a train of evils which are now rapidly developing themselves. ... How vast the number of those who have been driven from their employments to make room for the under-bidding competition of the foreign laborer! The American mechanic cannot live upon the pittance demanded by his European competitor. It is not his custom, ... it is degrading to his sense of self-respect.
> Thus the personal interests of the American mechanic are submerged, his rights neutralized, and his hopes thwarted by excessive immigration of the poor of Europe. These are the direct effects. Indirectly, the effects assume a different phase. The introduction of this degraded element into the industrial arena of the country, is in itself calculated to promote caste, and stimulate a puerile aristocratic taste among the rich. (13)

This document shows first of all that nativism was in part a reaction to the changes brought about in society by industrialization, a reaction -- shared by some skilled workers -- which longed to turn the clock back to a less complicated society composed of independent small farmers and artisans. Second, it provides a striking early illustration of the ideology of "classlessness," of American "exceptionalism," of the promises of social mobility and opportunity. Also, it reflects, albeit in a twisted way, consciousness of the growing conflict between rich and poor, capital and labor, thought to have its source in excessive immigration. Finally, it voices throughout the nativistic fear that assimilation of new immigrant groups was bound to fail and that consequently their loyalty to "American" institutions was highly suspect.

This nationalistic opposition to an apparently threatening internal minority[14] was not only aimed at workers. It was also directed specifically against those progressive immigrants who hoped to put their radical democratic ideals into practice in the United States. The specter of anti-radical nativism had already raised its head as early as 1798, when the Federalists, the party of rank and privilege, enacted the notorious Alien, Sedition and Naturalization Acts directed in part against sympathizers with the French Revolution and English, French and Irish immigrants described by one Federalist as "the most God-provoking Democrats this side of Hell."[15] With the election of Thomas Jefferson to the Presidency in 1800 and the ensuing eight years of Jeffersonian Democracy, these laws were repealed and broad reforms were introduced (including the removal of property qualifications for voting), thus giving rise to the general rejoicing expressed in the popular song of the time, "Jefferson and Liberty:"

> The gloomy night before us flies,
> The reign of terror now is o'er;
> Its gags, inquisitors, and spies,
> Its herds of harpies are no more!
>
> No lordling here, with gorging jaws
> Shall wring from industry the food;
> Nor fiery bigot's holy laws
> Lay waste our fields and streets in blood!
>
> Here strangers from a thousand shores
> Compelled by tyranny to roam,
> Shall find, amidst abundant stores,
> A nobler and happier home.
>
> Rejoice, Columbia's sons, rejoice!
> To tyrants never bend the knee,
> But join with heart, and soul, and voice,
> For Jefferson and liberty! (16)

Anti-radicalism waned for a time, but this strain of nativism began to revive with the arrival of progressive German immigrants and political exiles. The following statement from a Whig newspaper in 1846, directed against a German land reform group in New York City called the Sozialreformassoziation, is a prototype for succeeding expressions of hostility towards foreign radicals: they are accused of attempting to introduce "Un-American" ideas and politics into the country, and of doing this in a language other than English:

24

Wir müssen bekennen, dass wir sehr erstaunt sind, mitten in der Stadt
New York einen Fremden in einer fremden Sprache eine Rede halten
zu hören, worin er seine besonderen Grundsätze befürwortet. Es ist
in der Tat ziemlich weit gekommen, wenn Männer, die nicht die Sprache
von Amerika sprechen können, darüber schwatzen, was die Politik der
Amerikaner sein sollte, und wenn in deutscher Sprache zu Deutschen
gesprochen wird über unsere Gesetzgebung, so halten wir das für eine
grenzenlose Unverschämtheit.
Wir nehmen das niedergetretene Volk aus der Fremde auf; wir geben
ihnen Privilegien und Rechte, die sie nie vorher hatten; sie werden
genährt, gekleidet, sie erhalten ein Obdach, wir gewähren ihnen
Stimmrecht; aber es heisst in der Tat den Spass zu weit treiben, in
unserem Staat die Grundsätze irgend einer 'deutschen Verbindung'
einführen zu wollen. Mögen diese Reformer wenigstens zuerst unsere
Sprache lernen, ehe sie unsere Gesetze zu ändern suchen. (17)

Such nativistic utterances became much more strident and violent[18] with the advent
of the German Forty-Eighters, who, as the historian Carl Wittke states, antagonized
the Know-Nothings by their enlightened attitudes towards "religion, Americaniza-
tion, the Puritan Sabbath, temperance legislation, and radicalism in politics and
economics."[19] The materialism and atheism of these so-called "disciples of Heine"
were attacked by nativists as a threat to "our American, home-bred ideas of
liberty." With respect to their supposed political and economic goals, one nativist
writer spoke out against immigrants who "come with their heads full of a division
of property," and "socialists [who] are silently making an impression on the people
of our great cities, where all the seepings of the country are gathered into one great
mass of ignorance and corruption."[20] This fear of the "socialists" (meaning radical democrats, not Marxian socialists in a later sense) is clearly connected to the
economic concepts of nativists such as Thomas R. Whitney, who expressed the fear
that German "red republicans" might be able to ride "the blood-red waves of Revolution" to power in the United States.[21] Indeed, the elements of political, religious
and cultural antagonism establish a pattern here which is intensified in later attacks
against German-American radicals, culminating in the hysteria following the Haymarket bombing in 1886, and which is also evident in attacks on radicals of other
nationalities and language groups.

In brief, then, the situation facing the immigrant Forty-Eighters with respect to the
formation of the American working class and the beginnings of the labor movement
was characterized by the evolution of the following areas of economic, political and
cultural conflict: 1) Most broadly speaking, the problem of assimilating the various
immigrant groups into an English-speaking, rapidly industrializing society, 2) The
clash between the development of modern industry and pre-industrial, agrarian
ways of life, 3) Resistance to industrialization, first in the form of maintaining and
asserting non-rationalized work habits, and then, as capitalism became firmly
entrenched, increasingly through organization of labor parties and unions among
skilled workers, 4) The nativist reaction against Catholic and non-English-speaking
immigrants, most relevantly here against radicals, workers and the poor. These

were all vital components of the experience of Germans in the United States in the 1840's and 1850's, and continued to be crucial factors after the Civil War in the encounter of every immigrant group with American society.

2. FROM THE FORTY-EIGHTERS TO THE CIVIL WAR. THE BEGINNINGS OF SOCIALIST ORGANIZATION IN THE UNITED STATES, 1848-1861

During the 1850's, the German-American political scene was dominated by exiled participants in the 1848 revolution, who both greatly expanded and consolidated the public institutions and means of communication within the ethnic group and also began to assert its vital interest in the public affairs of the nation, thus strengthening its self-identity and influence.[22] Many of the exiles had been among the foremost journalistic talents of the Vormärz, and they immediately began to employ their skills in the service of their liberal tradition by establishing newspapers and journals of high quality which soon became widely read and which, in many cases, thrived until well into the twentieth century. It is possible to discern various trends in the German-American press of this decade which, however, are not absolutely distinct, voicing as they all did a pervasive republican, anti-clerical outlook. Of the papers founded or made secure and viable by forty-eighters which were aligned with the established parties and which supported the Union in the Civil War, perhaps the most important were the New York Staatszeitung (published from 1834-1954) and Belletristisches Journal (1852-1911), the Illinois Staatszeitung (1848-1922), and the St. Louis Anzeiger des Westens (1835-1912) and Westliche Post (1857-1938). Other groups also realized the indispensability of creating their own public forums. The Freidenker were represented most notably by Karl Heinzen,[23] who edited the Boston Neu-England Zeitung (1846-1853) and then Der Pionier (1854-1879). These societies also published the Milwaukee Freidenker (1872-1942). The Turn-Zeitung was the official organ of the Sozialistischer Turnerbund from 1851 to 1861, when most of the gymnastic societies dissolved as their members joined the Union Army.[24] Although all of these papers were opposed in varying degrees to the institution of slavery,[25] one abolitionist paper deserves particular mention, the San Antonio Zeitung (1853-1856), "ein sozial-demokratisches Blatt für die Deutschen in West-Texas," published in this slave-holding state by Adolf Douai. Under pressure from attacks in the English press and threatened by mob violence, Douai was forced to flee to the north, where he became one of the most prominent German-American socialist journalists after the war.[26]

A world is in order on the meaning of the terms "sozialistisch," "sozial" or "sozial-demokratisch" as they are used here. These various groups considered themselves to be radical democrats, not scientific socialists or communists; they desired a state based on equality for all but did not understand the proletariat to be the revolutionary agent in society. In this vein, the Sozialistischer Turnerbund defined its concept of socialism early in the 1850's as follows:

> Eine demokratisch-republikanische Verfassung, ein "Allen" garantierter Wohlstand, bestmöglichste und unentgeltliche Erziehung nach den Fähigkeiten eines Jeden, die Beseitigung aller hierarchischen und privilegierten Gewalten. (27)

And Adolf Douai, writing in his San Antonio Zeitung in 1853 on "Die Sozialdemokratie, ein Glaubensbekenntnis," defined socialism rather vaguely as "die mög-
lichste Gleichheit der Einzelnen in Freiheit, Wohlstand und Bildung."[28] As in his
later writings, he went on to stress the prime importance of centralized, secular
education in attaining this goal of equality. Putting these views into practice, such
forty-eighters founded "freie Schulen" which were sometimes, though not always,
connected to workers' societies and provided children with non-religious, German-
language instruction in several subject areas. Politically, these radical democrats
were often active in the Sozialreformvereine which supported land reform and the
Free Soil Party.

Therefore, almost all of these immigrants -- even the "socialists" -- who were
active in public affairs and journalism believed that their ideals could be realized
within the political system of the United States, although most saw that a protracted
struggle would be necessary to overthrow the odious institution of slavery. After
a short period under the sway of Gottfried Kinkel's tour of 1851, when some of the
more influential forty-eighters concentrated on raising money to support the eventual revival of revolution in Germany,[29] they saw that this was a hopeless cause,
ans the vast majority turned their energies towards reform in the United States.
As one former revolutionary stated in 1855,

> We must not look upon ourselves as refugees in America. This nation
> is not our land of exile. Here one can fight as vigorously as in Europe
> for our highest and most sacred ideals, and the battle for the realiza-
> tion of those ideals is rightly ours. (30)

The forty-eighters now affiliated themselves en masse with the newly-founded (1854),
anti-slavery Republican Party, and becoming increasingly involved in electoral politics, they provided a crucial portion of the vote which elected Lincoln President
in 1860.[31] A cohesive and influential presence of the German-American ethnic
group had been established by spokespersons who attempted to further desired
reforms by integrating the ethnic group into the American political process.

However, a small number of forty-eighters pursued more radical paths, the utopian communists and those socialists influenced by the principles of the Communist
Manifesto. It was within these circles that independent working class political and
economic activity gained a solid foothold within the German-American ethnic group,
that class solidarity began to be asserted over ethnic solidarity, although the diverse societies of skilled workers were still closely entwined with the various
groups referred to above.

Utopian communities, as a response to the growing contrasts between rich and poor
created by industrialization, had been flourishing in the United States, with its vast
tracts of free land, during the first half of the nineteenth century.[32] These attempts
at shaping a self-sufficient, collective way of life took many different forms, from
the religious sects like the Rappites and Shakers, to the Owenite communities of
the 1820's, the Fourierist phalanxes of the 1840's, and the growth of producers'

and consumers' cooperatives in the 1840's and 1850's modeled along the lines of the social workshops proposed by Louis Blanc in France and continuing an older tradition of artisan and peasant or farmer solidarity.[33] The outstanding advocate of utopian communism within the German-speaking community was Wilhelm Weitling, a tailor who first came to the United States in 1846, returned to Germany to participate in the 1848 revolution, and settled permanently in America in 1849, where he remained until his death in 1871. Weitling had constructed his vision of the future and his theories in three works written during the period of the Vormärz, Die Menschheit, wie sie ist und wie sie sein sollte (1838), Garantien der Harmonie und Freiheit (1842), and Das Evangelium des armen Sünders (1845). In the paper he published in New York from 1850 to 1855, Die Republik der Arbeiter, he continued to expound on his program of producers' and consumers' cooperatives, laborers' exchange banks, and communal, cooperative colonies as the answers to the social question. Weitling's utopianism was characterized by two things. On the one hand, it was part of the tradition which made a moral appeal to the communistic tendencies of primitive Christianity: instead of a world dominated by the evils of greed and self-interest, there should be a return to communal property, brotherly love, and harmony with nature. On the other hand, his system of economic production was to be based on the cooperative efforts of skilled handicraft workers residing with their families in colonies. This Handwerkerkommunismus (which was current among groups of workers in Europe, particularly Switzerland, in the 1840's), was an attempt to overcome the insecurity and unsettling of artisans caused by the growth of industrialization. It also reflects the as yet underdeveloped state of industry, however, for it seemed to Weitling and his followers that industrial expansion and its concurrent evils could be avoided and checked by a withdrawal to colonies isolated from the society surrounding them, by a return to preindustrial patterns of work and leisure. The superiority of communal life would then become so manifest, they believed, that the cooperative system would rapidly spread and utopia would be established on earth. After settling in America, Weitling attempted to put his ideas into practice in 1851 by affiliating his New York Arbeiterbund financially with the colony of Kommunia, Iowa, and by commuting between the two places to instruct the colonists in his plans for communal organization. Kommunia eked out its existence until 1855, when, rent by internal quarrels and plagued by financial difficulties, the colony disbanded -- its collapse also contributing to the demise of Weitling's Arbeiterbund and his Republik der Arbeiter because of the substantial amount of money he had invested in the colony.

Although Weitling's energies were always directed ultimately towards the establishment of cooperatives and communal colonies, he was one of the very few utopian communists who also took part in establishing unions or "associations" among skilled workers. Although he believed strikes and electoral involvement to be ineffective in the long run in substantially altering the uneven balance between rich and poor, he still participated in the union activity in New York in the early 1850's, especially in his own craft of tailoring, and in the Republik der Arbeiter he urged workers not only to organize into unions but also to support him and his paper's program. Progress was encouraging. During the wave of strikes in New York City in the spring of 1850, about twenty crafts organized,[34] and, influenced by the only German labor paper in New York, united into the Zentralkommission der Vereinigten Gewerbe (Central Committee of the United Trades), a body dedicated to Weitling's principles and represented by him in the city's Industrial Congress.[35] Always thinking in more expansive terms, Weitling immediately conceived the idea of a national Arbeiterbund (Workingmen's League) composed of workers' organizations in cities around the country which would support his plans for social reform. In October of 1850, the Zentralkommission of New York and the Deutsch-amerikanischer Arbeiterverein of Philadelphia, at Weitling's initiative, convened in the latter city the first national convention of German-American workers, with the express purpose of creating such an Arbeiterbund. This Congress represented about 4400 skilled workers from many parts of the country, with the New York membership accounting for about 1/5 of the total, and certainly marked the high point of Weitling's influence in the United States.[36] In the constitution of the newly-founded Arbeiterbund, written by Weitling himself in 1852, the association is described as "eine nach den Interessen gleicher Verhältnisse geordnete gegenseitige Tausch-, Kolonisations-, Assoziations- und Unterstützungsgesellschaft."[37] It was structured as a mutual insurance and benefit society, but also aimed to establish producers' and consumers' cooperatives, workers' halls, a workers' exchange bank, and a colonization society. During its first two years of existence, the Arbeiterbund seemed to thrive, and the local Vereine associated with it poured their energies and funds into creating the sorts of cooperative ventures that Weitling envisioned. Individual chapters were able to establish themselves as centers of the German-speaking working class community primarily through two sorts of organizations: producers' and consumers' cooperatives, and Arbeiterhallen -- although the first Arbeiterbildungsvereine in the United States were also founded in the 1850's.[38] The Arbeiterhallen served as social and cultural centers, as meeting places for labor groups, and as mutual insurance societies. In New York, St. Louis, Philadelphia, Detroit, Baltimore, New Orleans and other cities these halls supported dramatic and singing societies, furnished reading and social rooms and occasionally provided lectures and debates. These local Vereine continued to exist and even thrive after the onset in 1853 of the decline of the Arbeiterbund, thus representing the first continuous presence in most major cities of cooperative ventures among German-American workers. Indeed, the effectiveness of the Arbeiterbund was greatest on the local level, rather than in its function as a national organization, a pattern which holds true for subsequent German-American political efforts.

The reasons for the dissolving of the first national German-American workers' organization are diverse. Internally, Weitling's attempts to exercise absolute control in pursuit of unrealizable goals and his neglect of immediate, pressing economic issues affecting members, coupled with financial irregularities, led to dissension, while externally, the Arbeiterbund was disrupted by the economic crises of 1854 and 1857, which affected all labor organizations. Also, conservative political and religious groups attacked the utopians in general and the Arbeiterbund in particular in tones which often reflected the strident nativism of the day. For example, the New York Herald lumped together socialism, Fourierism and infidelity as foreign "theoretical nonsense" and denounced (utopian) socialism as "nonsense, humbug, cant, hypocrisy, rascality and visionary,"[39] while in Detroit, the

Catholic church condemned the Arbeitervereine.[40] Finally, the Arbeiterbund began to lose some of its members to a rival central workers' organization founded in New York in 1853, the Allgemeiner Amerikanischer Arbeiterbund.

While Weitling's utopianism responded to social inequality by downplaying the importance of voicing immediate demands through electoral politics or trade unions and by championing a system of handicraft economy, the second group of forty-eighters who went beyond the standpoint of the radical democrats to side with the working class proceeded from the assumption that the spread of industrialization was inevitable and that therefore workers had no choice but to accept this and organize politically and economically to defend their own interests and improve their immediate situation. The most important figure among this group was Joseph Weydemeyer, a socialist journalist and member of the Communist League who arrived in New York in 1851. Already before Weydemeyer's departure for America, Marx had written to him on the importance from a European perspective of establishing a revolutionary press in America: "If you can stay in New York, you are not far from Europe, and with the total suppression of the press in Germany, it is only from over there that a battle can be waged in the press."[41] Continuing an old feud against utopian communism from the Brussels Communist Correspondence Committee of 1846, Marx also cautioned Weydemeyer against buying the Republik der Arbeiter "from the wretched Weitling" as he thought this would mean losing "the great reading public" for the sake of a handful of apprentices.[42] Acting as the "literary agent for Marx and Engels," whom he had met in London and with whom he corresponded until his death in 1866, Weydemeyer immediately began to publish a journal in January of 1852 called Die Revolution, described on its masthead as a weekly under the "collaboration of the editors of the former Neue Rheinische Zeitung, Karl Marx, Friedrich Engels, Ferdinand Freiligrath, etc."[43] Unfortunately, however, in spite of the stellar list of contributors, the journal was able to survive for only two issues since it did not attract enough subscribers to sustain itself financially -- the second issue being the first publication anywhere of Marx's Eighteenth Brumaire of Louis Bonaparte. After the failure of Die Revolution, Weydemeyer continued to contribute to other radical democratic papers such as the New York Turnzeitung and the Boston Neu-England Zeitung. By March of 1853, however, he was able to establish another paper, Die Reform, co-editing it with G. T. Kellner, an exiled journalist who had published the radical paper Die Hornisse in Kassel during the revolution. Die Reform, which became the official organ of the Allgemeiner Amerikanischer Arbeiterbund and is thus the principal source for the history of this organization, managed to exist as a weekly and then as a daily until April of 1854, claiming in May 1853 to have a circulation of more than 2000 in various states. Described by Marx as "an honest paper, something rare in America, and a workingman's paper,"[44] its content consisted of official statements and announcements, theoretical articles such as Weydemeyer's series of "Nationalökonomische Skizzen," reports on current events and the condition of the working class in the United States and abroad, and a "Belletristisches Sonntagsblatt" which unfortunately has not been preserved. Die Reform was not to be spared the tirades of nativists. In December of 1853 the New York Herald attacked the radical German press in these terms:

Sie reizen die Leidenschaften dieser erregbaren Race zu Exzessen
auf, und treiben die Demokratie über die Grenzen des amerikanischen
gesunden Urteils hinaus in die gewaltsame Extreme des roten Republi-
kanismus der europäischen Theorien. (45)

Die Reform replied to these accusations by formulating what it believed its mission
to be, showing that it was oriented towards having a real effect in the United States:

Kein englisch-amerikanisches Blatt hat die Courage, dem Pfaffentum
und Glaubenstum den Krieg zu erklären. Dieses Amt hat die radikale
deutsche Presse dieses Landes und sie allein besitzt die Waffen dazu
und versteht sie zu führen; und diese Waffe heisst: deutsche radikale
Bildung und Aufklärung. (46)

Such sentiments were widespread among the free-thinking, enlightened democrats
in exile, and in this respect, Die Reform reflected a broad, persistent opposition
among German immigrants to the pervasiveness of the Puritan heritage.

On March 20, 1853, about 800 German-American workers attended a meeting in
Mechanics' Hall in New York City to form the Allgemeiner Amerikanischer Arbeiterbund, in response to a call issued by the Proletarierbund, a tiny club which Weydemeyer had gathered together in the summer of 1852.[47] This new league intended
to be the organizing center for an independent workers' party, as its constitution
stated:

Der Amerikanische Arbeiterbund erstrebt die Organisation der Arbeiterklasse zu einer festgeschlossenen und selbständigen politischen
Partei zur Durchführung und Geltendmachung der Rechte der Arbeiter. (48)

The platform of the Arbeiterbund, published in Die Reform, included demands for
speedier naturalization, free access to the courts, land reform, compulsory and
free schooling, an end to child labor, the ten-hour day, and, reflecting the resistance to the physical and spiritual disciplinary forces of industrialization and Pu-
ritanistic religion, the repeal of all laws

die den Arbeiter jedes Genusses berauben oder ihm denselben ver-
kümmern wollen, und die hiedurch die natürliche Freiheit beeinträchti-
gen, wie z.B. Gesetze über Sonntagsfeier, Verbot geistiger Getränke,
etc. (49)

These programmatical demands show that the Arbeiterbund was attempting to re-
spond concretely to urgent problems facing workers in the United States, rather
than proclaiming an "imported" European dogma which had nothing to do with
American society -- a charge which was often leveled from various quarters
against immigrant radicals. In its "Prinzipienerklärung" the League invoked the
justification for revolution given in the Declaration of Independence and voiced the

disillusionment felt by immigrants who continued to experience oppression in the New World:

> Amerika ist frei vom fürstlichen Joche, hat keine auf Geburtsvorrechte begründete Stände; das verhindert aber nicht, dass der Besitzlose, derjenige, der nichts als seine Arbeitskraft einzusetzen hat, hier wie jenseits des Ozeans unterdrückt und ausgebeutet wird. Der Unterschied ist nur, dass es dort von monarchischen, hier von republikanischen Bourgeois geschieht. (50)

The Declaration went on to explain that the development of industry in America had created the class of propertyless workers and the flooding of the labor market which brought about so much misery. Therefore, workers were exhorted to unite to shorten the working day and assume political power.[51]

However, such oneness of purpose would entail breaking down the barriers between workers which had contributed to mutual suspicion. An article in Die Reform entitled "Die Organisation der Arbeiter" reflected on the heterogeneous American working class, and voiced an extremely optimistic belief in its eventual solidarity, in one of the earliest statements on this dilemma of the American labor movement:

> Amerika ist der Boden, welcher den Völkern der alten Welt zuerst das Schauspiel der innigen Verschmelzung aller Nationen geben kann; das erhabene Beispiel, auf dessen Nachahmung allein das Glück jeder neuen Revolution in Europa beruht. ...
> Unter 'Solidarität der Völker' verstehen wir die Solidarität der arbeitenden Klassen. Die Bourgeoisie kommt nie zu einer solchen Vereinigung, denn ihr Lebensatem ist die ewige Konkurrenz, die ewige Vernichtung, die ewige Vereinzelung -- nicht bloss nach der Nationalität, -- nein, in Betracht jeder einzelnen Persönlichkeit, oder wie sie sich ausdrückt, jedes einzelnen Kapitals. Denn hier gibt es keine Menschen, sondern nur einen Menschen, das Ich, das Geschäfte macht, die übrigen Ichs sind Kapitale oder Geschäfte. (52)

Solidarity did not only imply cooperation between workers of different languages and ethnic groups, however, but because of the spread of female and child labor in the wake of industrial expansion, it also meant that men and women workers shared a common cause. In May of 1853, Mathilde Annecke, participant in the 1848 revolution and prominent advocate of women's rights in German-American circles,[53] reported in Die Reform that the Executive Committee of the Arbeiterbund had recently decided to support the organizing efforts of women workers and to encourage its affiliated men's associations to merge with women's Vereine which had joined together around similar issues.[54] Annecke viewed this as a positive step, asserting that women deserved equal pay and an equal chance at employment and that for the first time, this had been recognized by the workers' movement. A month later, in the first evidence to be found of a German-American women workers' organization, Die Reform reported that a small Frauenverein had been created in New York

City, largely due to the efforts of Annecke.[55] It hoped to provide for contact and support among women of different occupations, material support in sickness and health, "Bildung" and mutual instruction through lectures, and the establishment of schools and institutes to train women in occupations which would be more profitable than those they were already engaged in. Although the Frauenverein was cooperating with "rechtlich und freidenkenden Männern," it also asserted the necessity of independent action in its Aufruf:

> Die Zweckmässigkeit und Zeitgemässheit einer solchen Vereinigung wird gewiss allen denjenigen unserer Schwestern einleuchten, welche gewohnt sind, selbständig zu denken, und sich nicht als die blossen Anhängsel der Männer betrachten. ... Schwestern! Erwartet nicht von den Männern, dass sie Eure Lage verbessern werden, so lange Ihr selbst nicht mit Hand anlegt. Sie werden Euch im Gegenteil so lange als nichtberechtigt halten, als Ihr nicht für Euer Recht selbst einstehet. (56)

Later reports in Die Reform on Women's Rights Conventions indicate that while the Arbeiterbund wanted to incorporate women workers within itself, it was also quite skeptical of anything hinting at an autonomous position.

The Arbeiterbund, made up of Wardvereine which any worker could join, some unions of German-American skilled workers,[57] and a few other groups, enjoyed only a brief existence. In spite of its ambitious program, it seems to have been able to function in reality primarily as a mutual aid society, and by the time Die Reform ceased publication during the depression of 1854, the organization existed in name only. Several attempts were made by New York reform groups to revive it after Weydemeyer moved to Milwaukee in 1856, but the crisis of 1857 -- the first capitalist economic crisis to assume worldwide proportions -- contributed to the disintegration of unions and made political organizing insurmountably difficult for the time being. During the economic upswing in the two years preceding the Civil War, German-American workers were able to revive their unions to some extent -- again mainly in New York City[58] -- but all independent political activity came to a standstill in the face of impending civil war.

Some historians who have had an interest in legitimating the "correctness" of strategies developed by "Marxist" German-Americans, beginning precisely with Weydemeyer, have posited a clear-cut, unambiguous distinction between his emphasis on economic and political activity and a concept of socialism geared more towards cooperative ventures as Weitling envisioned them.[59] While this fundamental break between the two men was certainly true personally, it was only partially true with respect to the organizations they were affiliated with and their real function within the German-American community. Weitling's Republik der Arbeiter was a beginning impetus to the development of communication among German workers around the country, and the network of cooperative organizations which either existed independently of his endeavors or which were formed as a result of his journalistic efforts and speaking tours were an expression of artisan solidarity, resistance to the changing nature of work, and preservation of familiar work habits. Indeed, the early advocates of a political and economic labor movement, such as Weydemeyer, were able to build on already existing receptivity to cooperative social and political goals, though there were always disagreements about the importance of such associations which thrived outside the narrowly defined labor movement. The tiny group of socialists around Weydemeyer were thus embedded in a much broader working class (as opposed to socialist) culture which had been shaped according to an older tradition of artisan solidarity and utopian communism, and which, as far as the Germans were concerned, both preserved European traditions and altered them to correspond to the experience of immigrant workers, and had the function of helping to establish the beginnings of class solidarity within the German-speaking ethnic group.

3. FROM THE END OF THE CIVIL WAR TO THE DISSOLUTION OF THE FIRST INTERNATIONAL: 1865-1876

> From the commencement of the titanic
> American strife the workingmen of Europe
> felt instinctively that the star-spangled
> banner carried the destiny of their class.
> The contest for the territories which opened
> the dire epopee, was it not to decide whether
> the virgin soil of immense tracts should be
> wedded to the labor of the emigrant, or
> prostituted by the tramp of the slave driver?
>
> (Congratulatory message of the
> First International to Lincoln upon
> his reelection, Jan. 7, 1865) (60)

With the victory of the Union over the slaveholding Confederacy in 1865, the greatest obstacle to the growth of Northern industry had been destroyed, and the conditions for the formation of a large immigrant working class -- and thus for the sharp-
ening of the conflict between labor and capital -- had been created. The utilization
of slave labor had limited the possibilities of industrial expansion in the South and
in newly founded western states, and wealthy Southern planters had been able to
gain the passage of legislation favorable to their interests in Congress. But after
the secession of the rebel states, Congress passed a series of laws which committed the nation to an industrial policy, having realized the crucial role that the development of Northern industry would play in winning the war. A national banking
system was established, immigration laws were relaxed to permit large-scale
importation of contract labor (workers who were practically indentured servants
and who were exempt from the draft), and the tariff on imports was more than
doubled. These laws continued in effect after the war, thus stimulating industrial
growth. Concretely, the war brought about a phenomenal expansion in a number of
industries and removed the restraints of pro-agrarian policies from others. The
closing of traffic on the Mississippi River redirected Midwestern business east-
ward, stimulating east-west railway construction. Between 1860 and 1870 railroad
mileage increased by about 80%, and there was an increase from 30,626 miles in
1860 to 125,739 miles in 1884. Accordingly, the production of iron and steel increased many times over, and the amount of coal mined grew from 14 million tons
in 1860 to 100 million in 1884. The shortage of civilian workers hastened the mechanization of farming, leading to the widespread use of the harvester and the cul-
tivation of rich lands in the west. The requirements of supplying the army neces-
sitated far-reaching developments in industries such as meat-packing and canning,
boot- and shoe-making, and clothing. In the decade from 1860 to 1870, the value
of manufactured products almost doubled. The United States, which ranked fourth
in world industry in 1860, had taken first place by 1894, producing about one-third
of the world's manufactured goods.

In this "Gilded Age,"[61] with the rapid spread of mechanization, the laboring population also underwent an accelerated transformation. Unskilled and semi-skilled factory workers threatened the position and security of skilled workers, who in turn became more and more convinced that unions were the appropriate means of furthering their own particular interests. The period after the Civil War, until the onset of the devastating depression in 1873, saw a revival of trade union activity and the significant, though temporary unification of workers of different trades into the National Labor Union, which lasted from 1866 to 1872. It has been estimated that in 1873 about 300,000 workers belonged to trade unions, although the effect of the depression was that only 50,000 remained in 1878.[62] (Still, the figure of 300,000 contrasts markedly with the situation in Germany, where, as the historian Vernon Lidtke states, "craft unions were hardly known in the sixties," and the Gewerbeordnung of the seventies "severely restricted the unions in their pursuit of economic gain."[63] In 1877, about 49,000 workers belonged to trade unions in Germany). The labor press also expanded many times over: approximately 120 journals of labor reform appeared during the decade of 1863 to 1873.[64]

The skilled German workers were among the most active in organizing their trades and were able to form coalitions on the city level. In New York these were the Deutsche Arbeiterbund with its paper the Arbeiter-Zeitung (1864-1865), which advocated Schulze-Delitzsch's system of cooperatives, and the National Labor Union affiliate, the Arbeiter-Union which had as its official organ a paper (1868-1870) of the same name, edited by Adolf Douai and championing the American Edward Kellogg's proposals for monetary reform. In Chicago, the other important center at this time of organized German workers, the Arbeiter Centralverein published Der deutsche Arbeiter (1869-1870). Although all of these associations were short-lived, nevertheless, a presence of trade unions had been reestablished after the war which would strengthen immensely and continue unbroken until the assimilation of the language group made separate organizations unnecessary. A detailed discussion of German-American unionism would go far beyond the scope of this survey, but the important influence of German language branches in Central Labor Federations of the major Northern and Midwestern cities and later in the American Federation of Labor (AFL) should at least be kept in mind.

Few forty-eighters moved beyond the confines of the major political parties after the war to participate in the budding socialist movement among German immigrants. Weitling had long since withdrawn from politics, and Weydemeyer, who became a Union officer and was placed in command of St. Louis, died of cholera in 1866. However, in 1867, the New York Kommunisten-Klub -- originally established in 1857 -- was reorganized in hopes of being able to carry on its goals as an educational society.[65] It required that all its members "strive to abolish the bourgeois property system," and sought, as it set forth in its Statutes,

> by any means it might consider appropriate, by private conversation, public meetings, correspondence with American and European communists, the circulation of appropriate newspapers and books, to spread propaganda for its objectives. (66)

Members of this club and of the <u>Allgemeiner</u> <u>Deutscher</u> <u>Arbeiterverein</u>, a Lassallean group in New York which also functioned as an educational society,[67] united in 1869 to become a local of the National Labor Union and Section 1 of the First International (International Workingmen's Association -- IWA) in the United States.

The IWA had been founded by British and French labor groups in London in 1864 as a broad-based organization which promoted international cooperation between workers on economic and political issues. By the time the first sections were established in the United States, it had become a respected and feared power in Europe, and was widely believed to be the power behind the upheaval of the Paris Commune -- which Friedrich Engels described as its "great success:" "The Commune ... was beyond doubt the child of the International intellectually, though the international did not lift a finger to produce it."[68] Events in Paris and large anti-war demonstrations sponsored by Internationalists and freethinkers in New York[69] caused the American press to take note of the International, which it often did in nativistic, paranoiac terms, estimating its size (never more than 5000 members in America) from one to seven million. Thus, the New York <u>Journal</u> <u>of</u> <u>Commerce</u> stated that the "communism" of the International appealed only to "men of foreign birth"[70] in America, and Carl Schurz traced its origins to Sicily, implying a connection with organized crime.[71]

But the charge of appealing only to "foreigners" was leveled against the German-American Internationalists from quite another quarter when they organized a Central Committee with Friedrich Sorge as Corresponding Secretary for the United States in 1871, from Marx and the General Council of the International in London. In their opinion, the almost exclusively German North American Federation consisted of "no branches of U.S. workmen ... but only branches formed by Foreigners residing in the U.S."[72] Sorge disagreed vehemently with this, and his reply highlights the particular problems facing those who sought to unify such a diverse, heterogeneous working class:

> Workingmen from other countries arriving here do not come with the intention of residing but temporarily here; they are in nowise regarded as <u>foreigners</u> or simple residents, but as citizens, the only distinction being made by calling them sometimes adopted citizens; ... they form an important and considerable part of this country's Trades Unions & Labor Societies ... whilst some of the most powerful and best Trades organizations in the U.S. consist almost exclusively of socalled 'Foreigners,' viz. the Miners and Laborers Benevolent Association, the Cigarmakers International Union, the Cabinetmakers Societies, the Crispins, etc. etc. The term 'foreigner' therefore does not apply to us at all. (73)

While the importance of immigrant workers in trade unions cannot be overestimated, Sorge neglects two crucial problems here: nativist reaction and, perhaps more importantly at this time, the lack of cooperation of the German-dominated International with "native" American reform movements. Indeed, this latter source of conflict was to spell the death of the International in the United States after it fell apart into two irreconcilable factions -- German and American.

In 1872, at the Hague Congress of the International, Engels proposed that the seat of its General Council should be immediately transferred to New York to be beyond reach of the reaction in Europe after the downfall of the Paris Commune and to thwart the attempts of anarchists to gain a majority on the General Council. Friedrich Sorge became secretary of the General Council in New York, and from this time on, the United States was the only country in which the International was able to maintain an organized presence. In the United States, the International's influence was felt in the labor movement in two fields of activity: through its involvement with trade unions, particularly the National Labor Union, and by attempts to spread the principles of socialism through educational, public activities, mainly among non-English-speaking immigrants. Accordingly, the International sponsored large workers' festivals in the New York area and demonstrations in support of the Paris Commune and French exiles. It established an official newspaper in New York, the (Neue) Arbeiter-Zeitung (1873-1875), which reached a circulation of 3000. Other papers which published official announcements of the International and which sometimes were fundamentally at odds with Sorge and the Central Committee were published by its German, French and English-speaking sections.[74] The International promoted the demand of the eight-hour day, and, in the face of widespread suffering brought about by the unprecedented depression of 1873, was prominent in rallying demonstrations of the unemployed in Chicago and New York. In the latter city, these demonstrations culminated in the brutal attack by police on 10,000 workers assembled at Tompkins Square on Jan. 13, 1874, which the New York Times lauded as the defeat of the foreign Communists.[75]

After the flurry of intensive organizing around the pressing problem of unemployment in 1873, the International rapidly declined. Early in 1874, it was reported as having only a few hundred members, and of its 23 sections, 16 were German, four French, two American, and one Scandinavian. For the last two years of its existence, the International was rent by internal dissent and struggles for control of the Neue Arbeiter-Zeitung -- to the point that Sorge offered to resign as General Secretary. To chronicle these hair-splitting disputes - so characteristic of political groups existing in a theoretical vacuum, removed from contact with the masses of people they claim to represent, and exacerbated here by the ethnic and language ghetto -- would add nothing of substance to the discussion of German-American socialism.[76] However, one controversy which transpired within the International in 1871-1872 and finally split it in two bears recounting because it highlights several inherent problems in the socialism of that day which German socialists continued to face in the United States and which, even today, are still burning issues.

If the conflict within the International in Europe had been between the anarchists grouped around Bakunin on one side and Marx and his adherents on the other, in the United States the conflict took the shape of a clash between the American Section 12 of Victoria Woodhull and the Germans around Sorge, between the promoters of women's rights, spiritualism and universalism on the American side and the defenders of working class hegemony in the International. Standing in the long tradition of American democratic reformism -- which contrasted sharply with the clash in Europe between monarchy and an increasingly assertive working class -- the Americans in Section 12 did not view the emancipation of labor as their primary, foremost goal, but integrated it into their platform of wide-ranging reforms, stressing women's rights. In a manifesto published in <u>Woodhull</u> & <u>Claflin's</u> <u>Weekly</u>, they defined the goal of the International as "the political equality and social freedom of man and woman alike" and "the establishment of an Universal Government, based primarily on equality of rights and reciprocity of duties in the matter of production and distribution of wealth."[77] The members of Section 12 clearly believed that the winning of equal rights for women was a prerequisite for any change in the balance of power between capital and labor, and Victoria Woodhull reiterated these tenets as Presidential candidate of the Equal Rights Party in 1872 (linking the oppression of women and Blacks, this party chose Frederick Douglass as her running mate). This emphasis on the "social question" to the neglect of trade union issues such as hours and wages antagonized German Internationalists who were quite deterministic in their economic outlook and who tended to have conservative views on family life, the place of women, and social propriety. In short, their views on women's rights can be characterized as embodying that "proletarian anti-feminism" which Werner Thönnessen has described in his study on women and German Social Democracy.[78] Relegating women's rights to the status of a "secondary contradiction," they thought that through the emancipation of the working class, women would also be emancipated automatically, and they rejected the necessity of a separate women's movement, giving it the ideological label of "bourgeois." Thus, with respect to women's suffrage, the leading German section of the International in New York stated programmatically: "The granting of the right to vote to women does not concern the interests of workers. It is the duty of the workers to include women in the social struggle to help to liberate the workers and with them all mankind."[79] And in a meeting of the same section, the American reformers were castigated by a prominent member, Friedrich Bolte, a cigarmaker who was indignant at their flaunting of "free love:"

> All this talk of theirs is folly, and we don't want their foolish notions credited as the views of this society [i.e. the International]. This nonsense which they talk of, female suffrage and free love, may do to consider in the future, but the question that interests us as workingmen is that of labor and wages. (80)

Such fundamental differences of opinion on whether the emancipation of women or of labor was the primary concern of the International could not coexist for long within the same organization, and late in 1871 the International divided into rival factions, each led by a Federal Council and each claiming legitimacy. Both appealed to the General Council in London for recognition. Marx sided with Sorge and the German sections, writing to Bolte that the allies of the American Section 12 were "full of follies and crotchets, such as currency quackery, false emancipation of women, and the like."[81] Finally, at the Hague Congress of the International in 1872,

Section 12 was expelled, and a rule introduced by Sorge was upheld that three-fourths of the membership of sections had to be wage workers. The International then entered upon an irreversible decline, undoubtedly caused in part by this dissension.[82]

The course and outcome of this confrontation were to prove typical of the intransigent attitude of many politically active German-American socialists in the next fifteen years. This was the most extensive debate of this period which took place between the advocates of an independent labor movement fashioned after the European model and native American reformers, and the result -- while a moral victory for those who stressed the primacy of working-class emancipation -- had the effect of consigning precisely these ideas to the ghetto of the German-speaking language group. This reflects a separation and insulation between the development of German-American socialism and contemporary trends in American society, namely, feminism and the continuing strain of agrarian radicalism, which was not only a matter of language differences, but also an expression of different traditions and interests. In all fairness to the German sections of the International and Sorge, it deserves to be stated that they participated in unions of mainly English-speaking workers (the National and International Labor Unions), while some of their successors did not even condescend to do that. Nevertheless, truly legitimate concern with issues of immediate import to labor usually was carried to the extreme of political sectarianism by the Germans. Their conservative outlook on social questions and their suspicion that these were merely "diversionary tactics" aimed at confusing the proletariat led them to refuse to participate in reform movements which had widespread support but which did not measure up to their standards, and a few years later, would lead them to expend enormous amounts of energy in running their own candidates in elections which they had no hopes for winning.

When Friedrich Sorge offered to resign as General Secretary of the International in 1874, Engels wrote him that with his resignation

> the old International is entirely wound up and at an end anyhow. And that is well. It belonged to the period of the Second Empire, when the oppression throughout Europe prescribed unity and abstention from all internal controversy for the labor movement, then just reawakening. ... Now its prestige is exhausted [in America] too, and any further effort to galvanize it into new life would be folly and a waste of energy. (83)

Two years later, about a dozen delegates representing the remnants of the organization which had once appeared to the bourgeoisie as a grave threat met in Philadelphia to conduct the final meeting of the International. Including Sorge, Otto Weydemeyer (the son of the forty-eighter), and August Otto-Walster as a representative of the German Social Democrats, this conference dissolved the IWA with a declaration of hope in the future of socialism:

Die Internationale ist tot! wird die Bourgeoisie aller Länder von neuem ausrufen, und mit Hohn und Freude wird sie die Beschlüsse der Konferenz als die dokumentierte Niederlage der internationalen Arbeiterbewegung in die Welt posaunen. ...

Die Genossen in Amerika geben Euch das Versprechen, dass auch sie die Errungenschaften der Internationalen dieses Landes wahren und pflegen werden. (84)

4. "STRIKERS, COMMUNISTS, TRAMPS AND DETECTIVES:" THE WORKING-MEN'S PARTY OF THE UNITED STATES, 1876-1877

The members of the International were not the only active German socialists in America during this period. At the same time, German immigrants influenced by the ideas of Ferdinand Lassalle, who had been connected with his Allgemeiner Deutscher Arbeiterverein (ADAV, founded 1863) or with the Eisenach party of August Bebel and Wilhelm Liebknecht, the Sozialdemokratische Arbeiterpartei (SDAP, founded 1869), were engaged in creating small parties after the German models, most importantly in New York and Chicago.[85] The Sozial-Demokratische Arbeiterpartei (Social Democratic Workingmen's Party), centered in New York, was founded in 1874 by Lassalleans who believed in the primacy of political action in establishing the "people's state" and who believed that trade unionism would be of no avail against the "iron law of wages." The official paper of this party, the Social-Demokrat (1874-1876), which took over its title from the earlier Lassallean paper in Berlin, had a circulation of 1500. Also founded in 1874, the Arbeiterpartei von Illinois (Workingmen's Party of Illinois) owed the impetus for its creation to the meetings of the unemployed held during the crisis of 1873. Although indebted to Lassalleanism, its program was a mixture of demands it thought likely to appeal to farmers and various reform groups, as well as industrial workers.[86] Its official organ, the Vorbote, began to appear in 1874 and was one of the longest-lived German-American socialist papers: going through many ideological metamorphoses, it survived until 1924.

In the two years after their founding, realizing their similarities, these parties discussed the possibility of merging. Also, after some abortive attempts at running candidates in local elections, experience was leading the Lassalleans within these parties to become less intransigent in their stand against trade unionism -- after all, unions in America had been able to make more significant gains and were much larger than in Germany -- and to become more receptive to cooperation with Internationalists who believed that these parties should abstain from such hopeless political activity for the time being. This continuing rapprochement, plus the impetus which came from the example of the unification of the Lassalleans and Eisenachers at Gotha in 1875, culminated in a Unity Congress of socialist organizations held in Philadelphia four days after the dissolution of the International, in July of the Centennial year, 1876. At this conference, the delegates completed the merging of four organizations: the Arbeiterpartei von Illinois (593 members) the Sozialdemokratische Arbeiterpartei (1500 members), the Sozialpolitischer Arbeiterverein of Cincinnati (250 members), and 635 former members of the International.[87] The new party was named the Arbeiterpartei der Vereinigten Staaten (Workingmen's Party of the U.S.A., WPUSA) and had a total of about 3000 members. Although headed by a native American, Phillip van Patten, the composition of the party was overwhelmingly German, as a few statistics will show: of 55 sections reported in October, 1876, 33 were German, 16 English-speaking, 4 Bohemian, 1 Scandinavian, and 1 French. A year later, only 23 of the 82 sections were English-speaking.[88] The WPUSA took over the press of its predecessors: the German papers were the Vorbote in Chicago and the New York Social-Demokrat, the latter edited by August Otto-Walster and renamed Arbeiter-Stimme (1876-1878), and the official organ for English-speaking workers was the Labor Standard, edited by J. P. McDonnell, an Irish socialist.[89]

This party is best known for its brief but spectacular prominence in the national railroad strike in the summer of 1877, when its St. Louis section virtually controlled the city for several days, giving rise to fears of an "American Commune" among industrialists and in the press.[90] This first nationwide strike ever was the climactic response to four years of economic depression. By 1877, as the historian Philip Foner states,

> three million workers were unemployed, and at least one fifth of the working class was permanently unemployed. Two-fifths worked no more than six to seven months in the year, and less than one fifth was regularly employed. (91)

The extreme severity of the depression meant that wages were drastically reduced and hours lengthened for those who were still employed: the wages of textile workers fell by 45%, those of furniture workers by 40-60%, those of railroad workers by 30-40%.[92] The real significance of these dry statistics was the misery caused by the sudden plummet in the standard of living, which led to widespread disillusionment with the American economic system: what the independent artisans of the antebellum period feared most had become indisputable reality. Accordingly, papers sympathetic to labor such as the Pittsburgh National Labor Tribune questioned the meaning of the Centennial celebration of freedom when industrialization appeared to be destroying all possibilities and hopes for self-sufficiency:

> The dreams have not been realized. ... The working people of this country ... suddenly find capital as rigid as an absolute monarch. ... Capital has now the same control over us that the aristocracy of England had at the time of the revolution. (93)

In some localities, strikers expressed their consciousness of these fundamental conflicts by proclamations and actions which went beyond immediate demands for economic redress, aiming at transforming structures of power.

The strike, which began in West Virginia on July 16, was at first a reaction of railroad workers to the announcement of still more wage cuts after four years of depression living. While some of them were organized in several unions at this time, the strike was not directed centrally or nationally, but spread spontaneously. Within a few days, 100,000 workers were on strike throughout the country, affecting most of the transportation system. In some cities, workers in other industries who had similar grievances joined the railroad workers in walking off the job and demanding higher wages and the eight-hour day. The strike was marked by violence and the use of militia, the National Guard and federal troops -- especially in Pittsburgh, where strikers burned railroad cars and the depot in retaliation for the

44

shooting of over twenty of their number. It was the use of force which finally ended the strike about ten to fourteen days after it had begun in different cities, and only limited gains were achieved.

In St. Louis, the nature of the strike as a social rebellion was most apparent, as it escalated here into the first general strike the country had known. Second only to Chicago as a Western railroad center, St. Louis felt the full brunt of the strike. Railroad workers in East St. Louis were soon joined by workers from other industries (the Germans being the largest foreign-language group), who all came together in nightly mass meetings of 10,000 or more, organized by an Executive Committee composed almost solely of members of the WPUSA. Accounting for about one-fourth of the national membership of the party, the St.Louis sections consisted of about 600 in the German, 200 in the English, 75 in the Bohemian, and 50 in the French.[94] Although it can in no way be maintained that the WPUSA instigated the strike, its members were able to persuade fellow unionists in other trades to join the railroad workers, and, through the Executive Committee, were able to direct the general strike for the eight-hour day and an end to child labor. On the night of July 25, after announcing at a mass meeting that the strike should continue until the workers could take over control of the government, the Executive Committee assumed effective control of the city, decreeing which economic activities would be allowed or forbidden. More factories were closed, but certain necessary services such as a flour mill were permitted to operate. But the mayor, fearing the power of what he described exaggeratedly as "30,000 armed socialists,"[95] had requested the aid of federal troops, and by July 28, the strike had been crushed by the St. Louis police, units of citizens' militia, and three companies of United States Infantry, and all the members of the Executive Committee had been arrested.[96] St. Louis newspapers proclaimed the end of the "first American Commune."[97]

This slogan was typical of a new wave of anti-radical nativism resulting from the sensational publicity given earlier to the Paris Commune, from the sudden violence of the railroad strikes, and from the involvement of the WPUSA, which was defamed in many accounts, along with the "Internationalists," as the sinister, guiding hand behind the national upheaval. If anti-radical nativism before the Civil War had been aimed against "radical republicans," it now assumed a distinctively modern aspect, for the threat to "American" institutions was now viewed as emanating from the uprising of labor, from the full-blown conflict between the interests of labor and capital in industrial society.[98] Many newspaper editorials in cities affected by the strike and even some book-length accounts and novels gave voice to this hostile point of view. Thus, Allan Pinkerton, head of the notorious detectives' agency which served practically as an employers' secret police and was instrumental in breaking this and other strikes, described in his book Strikers, Communists, Tramps and Detectives (1878) the link between events in Paris and America in the following way:

> The city [Paris] fell an easy prey to a horde of bad men, the worst
> of its vile elements, and human beings so devoid of all conscience,

45

pity, or consideration, that it is hard to look upon them as possessing
the least of human attributes. But this is the class, the world over,
who are at the bottom of all troubles of a communistic nature. They
were the _real_ cause of the great strikes of '77, and their prompt and
utter extermination, in this and all other countries, is the only method
of removing a constant menace and peril to government and society.
...
When bloodshed was stopped in Paris, many of that city's Commune
sought refuge in the United States, and from that day to the present,
journals in various parts of this country have circulated their peculiar
views. It is certain that their societies have been gradually increasing,
and that in the mobocratic spirit, the outrage and pillage of July 1877,
are plainly seen the outcroppings of this foreign-born element. (99)

The National Republican of Washington, D. C. editorialized on the "American Commune," saying that it was "manifest that communistic ideas are very widely enter-
tained in America by the workmen employed in mines and factories and by the
railroads. This poison was introduced into our social system by European laborers."[100] The New York Times simply announced on July 25: "The City in Pos-
session of Communists,"[101] and the New York Herald railed against foreign dem-
agogues who "have imported ideas and sentiments which have repeatedly deluged
France in blood. The railroad riots ... were instigated by men incapable of understanding our ideas and principles."[102] The Chicago Tribune, in condemnation of
events to the south, wrote: "The cool audacity and impudent effrontery of the Communists have nowhere shown so conspicuously as in St. Louis," and the Chicago
Inter-Ocean, reporting on events in its own city in an article with the headline
"Women's Warfare: Bohemian Amazons Rival The Men In Deeds of Violence,"
chronicled "this curious repetition of the scenes of the Paris Commune." The
Philadelphia Ledger also made the association with foreign communists, asserting
that "when the whole history of the uprising comes to be known, it will be found
that the secret inspiration of it will be discovered in the famous International Society, which played such havoc in Paris when they had the upper hand there."[103]
But it is Pinkerton again who represents perhaps the most paranoid expression of
fear of the involvement of the "International" in the strike (and this fear is skill-
fully manipulated in his book to justify the need for a repressive agency like his
own):

> On every railroad that was held by lawless men, in every city where
> violence reigned, and through every excited assemblage where law
> had been trampled under foot, this accursed thing [the International]
> came to the surface. If its members did not actually inaugurate the
> strikes, the strikes were the direct result of the communistic spirit
> spread through the ranks of railroad employees by communistic
> leaders and their teachings. When they were fairly begun, the com-
> munists commenced to grow bold and defiant, and showed their hands;
> and when the strikes were well under way, every act of lawlessness
> that was done was committed by them. They held an undeniable and

easily defined relation to every instance of outrage, and they are unqualifiedly responsible for the millions of dollars in property destroyed, and the hundreds of lives sacrificed. They are a class of
human hyenas worthy of all notice and attention. (104)

Through these and similar attacks, therefore, some sectors of public opinion were
able to denounce the strikers and dismiss their demands as the fabrications of
"foreign" radicals and workers who deserved whatever fate they might receive at
the hands of "American" armed authorities.

In spite of the notice excited by foreign radicals, however, the short duration of
the strike and the relatively swift restoration of the status quo encouraged other
voices of public opinion to take a more benevolent view and recognize the grievances which led to the strike as at least partly legitimate and as arising from
conflicts caused by rapid industrialization. It seems that the prevailing opinion
shortly after the cessation of violence was one of self-confidence: that the nation
was too secure to be threatened by temporary crises, and that ways could be
found -- whether welfare measures or techniques of repression such as the black
list -- to pacify and integrate the working class.[105] Thus, there was no attempt
to suppress the WPUSA, as might possibly have been expected. In this regard, it
seems that the language barrier, which caused the socialists so many headaches,
also gave them paradoxically a certain kind of Narrenfreiheit. It both hindered them
from entering into public political debate and increased their freedom from super-
vision and control. Therefore, in spite of the brief panic, the major virulent manifestations of anti-radical nativism were yet to come.

In the months immediately following the strike, dissatisfied with the limited gains reached through their efforts, the advocates of independent political action became more vocal within the WPUSA, and ran candidates in several cities around the country in the fall elections. In a few races, the labor party met with surprising success: for example, it polled two-thirds of the vote in Louisville to elect five out of seven representatives to the state legislature.[106] However, many of the former Internationalists, including Sorge and Otto Weydemeyer, believed that this political involvement was quite premature, and so when they turned their efforts toward the International Labor Union, the party which they left placed primary emphasis for the time being on participating in elections rather than on trade unionism. In December of 1877, at its convention in Newark, the WPUSA changed its name to Sozialistische Arbeiterpartei (SAP, or Socialist Labor Party, SLP), and it was this organization, along with the anarchists' "Black International," which attracted German-American socialists throughout the next decade.

Broadly speaking, then, there were three directions in German-American socialism which evolved as responses to the experience of the 1877 strike: those socialists who advocated political participation, those who continued to emphasize rebuilding the trade unions, and those who believed that only violent confrontation could overthrow a system whose brutality had become so manifest in repressing the strikers. The labels affixed to these three trends by many labor historians -- "Lassallean," "Marxist," and "anarchist" -- while accurate in some respects, tend to imply that these radical German immigrants simply held fast to inflexible doctrines learned in Europe, and that there were precise, clear divisions with respect to both ideology and practice between the three groups. However, if we begin to analyze their real, daily political involvement within the larger labor movement and their own ethnic group, a different, more complex picture emerges which suggests that they were arriving at varying strategies because of conflicting interpretations of the American experience, and this, in turn, has implications for understanding why socialism developed as it did in the United States.

Concretely, then, the SAP's attempt to establish a viable socialist movement in the United States centered around several areas of activity: around elections, trade unions, its press and the distribution of socialist publications, and, existing on the fringes of the party and not recognized officially by it, a vital subculture. On the other hand, it also undertook projects to provide publicity and material support for the Social Democratic Party in Germany. The forms all these spheres of activity took were decisively shaped by the German composition of the party. It has been estimated that during the first twenty years of its existence, an average of 80% of the members of the SAP were native Germans. In 1891, fifteen years after its founding, 88 of 100 sections were German, the next largest group was composed of Jewish socialists, and the number of native Americans was miniscule.[107] Indeed, this state of affairs led contemporaries and some historians to describe the SAP as a "German colony" in New York, where the bulk of its members lived.

The most deleterious effect of the foreign-language makeup of the SAP was on the party's attempts to participate in elections. After a few local successes in 1878 (still riding on the popularity of the WPUSA after the railroad strike), the SAP continued to enter its candidates in local, and beginning in 1892, even in national, Presidential elections -- its most extensive slate, including many naturalized Germans, was always in New York[108] -- but the fact that its membership was overwhelmingly non-English-speaking was an insurmountable obstacle. Plagued with the problem of effectively reaching English-speaking voters and other language groups, the party's success at the ballot box was prevented among other things by this exclusivity and the consequent difficulty of entering into public debate, and by the widespread feeling (running throughout American politics) that a vote for a tiny third party was a wasted vote. In spite of the insuperable difficulties encountered in running its own candidates, however, the SAP generally did not pursue the alternative strategy of entering into coalitions with other progressive third parties which were attracting more English-speaking workers, as a means of reaching beyond the German ethnic group. Aside from quite limited cooperation with the Greenback-Labor Party in 1880[109] and more enthusiastic involvement with the United Labor Party in New York City in 1886, the SAP was opposed to such alliances. In the interests of "Reinhaltung der Partei,"[110] from which they undoubtedly derived a certain sense of legitimacy and will to carry on, these socialists consciously narrowed their field of political influence. Specifically, they did not integrate into their economic theory and their concrete practice the indigenous tradition of agrarian radicalism which had coalesced with labor in some areas, just as the Germans of the First International had pulled away from the National Labor Union when it began to be dominated by agrarian reformers championing Edward Kellogg's system of currency reform.[111] In a pamphlet written for English-speaking workers entitled Socialism and the Worker, Friedrich Sorge had already argued in 1876 against farmer-labor alliances in the same fashion that he and other Internationalists refused to consider specific issues of women's rights, stating that "whoever works for a living has the same interests that the wages-laborer has, and should assist the latter in his struggle for the right of labor against the encroachments of capital."[112] This pattern was to continue in the SAP for the following twenty years until the 1890's, when, even though its American membership was increasing, the party officially opposed cooperation with the Populist farmers' movement and suspended party sections which violated this constitutional decree. Writing in 1896, the well-known journalist and Populist Henry Demarest Lloyd criticized the SAP as doctrinaire and "foreign," saying that

> At this moment the most distracted and helpless body of political radicalism in the world is, perhaps, that which in the United States has no place to lay its head. ... Our Socialist Labour Party, of German Marxians, has never taken hold of the Americans and never will. (113)

With respect to their failures at electoral politics in spite of their energetic, tenacious commitment, this is an accurate, if harsh assessment of the SAP of the "German Marxians" in the first twenty years of its existence. Measured according to the standard of electoral gains, therefore, the political achievements of this party were minimal, indeed.

In 1881 the National Executive Committee of the SAP proudly reported that "in almost all the industrial towns of the nation" trade unions were headed by socialists.[114] While some room for exaggeration must of course be taken into account, German-American socialists could rightly take credit for more successes in union organizing than in the area of electoral politics. Again, it is important to draw the distinction here between the theoretical positions of "Lassalleans" and "Marxists" and the concrete efforts of party members and sympathizers within the unions. As the historian Hartmut Keil has shown, even though many socialists questioned the limited goals of trade unionism, both groups recognized the necessity for strong unions in the 1880's, and accordingly they joined and founded unions of skilled workers and attempted to carry out education towards more long-range perspectives. According to Keil, in New York City, the city with the largest number of organized German workers, "every German union and almost every other union with a predominantly German membership or a strong minority of Germans was founded by socialists who also held key positions in those unions. Examples are the furniture workers, the German-American Typographical Union, the Bakers, Brewers, and Cigarmakers."[115] These German unions formed a central trade council, the Vereinigte deutsche Gewerkschaften, which was represented in the Central Labor Union (CLU) of New York City -- in 1886 the largest central labor federation in the country with 207 unions and 150,000 members representing many different language groups.[116] The CLU did not immediately throw its weight behind candidates for city office upon its founding in 1882, but four years later its members were the main source of organizational and material support for the United Labor Party and its mayoral candidate, Henry George. The influence of socialist-oriented, German-speaking unions in this turn towards politics is described as follows in the autobiography of Abraham Cahan, prominent SAP member and editor of the socialist Yiddish newspaper, the Jewish Daily Forward:

> The realization spread that the political struggle was as essential as the economic struggle. Even the native workers were moved by the spirit of class struggle. But only the German delegates to the CLU understood what had to be the ultimate, socialist goal of that struggle. (117)

German unions in New York also initiated the organization of national unions: for example, the furniture workers and bakers.

What circumstances made it possible for German workers to be so well-organized into unions at this time? The answer must be sought in the character of the German working class population of New York City, and seen in the context of steadily increasing immigration from Germany which reached its peak in 1882. As Keil has outlined, there were three characteristics of German immigrant workers which fundamentally influenced the course of development of the union and socialist organizations. First, the majority were skilled and artisan, from the industrial centers of Germany, and therefore -- in the American context of a division of labor along ethnic lines -- they predominated in occupations such as bakers, brewers, butchers, furniture workers, piano makers and cigar makers. The factor of a common language furthered organization in trades such as these, although obviously it was a hindrance in other ways. Second, many had experience in the workers' movement in Germany and continued unabatedly to carry on their organizing activities in the United States. Finally, their familiarity with the tradition of German Social Democracy led them to question the limited goals of American unionism and sometimes even to found alternative unions. This socialist orientation was intensified after 1878 with the arrival of Social Democrats who had been exiled under Bismarck's Anti-Socialist Laws and who concentrated in the New York area. Consequently, it can be maintained that the high level of trade union organization among German workers in New York resulted from the nature of their work in the skilled trades and from their socialist perspectives and experience. If we study the involvement of German-American socialists with unionism, it becomes clear that this was one area of activity in which they effectively concentrated their efforts on bettering American conditions -- though focusing on their own language group -- and thus that in this sense they broke through the boundaries of existence as a "German colony."

The foreign-language makeup of the party also determined the nature of its publications and public forums, and the sort of press it was able to support. Despite repeated attempts, the SAP was unable to sustain an English-language paper until after 1890, when Daniel DeLeon became editor of The People. However, as a compensation, its German-language press thrived, and the editors of these papers were among the most articulate and influential of German-American socialists. Reflecting the weak national organization of the party and the fact that in some states such as New York it was illegal for a political party to own and publish a newspaper, [118] the papers in various cities which were sympathetic to the SAP were privately owned by organizations such as the Socialistic Co-operative Publishing Association of New York. These papers, which were designated as official organs of the party, meaning that they published all its reports, announcements and correspondence, were concentrated in New York and included, most importantly, the New York Volkszeitung (published from 1878-1932, with a circulation of 8000 in 1878 and 19,000 in 1890, and edited by the well-known New York socialists Alexander Jonas, Adolf Douai, Sergius Schewitsch and Hermann Schlüter) and its weekly edition, the Vorwärts (1877-1932). Both of these papers transferred their affiliation to the Socialist Party after 1901. Other German papers affiliated with the SAP at this time included the New York Sozialist (published from 1885-1892 and edited by the playwright and poet Wilhelm L. Rosenberg and for a short time in 1885 by the worker-philosopher Joseph Dietzgen, this paper provides a goldmine of information on local party sections around the country), and the St. Louis Volksstimme des Westens (1877-1880, edited by the former Eisenacher August Otto-Walster, socialist novelist and writer of plays for workers' theaters). The SAP also received support and publicity from many German-language papers which were official organs of central federations of trade unions, such as the Philadelphia Tageblatt (1877-1944). In Chicago, where the Social-Revolutionary movement grew rapidly early in the 1880's, the SAP did not maintain an official paper, but reports on its activities could be found in the independent Arbeiter-Zeitung and its Sunday (Fakkel) and weekly (Vorbote) editions. The importance attached by the SAP to the building up of a party press can be seen from the lengthy discussions of its publications at the biennial or triennial party conventions. At these national meetings, the party not only encouraged the fastest possible growth of daily and weekly newspapers in various languages, but also emphasized the necessity of massive distribution of pamphlets in German and English to familiarize workers with socialist theories. As would be expected, they were more successful with the German brochures, which included among other things short works by Lassalle, Marx, Liebknecht, Sorge, and Volkszeitung editors Douai and Jonas on the fundamental principles of socialism. In 1885, the party reported that 160,000 pamphlets had been distributed in the preceding two years, and shortly thereafter it founded its own publishing firm and center for literature distribution, the New York Labor News Company. Already by 1883, the National Executive Committee had admitted that so far the SAP was chiefly a "propagandistic" party,[119] but in 1885 this was assessed positively as precisely the party's strength:

> Der Fortschritt des Sozialismus in den Vereinigten Staaten beschränkt sich nicht auf die direkten Erfolge der Sozialistischen Arbeiter-Partei. Wenn in Hunderten von Arbeitervereinen sozialistische Ideen sich einbürgern, wenn in 100 Arbeiterzeitungen sozialistische Forderungen verfochten werden, wenn ein allmählicher Umschwung der Volksmeinung zugunsten des Sozialismus unverkennbar ist; so ist das, abgesehen von der Logik der ökonomischen Entwicklung, ein Verdienst der hartnäckigen Agitation der Sozialistischen Arbeiter-Partei. (120)

While the creation of an independent socialist press was certainly of inestimable value to the labor movement, it should also be seen in the context of providing alternative forums and means of communication within the German ethnic group. No more bitter enemies were to be found than the socialist papers and well-established German "bourgeois" papers such as the New York Staatszeitung (with a circulation of 50,000 in 1880) and the Illinois Staatszeitung (with a circulation of 8400 in 1880). On the level of content, the socialist papers provided information on local, national, and international events of interest to labor, as well as scientific, historical and literary columns reflecting a perspective not to be found elsewhere. On the level of editorial policy, of course, the socialist and bourgeois press often took diametrically opposed stands on concrete issues facing the German-American community, for example, on support for strikes, endorsements for political candidates, or social welfare measures. The division of the ethnic community into classes is nowhere more clearly reflected than in the wide range of differing, clashing standpoints voiced through its press. This may seem like an obvious fact, but it is worth stating because it has been the general tendency in the field of German-American studies to conceal this diversity in favor of a distorted, one-dimensional picture of a unified, harmonious (read: conservative) ethnic group.

On Dec. 1, 1878, it was reported in the <u>Christian Union</u>, edited by the flashy former abolitionist, now anti-labor orator Henry Ward Beecher, that

> Several more expulsions of Socialists have been ordered by the German government. So it ought to be. We advise the American people to make certain that none of these expelled Socialists are welcomed in this country where they will spread their poisonous virus. (121)

This editorial was reprinted in the <u>New York Tribune</u> (owned by railroad magnate and "robber baron" Jay Gould, one of the chief targets of the 1877 strike), which went on to call for the expulsion of German socialists already in the United States.[122] However, in spite of these hostile voices, New York City remained the preferred point of destination for many Germans who fell under the ban of the <u>Sozialistengesetze.</u> In the period from 1878-1890, the activities which the SAP undertook to provide publicity and material support for the German Social Democratic Party (SPD) centered around resistance to the Anti-Socialist Laws, beginning with protest meetings around the country in January, 1879, which focused on the German situation and the danger of repression (termed "Bismarckism") in America after the use of the army and militia in the 1877 strike.[123] This was the concrete manner in which both the party's internationalism and its orientation towards the German political scene were expressed.

Just as socialists -- many of them German and French political exiles -- living in America had earlier raised money and provided other aid for Communards fleeing the reaction in Paris (or deported to the French penal colonies), German socialists and unionists in New York immediately formed support committees as soon as exiles began to arrive.[124] These committees, which appear to have been most active in the years 1878-1882, collected and distributed money among the exiles, tried to help them finance the immigration of their families, and also attempted to secure them jobs. The limited resources of the SAP made these tasks quite difficult, and it warned against massive immigration to the United States, while recognizing that individuals often had no alternative since they no longer had any possibility of employment in Germany.[125]

In addition to the help it gave individuals, the SAP also contributed directly to the SPD by raising money for its <u>Reichstag</u> election fund (more than ℳ 4000 in 1885 and more than 40,000 M. in 1887)[126] and for its press, by sponsoring events such as large concerts and fairs with the proceeds going to the SPD, by encouraging members to collect contributions, and by sponsoring tours of several prominent German Social Democrats. At its Wyden Convention in 1880 the SPD had decided to send a deputation to the United States to inform German-American workers of the plight of the SPD and to collect funds for the approaching <u>Reichstag</u> election. The first such tour took place in the spring of 1881, when <u>Reichstag</u> deputies Friedrich Wilhelm Fritzsche and Louis Viereck (who later were expelled from Berlin and Leipzig respectively under the <u>Kleiner Belagerungszustand</u> and immigrated to the United States) spoke in New York and other major cities.[127] In a leaflet which was

forbidden to be distributed in Germany, the deputies addressed their "Gesinnungsgenossen" in America on the purpose of their visit:

> Da man uns verhindert, die Mittel zu [dem Kampf gegen diese gewalt-
> tätige Politik] in Deutschland selbst aufzubringen, sind wir zu Euch
> gekommen, geleitet von der Ueberzeugung, dass Ihr nicht weniger
> Liebe haben könnt zur Freiheit des Volkes, dem Ihr selber entstammt,
> dass Ihr nicht geringere Opferfähigkeit besitzt, als dem gleichfalls
> geknechteten und um seine Befreiung ringenden Irland von seinen
> fern von der Heimath lebenden Söhnen dargebracht wird. [This refers
> to the Irish Fenians in New York who were working for Ireland's in-
> dependence]. (128)

They were successful enough that the President of the Berlin police, Guido von
Madai, after predicting their failure, found it worthwhile to include a report of
their tour in his semiannual secret report on the progress of the international socialist movement. Here he painted a picture of the willingness of German socialists
living in America to give moral and financial support at every opportunity to the
movement in Germany, as was demonstrated by the warm and enthusiastic reception given to the two deputies.[129]

In the fall of 1886, also speaking under the auspices of the SAP, Wilhelm Liebknecht, Eleanor Marx Aveling and Edward Aveling traveled through the United
States, speaking to large audiences in over forty cities from Sept. 27 to Dec. 19.[130]
Minister of the Interior Robert von Puttkamer had suggested to Bismarck that Liebknecht would probably be more explicit and open about the plans and the organizational state of the SPD in America than he could be in Germany and consequently
recommended that a spy from Pinkerton's Detective Agency be hired to shadow
him. Based on reports from the detective who followed Liebknecht through more
than two dozen cities, the Berlin Police Headquarters composed a detailed report
on his speeches, covering topics such as the situation of the party in Germany, its
goals and strategy, and the American scene.[131] Similarly, the German chargé d'af-
faires in Washington reported to Bismarck on the tenor of a speech given at a mass
meeting of over 5000 in New York, writing from his own perspective that Liebknecht

> erging ... sich ... in heftigen Schmähungen gegen deutsche Zustände
> und die Politik der kaiserlichen Regierung und fühlte sich anderer-
> seits bewogen, eine Lanze für die zum Tode verurteilten Chicagoer
> Anarchisten zu brechen. (132)

Not only did Liebknecht defend the Haymarket anarchists as victims of class jus-
tice (while insisting on the distinction between socialism and anarchism), he and
his traveling companions also visited them in their prison cells in Chicago, as the
Avelings described in their book on their American journey, The Working Class
Movement in America (1888).[133] From these reports and from articles in the
German-American and English language press, which stress the publicity sur-

rounding this tour and its impact on audiences, it becomes evident that the speeches were a source of educational and political impulses for socialists in the United States, as well as a means of raising money for the SPD and its press. While the SAP was able to send 16,000 M. collected during the tour to the Zürich Sozial-Demokrat -- over half of its needed operating expenses[134] -- the dissemination of socialist ideas was also furthered in America. Therefore, the activities aimed at financial support for the German party were also beneficial in the actual political context of the country the exiles had chosen.

There was one other way -- perhaps less successful than supplying funds, but nevertheless significant -- in which the SAP and other exiled socialists attempted to strengthen the movement in Europe and counteract the decrees of the Anti-Socialist Laws: through smuggling into Germany copies of German socialist publications printed in the United States. Already on October 25, 1878, a week after the passage of the Sozialistengesetz, in an editorial captioned "Es lebe der Sozialismus," the New York Volkszeitung vowed to resist the German "Gewaltherrschaft" in this manner:

> Die Agitation wird im Geheimen fortgeführt werden; was in Deutschland nicht gedruckt werden kann, wird im Auslande erscheinen ...
> Uns aber die wir noch im Besitz der Rede- und Pressfreiheit sind, erwächst aus der Knechtung der deutschen Presse die heilige Pflicht, mit verdoppelter Energie die Grundsätze unserer Lehre zu verbreiten und in unserer Mitte dem geächteten Gedanken Deutschlands ein Heim zu schaffen.
> Heute schon rufen wir unseren Genossen zu: Alles, was vor der Knute Eurer 'Liberalen' nicht sicher ist, schick es nur zu uns herüber. Hier wird Eure Stimme frei erklingen und wir bürgen dafür, dass Alles was Ihr hier redet oder druckt, jeder Bericht, den Ihr uns einschickt, dass Alles dies auf Tausenden, den Argusaugen Eurer Polizei unbekannten Wegen nach Deutschland gebracht und daselbst in Hunderttausenden von Exemplaren verbreitet werden soll.
> Sozialisten, Proletarier aller Länder! Die Reaktionäre haben Euch oft mit der tausendköpfigen Hydra verglichen. Beweise jetzt, dass sie recht haben! Beweist jetzt, dass der Sozialismus tausendköpfig und doch von einem Gedanken beseelt ist; dass jeder Versuch einen Kopf abzuschlagen, nur den Erfolg haben wird, dass Tausend andere Köpfe sich drohend erheben! (135)

It is difficult to ascertain how well the German-American socialists were able to keep their promise. One of the few contemporary reports, that of Berlin Police President von Richthofen (1889), states that few copies of foreign social-democratic newspapers such as the New York Volkszeitung came into Germany.[136] In 1885, Police President von Madai maintained that 4500 copies of Johann Most's New York anarchist paper, Freiheit, were mailed to Germany biweekly.[137] Nevertheless, the list of proscribed periodical and non-periodical publications from the United States reads like a catalog of all the major and many of the obscure German-American socialist newspapers, books and pamphlets.[138] To survey some of this printed matter which was prohibited from crossing the borders of Germany: it included newspapers such as the Chicago Arbeiter-Zeitung and Fackel, the New York Volkszeitung, Most's Freiheit, the Philadelphia Tageblatt and at least two Czech papers, books on politics and economics, such as a New York edition of Lassalle's collected works and several pamphlets by Most, official publications of the SAP, and a few volumes of poetry and plays.

Leaving aside the matter of a socialist subculture for the moment, this brief survey of the main activities of the German-American socialists of the SAP clearly cannot provide as yet a definitive statement on the extent to which they were really responding to American events and conditions or merely preserving and clinging to theories which they were unable to connect with concrete interests and goals. At this point it can only be said that their strategies were a contradictory interweaving of both tendencies, made more complex by the isolation of the foreign language ethnic group, which nevertheless had common interests with the working class as a whole, the pronounced local character the socialist movement had in a country where distances were great and centralized direction was weak or lacking altogether until much later, and the exile situation of many active socialists, which sometimes led them to become preoccupied with events in Germany and sometimes pushed them into the most extreme stances.

6. SOCIAL-REVOLUTIONARIES AND ANARCHISTS, 1877-1886

The third trend in German-American radicalism which developed after the 1877 strike centered in Chicago and has been loosely termed "anarchist," though it called itself "sozial-revolutionär." Disillusioned by the decline in votes suffered by the SAP after 1878 and by attempts of corrupt politicians in Chicago to prevent legally elected socialists from assuming office, many members of the SAP began to have serious doubts about the official strategy of participating in electoral politics. The other source of dissension within the party which led to the development of a separate Social-Revolutionary movement was differences of opinion over the use of force in the labor movement. Already as early as 1875, a "Lehr- und Wehr- verein" (Educational and Defense Society) had been formed in Chicago, but it was the brutal treatment of workers by police and militia during the 1877 national strike which spurred on the growth of these societies of armed workers in Chicago and other cities around the country. The self-defense movement spread primarily among Germans: outside of Chicago after 1884, there were armed groups in De- troit, Cincinnati, St. Louis (2), Omaha, Newark, New York (2), San Francisco, Denver, and other cities.[139] In Chicago, uniformed workers marched in demonstra- tions with shouldered rifles until a state militia bill and the Haymarket affair put an end to this form of resistance. When these societies first sprang up, most members of the SAP appeared to believe that they were necessary to defend workers' consti- tutional rights. At an 1878 festival in Chicago to raise money for rifles and a library of military writings for one armed group of 450 men, attended by 8-10,000 peo- ple, one of their most ardent defenders, Gustav Lyser, stated their purpose:

> Der Lehr- und Wehrverein will die Press-, Rede- und Versammlungs-
> freiheit schützen, er will die Rechte hoch halten, welche uns die Con-
> stitution gewährt. ... Er lehrt seine Mitglieder, welche Pflichten sie
> dem Staate gegenüber zu erfüllen haben, welche Verpflichtungen aber
> auch der Staat seinen Bürgern gegenüber nie ausser Acht lassen
> soll. (140)

Similarly, the New York Volkszeitung, official organ of the SAP, while urging work- ers to be patient and adopt peaceful means of propaganda, nevertheless supported the "Lehr- und Wehrvereine" as a counterbalance to the citizens' militia, which enlisted few workers, and as an expression of the constitutional right to bear arms, stating:

> Sie zu entwaffnen, hat der Staat kein Recht, und einen Missbrauch von
> ihren Waffen zu machen, das wird den Lehr- und Wehrvereinen nicht
> einfallen. ... Welche wahnsinnige Furcht doch der Geldsack vor den
> Arbeitern hat! Man sollte meinen, wir lebten in Europa! (141)

However, soon the SAP's National Executive Committee began to distance itself bruskly from what it thought to be the confrontational, extremist tactics of the armed organizations, and late in 1878 it ordered party members to withdraw from them. The German socialist press in Chicago, the Vorbote and Arbeiter-Zeitung, which were independent of party affiliation, polemicized against this decree, and soon members and even whole sections were leaving the SAP. The first formal break over the issue of force came with the withdrawal of a group of New York members in 1880, who then founded a "Sozial-Revolutionärer Club" -- subsequently, more such clubs appeared in Chicago and other cities. By 1883, membership in the SAP had dwindled to 1500 (it claimed 10,000 in 1878), while in 1885, at their peak, the Social-Revolutionaries numbered around 7000.

What was the ideological direction taken by these clubs, which for a few years were the largest organized body of German-American radicals? In discussing this, the focus will be on Chicago as the most prominent center of their activity. In 1881, at a congress in London, the International Working People's Association (IWPA) -- also known as the "Anarchist," or "Black" International -- was revived, and this was the international organization which the German-American Social-Revolutionaries affiliated with. In 1882, perhaps the most influential German anarchist of the time, Johann Most, arrived in the United States, immediately began issuing his paper Freiheit in New York (as he had done in London after his exile in 1878), and embarked on speaking tours which won many new members for local clubs of Social-Revolutionaries. Most, who had been a SPD deputy in the Reichstag, had been imprisoned several times in Germany, and once in exile, turned towards communist anarchism and the "Propaganda der Tat" in ever more extreme fashion after his expulsion from the SPD in 1880.[142] The high point of his influence on German-American radicalism was 1882/3, when the Social-Revolutionary groups were expanding, but he continued to publish Freiheit, as well as pamphlets such as Die Eigenthumsbestie, until his death in Cincinnati in 1906. His encouragement of violent acts caused him to be jailed several times in New York, for printing instructions on the manufacture of dynamite and for praising in writing the assassin of President McKinley. This extreme standpoint was characteristic of only a few of the Social-Revolutionaries, however, most clearly of the club in New York, which was also a main source of financial support for Freiheit.

In 1883, Social-Revolutionaries held a national congress in Pittsburgh and issued their program as the Pittsburgh Manifesto, "to the Workingmen of America."[143] Written by Most along with the future Haymarket martyrs Albert Parsons and August Spies among others, this statement of principles was no different from that of the socialists in its analysis of capital, surplus value, crises and the exploitation of workers, but it incorporated the views of the London Conference with respect to force, viewing its utilization as necessary and unavoidable in the revolutionary movement to establish a new social order. By "force," the Manifesto meant the arming of workers in bodies such as the "Lehr- und Wehrvereine," however, there were some delegates, like Most, who encouraged individual terrorist acts. Also, while the delegates unanimously rejected participation in elections, a resolution introduced by representatives of the IWPA from Chicago was passed -- though opposed by Most and his supporters -- which called for taking part in trade union organizing. This proposal accorded with the real connections between the IWPA and the German working class in Chicago: it was very influential there within the

Central Labor Union, a central federation representing about 12,000 workers in 1885 and composed of unions with a high percentage of foreign-born members with radical leanings.[144] The Manifesto of the "Black" International in the United States which was welded together in Pittsburgh was, therefore, a non-synthesized program for revolutionary action which reflected uncertainty and disagreement over the strategy and ultimate goals of socialism and anarchism, and which, in keeping with its anti-authoritarian spirit, invested local sections with full autonomy. The only centralization deemed necessary was the creation of a National Information Bureau in Chicago and the designation of certain newspapers, including the Chicago Arbeiter-Zeitung, Fackel, Vorbote and Alarm (English) and Most's Freiheit as official publications.[145]

Seen in the larger context of the contemporary United States labor movement, the Social-Revolutionaries represented one of the most radical tendencies within the greatest concerted upheaval the country had yet known. The meteoric rise of the quasi-secret Knights of Labor during the depression of 1882-6 (from 40,000 members to over 700,000) and its successes in organizing skilled and unskilled workers across trade lines to win strikes reflected the growing discontent over 12 to 16 hour working days, low wages, and squalid living conditions.[146] In the midst of this upsurge, the Federation of Organized Trades and Labor Unions (later renamed the American Federation of Labor) recommended in 1884 that unions throughout the country go on strike for the eight-hour day on May 1, 1886. During the two years following this resolution, preparations were made for a general strike, and in Chicago, where the IWPA was thriving, its members and press entered unreservedly into the organizing effort after some debate over its revolutionary potential. As in New York, German radical workers were particularly influential in the Central Labor Union, including cigarmakers, butchers, metal workers, painters, printers and cabinetmakers. On May 1, 1886 (the first May Day) and the days following, when 350,000 workers across the country went on strike, Chicago, with 80,000 strikers and participants, could boast the largest number of any industrial center, [147] certainly thanks in part to the extensive efforts of its IWPA sections. And the strike achieved a significant measure of success: half of the workers gained the eight-hour day and most of the rest secured varying reductions in hours.

The strike for eight hours continued in Chicago after May 1, and a lock-out was the response at the McCormick Harvester Factory. On May 3, police killed several striking workers who were trying to prevent strikebreakers from entering the factory. Labor leaders and Social-Revolutionaries, including August Spies, editor of the daily Arbeiter-Zeitung, Albert Parsons, editor of the English IWPA organ Alarm, and Samuel Fielden, called a protest meeting against the police brutality for the evening of May 4 at the Haymarket in downtown Chicago. Just as the peaceful meeting was coming to a close, a group of 176 armed policemen marched on the crowd, but before it could disperse a dynamite bomb was thrown into the ranks of the police, killing one and wounding many more. The police then began to shoot aimlessly, killing workers in the crowd and some of their own men. To this day it is not known who threw the bomb.

The hysteria which raged in Chicago and throughout the country was the first in the series of "Red Scares" -- with few exceptions, public opinion was united, in contrast to 1877 -- which enjoy such a long and virulent tradition in the United States. It was as though this one violent act was the breaking point for the strains which had intensified with the formation of a large immigrant working class and the vast expansion of factories and cities in the previous twenty years. The cry for "law and order" and the search for a scapegoat led to the arrest and harassment of hundreds of labor leaders, and since the German Social-Revolutionaries had been in the forefront of trade unionism in Chicago, they were singled out especially by the police. The Arbeiter-Zeitung was raided and shut down briefly, and six of the eight men who were finally charged with conspiracy and murder were German "anarchists." After a packed jury rendered the guilty verdict, an international defense movement formed to support appeals to the Federal and Supreme Courts, but the decision was upheld. On Nov. 11, 1887, Parsons, Spies, Georg Engel (owner of a toy store) and Adolf Fischer (a compositor for the Arbeiter-Zeitung) were hanged. Louis Lingg, a carpenter and member of the CLU, had committed suicide or been murdered by the police, and Samuel Fielden (a Methodist minister and construction worker), Michael Schwab (of the editorial staff of the Arbeiter-Zeitung) and Oskar Neebe (a tinsmith and union organizer) were sentenced to life in prison. It remained for John Altgeld, then Governor of Illinois, to state in his message of 1893 pardoning the three men that all eight had been the victims of a biased jury and of a "judge who conducted the trial with malicious ferocity."[148]

The reaction of the press to the bombing was to call indiscriminately for the suppressing of all varieties of radicalism -- whether anarchism, socialism or communism -- and to vilify their adherents as foreigners, particularly Germans, spreading alien doctrines and importing class warfare to the United States. Such tones had already resounded more and more frequently in the early eighties. For example, in reference to the Knights of Labor, the New York Times stated that the methods of the

> strikers and boycotters ... are entirely un-American, and show that
> those who employ them have no real conception of what American
> citizenship is or implies. They are all based upon some pretensions
> of exclusive privilege to persons of a particular class or members
> of a particular association. (149)

However, after the events in May 1886, such relatively calm criticism yielded to stereotyped portrayals of the radical immigrant and hysterical demands for vengeance. The Cleveland Leader wrote: "The anarchist wolf -- unwisely permitted to take up its abode and propagate its bloodthirsty species in this country -- has fastened its hideous and poisonous fangs in the body corporate of the American people."[150] The Philadelphia Press: "The stain of this bloody crime in Chicago does not rest upon any American name or inspiration. ... It springs rather from a pestilent brood of socialist vipers, ... the enemies of general society."[151] The Albany Law Journal: "[The anarchists are] a few long-haired, wild-eyed, bad-smelling, atheistic, reckless foreign wretches, who never did an honest hour's work in their lives, but who, driven half crazy with years of oppression and mad with envy of the rich, think to level society and its distinctions with a few bombs."[152] One final denouncement: "The enemy forces are not American, [but] rag-tag and bob-tail cutthroats of Beelzebub from the Rhine, the Danube, the Vistula and the Elbe."[153]

The pervasiveness of these condemnations in the industrial centers of the North-east and Midwest indicates that the Haymarket Affair was the most important im-petus to nativistic sentiments in the late 19th century. As the historian John Higham states, "nativism, as a significant force in modern America, dates from that labor upheaval."[154] From the urban workers, petty businessmen and clerks who revived several of the secret fraternal orders of the 1840's out of fear of competition from cheap immigrant labor, to representatives of business circles who were struck by the predominance of foreigners in unions (in Illinois, immi-grants made up four-fifths of trade union membership in the 1880's)[155] and as leaders of radical groups, there was a waning of confidence in the unlimited capac-ity of American society for assimilation. For those who were at a loss to explain the rising tide of strikes, the Knights of Labor, and the mushrooming of city slums rivaling England's in their squalor, the immigrant provided a convenient scapegoat to explain why the widening gap between classes was leading to a "European" style of social unrest.

Concretely, this avoidance of grappling with the indigenous problems brought about by the expansion of capitalist industry (of which immigration was only one) led to attempts at passing discriminatory legislation against aliens and immigration re-strictions on "anarchists." Although the IWPA was dead as an organized force after 1886, events in the next decade kept images of labor unrest and violence in the public eye, and these were often associated with "anarchism:" the bloody Home-stead strike (1892) and Pullman strike (1894) during the depression of 1892-1897, European assassinations, and the attempt of the Russian self-proclaimed anarchist Alexander Berkman to kill Henry Frick, manager of the Carnegie Steel Company, during the Homestead strike. But it was the assassination of President McKinley in 1901 by Leon Czolgosz, who was native-born but whose tenuous associations with Berkman and Emma Goldman were enough to brand him an anarchist, which led to the first Federal laws aimed at excluding immigrants because of their be-liefs and associations. The Immigration Act of 1903, firmly supported by Presi-dent Theodore Roosevelt, barred entry and provided for deportation and refusal of naturalization to anarchists, that is, "persons who believe in or advocate the overthrow by force and violence of the Government of the United States, or of all government, or of all forms of law, or the assassination of public officials."[156] Once in effect, this law was little used, contrary to many predictions: up to 1921, only 38 persons were excluded under it, and only 14 were deported until 1919.[157] Nevertheless, a pattern had been set of viewing foreigners as the real agents of domestic unrest in what would supposedly be a peaceful society otherwise. This shifting of the blame culminated in the Red Scare deportations beginning in 1919 which were directed against the Union of Russian Workers, the Communist Labor Party and the Communist Party, in addition to anarchists, and which reached a height of 446 in 1921, under the tenure of future FBI chief J. Edgar Hoover as head of the alien radical division of the Justice Department.[158] The practices which run like a thread through the last hundred years of American history of denigrating radicalism as an importation foreign to "American" society and values and of using the presence of foreign radicals as an excuse to attack particular political organizations, parties or the labor movement as a whole can be traced back, therefore, to the upheaval of 1886 and the role of German-American radicals.

7. THE AFTERMATH OF THE HAYMARKET AFFAIR AND THE OUTLOOK FOR THE FUTURE: GERMAN-AMERICAN SOCIALISM IN THE 1890's

To return to the immediate aftermath of the Haymarket Affair, organized labor (and the SAP, as well)[159] was quick to distance itself from the methods of the Social-Revolutionaries, partly from real disagreement and partly out of fear of the sort of guilt-by-association reaction described above (though unions were also the main source of defense funds and protestors against the execution). In this vein, the General Master Workman of the Knights of Labor, Terence Powderly, declared that

> Honest labor is not to be found in the ranks of those who march under the red flag of anarchy, which is the emblem of blood and destruction. ... There is not a Trade-Union in America that will uphold those men in Chicago who have been engaged in the destruction of life and property. ... The anarchist idea is un-American, and has no business in this country. (160)

Despite such protestations, however, capital interests seized upon the opportunity to steer public opinion against labor, to strike back with lock-outs, the "iron-clad oath" and black lists, and to lobby for anti-labor legislation, particularly in Illinois.[161] Perhaps the most publicized example of the partiality of the legal system towards the employers was the Theiss boycott case in New York in 1886. In a suit brought there by George Theiss, the owner of a saloon, five members of the unions boycotting his establishment were sentenced to varying prison terms at hard labor. As the district attorney stated,

> This boycott business must be annihilated and stopped. These men of the Central Labor Union and the other Unions that have shown themselves opposed to the common good are like the Algerine pirates who extorted moneys and tributes without reason. This must be stopped at once. (162)

That this view was widely shared can be seen by the passage of anti-conspiracy and anti-boycott legislation in Illinois (the Merritt Conspiracy Law and the Cole Anti-Boycott Law, both in 1887) and in other states as well.

What was the response of organized labor to this offensive? Aside from distancing itself from terrorist acts, labor organizations in major cities, particularly in Chicago and New York, took the positive step in 1886 of forming United Labor Parties as an alternative to the dominance of employers' interests in the older parties. German-Americans were extremely active in these independent parties, through the Central Labor Unions, the SAP in New York and the supporters of the Social-Revolutionaries in Chicago. When the results were finally tallied in November, the new labor coalitions had scored unexpected gains. In New York, the mayoral candidate of the Independent Labor Party, Henry George, supported by the

CLU and the socialists, finished a strong second with 31% of the vote. In Chicago, the United Labor Party elected seven State assemblymen, one state senator and came within a hairbreadth of electing a Congressman. In Milwaukee, the People's Party carried the county, and elected the mayor, a state senator, six assemblymen and one Congressman. Labor candidates ran and were elected in other cities, as well.[163] The resonance of the elections ran throughout the American press and even to Europe, as Engels described shortly thereafter:

> In Europe the effect of the American elections in November was tremendous. That England, and America in particular, had no labor movement up to now was the big trump card of the radical republicans everywhere. ... The very fact that the movement is so sharply accentuated as a labor movement and has sprung up so suddenly and forcefully has stunned the people completely. (164)

Unfortunately, however, these labor coalitions did not hold together for long. In the fall of 1887, plagued by internal dissension (George, whose platform emphasized land reform, went so far as to have the socialists of the SAP expelled from his party)[165] and affected by the general waning of labor activity, their percentage of votes dropped drastically, and they were no longer a political force to be reckoned with.

With respect to its impact on German-American radicalism, the effect of the Haymarket Affair was complex. Sections of the Social-Revolutionaries rapidly disbanded and the IWPA was dead as an organized movement after 1886. But not to go beyond this obvious fact would be to remain on the surface level of events. First of all, the Germans who had participated in the movement of 1886 were still quite active publicly throughout the next decade. The papers issued by the Haymarket martyrs increased their circulation under editors such as Joseph Dietzgen and Max Baginski[166] (the Arbeiter-Zeitung from 5780 in 1886 to 15,000 in 1895) and continued to provide a forum for the German labor movement in Chicago. The Pioneer Aid and Support Association of Chicago, which had been created to assist the families of the executed and imprisoned men, was a unifying center for progressive unions and various clubs and associations of workers, sponsoring large demonstrations every Nov. 11 and benefits attended by thousands. That is, these public opportunities for expression provided alternatives and possibilities for self-articulation, chosen by German and English-speaking workers as channels for voicing their interests. Second, the larger labor movement was by no means dead. It remained highly visible through attempts at independent political action and particularly through intensive trade union organizing, and Germans continued their participation.

The effect of the events of 1886 on the SAP was similar, in that the party itself declined while the supportive network of relatively independent institutions around it, such as its affiliated press, remained intact and secure. This was perhaps even more difficult to cope with for a party whose sense of legitimacy and belief in eventual success were predicated upon the necessity of a tightly centralized organizational structure. Already decimated in its early years by the break with the Social-Revolutionaries, the SAP came out of the divisiveness of the Henry George campaign with about 1500 members nationwide and as much of a tendency as ever towards fruitless ideological hair-splitting and factionalism. As before, the debate within the National Executive Committee of the party was between the advocates of electoral participation and those who emphasized union activity within the context of the skilled workers of the AFL. After three years of acrimony, the latter group became the majority and held its own Congress in Chicago in 1889, naming its own Executive Committee. Asserting its legitimacy as the "real" SAP, the new group criticized its "Lassallean" predecessor -- which had in the meantime relocated its headquarters to Cincinnati and was also claiming to be the "real" SAP -- as led by "reactionaries,"

> welche sich krankhaft an die Tendenz anklammerten, die sozialisti-
> sche Bewegung, äusserlich mit der amerikanischen Flagge und mit
> amerikanischen Reden verbrämt, nach ihrem deutschländischen
> Muster zu modeln, deshalb die amerikanische Gewerkschaftsbewe-
> gung links liegen liessen oder von oben herab behandelten. (167)

It was this tiny group around Wilhelm Ludwig Rosenberg, head of the National Executive Committee from 1885-1890, to which Engels was referring when he wrote to Sorge in 1890:

> If the whole German Socialist Labor Party went to pieces ... it would
> be a gain, but we can hardly expect anything as good as that. ... I
> consider the decay of the specifically German party, with its ridiculous
> theoretical confusion, its corresponding arrogance, and its Lassalle-
> anism, a real piece of good fortune. Only when these separatists are
> out of the way, will the fruits of your work come to light again. The
> Socialist Law was a misfortune, not for Germany, but for America,
> to which it consigned the last of the louts. When I was over there
> [Engels visited the United States in 1888], I often marveled at the
> many loutish faces one encountered, faces which died out in Germany,
> but are flourishing over there. (168)

On the whole, then, the Germans who made up the larger group were convinced that the events of 1886 had shown definitively that a socialist political movement would have to be based firmly in the unions. As one German member of the SAP wrote in an article on "Die Gewerks-Union als Kampf-Organisation," (1888)

> In diesem Lande, auf Grund des natürlichen Verlaufes der Entwicklung,
> [bildet] die Sozialistische Arbeiterpartei eine Propaganda Abteilung
> der allgemeinen Arbeiterbewegung, während die gewerkschaftliche Be-
> wegung tatsächlich als die Arbeiterbewegung Amerikas und auch als
> die Basis ihrer politischen Kampforganisation zu betrachten ist.

And the writer continued: "Alles weitere besorgt die Zuspitzung der sozial-politischen Gegensätze -- Proletarisierung der Massen und Aufhäufung des Reichtums."[169] Therefore, this and similar statements in the press show that like the radicals in Chicago, the Germans of the SAP had concluded that working within the unions of skilled workers (meaning the AFL at the time) was an absolute necessity -- thus resolving for the time being one constant source of argument -- and that time would take care of the rest. They still believed that increasing impoverishment of the workers was inevitable, that this would necessarily create a class-conscious revolutionary proletariat, and that the demise of capitalism was imminent in view of these circumstances. During the 1890's, then, the SAP entered wholeheartedly into union work and into election campaigns -- which were not seen as mutually exclusive -- running its first Presidential candidate in 1892 (Simon Wing, who received a grand total of 21,164 votes) and paying special attention to the New York area with its faithful German and Jewish supporters.

During the 1890's, also, the German-American socialists relinquished their position at the head of the SAP for the first time. Although the majority of party members were still German, the figure who had the most to do with shaping policy after 1892 was Daniel DeLeon, editor of the English-language party organ, The People, frequent candidate for state offices in New York, union organizer and theoretician. DeLeon and other spokespersons criticized the pre-1890 party for its "exotic nature," describing it as a "propaganda body rather than a political party"[170] whose German members attempted "to make the Party in this country subordinate to the Party in Germany."[171] Their own tactics, however, were not designed to increase the following or influence of the party, nor to lead beyond the dilemmas in which the Germans had foundered. Conflicts between DeLeon's desire for a socialist union movement and the "pure and simple" unionism of Samuel Gompers and the AFL led the SAP to form a dual union to the AFL, the Socialist Trades and Labor Alliance (STLA). In turn, opposition to the STLA grew from its very formation within the SAP itself, coming mainly from German members of the AFL, particularly the brewery workers, and voiced through the New York Volkszeitung.[172] In the political realm, the SAP also continued the German-American tradition of not entering into coalitions, refusing officially to cooperate in a farmer-labor alliance with the Populists, or People's Party, in 1892 and 1896, and suspending sections which fused with other parties in municipal elections. As the report of the National Executive Committee stated in 1896 in reply to the protest of the suspended Section Cleveland (which maintained that it had joined forces with workers who were sympathetic to socialist principles, though not in name socialists):

> It is clear that if the policy of the party is to be shaped according to the decidedly vague notions of Socialism entertained by a multitude of workingmen who consider themselves sympathizers, so that the party will have to follow them through the whole labyrinth of errors in which they are certain to wander before reaching light, then we might as well give up the idea of having any fixed policy at all. (173)

DeLeon and his fellow torchbearers drove their uncompromising aloofness to such extremes that, as the historian Daniel Bell comments: "from 1895 on, the splits in the Socialist Labor Party were as regular as binary fission among the amoebas."[174] Finally, when the Socialist Party (SP) of America was formed in 1901 as a unification of the various socialist organizations which had grown up in the West around the American Railway Union of Eugene Debs and its successor, the Social Democratic Party, as well as a substantial group of dissidents from DeLeon's SAP, the SAP was the only socialist group in the country to remain outside the new party (which at its founding boasted 10,000 members, three-fourths being native-born Americans). Having learned precious little about the pitfalls of ideological rigidity from the twenty-year-long travails of the German-American socialists, the SAP (or SLP) ensconced itself within the walls of doctrinal purity, where it has remained as a tiny sect until this day.

In the decade of the 1890's, therefore, Marxist socialism ceased to be an almost exclusively German-American phenomenon, and 1901 marked an end to the era when for all purposes familiarity with socialism was confined to the German immigrant group. American socialism could no longer be accused of being an adjunct of German Social Democracy. However, certain problems which faced the German-American socialists in the 19th century continued into the twentieth, reflecting the diverse composition of the working class and the arrival of new immigrant groups from Southern and Eastern Europe, and posing formidable organizational tasks to the Socialist Party and, in the 1920's and 1930's, to the Communist Party as well. The foreign-language federations continued to be a vital, active constituent of American socialism. In 1917, at the time the United States entered World War I, 32,894 of the 80,126 members of the Socialist Party belonged to the language federations, which enjoyed considerable independence from the national organization precisely because of the language barrier, including South Slavs, Italians, Scandinavians, Hungarians, Bohemians, Germans, Poles, Jews, Slovaks, Ukrainians, Lithuanians and Russians.[175] As was the case with the 19th century Germans and their parties, this membership figure must be seen as vastly augmented by the socialist press and literature distribution in the various languages and the community presence of the Party. Similarly, at the 1925 convention, the Communists reported that the main bulk of the 16,325 members were foreign-born and that of their eighteen language federations, the largest were the Finns, Jews, South Slavs, Russians, Lithuanians and Ukrainians.[176] The Communists founded papers to compete with foreign-language press sympathetic to the Socialists (Der Arbeiter, published in New York from 1927-1937, became a bitter enemy of the more moderate Volkszeitung), and created their own social, educational and cultural networks within the communities.[177] Probably in all of these situations the tendency by participants in such organizations towards perceiving themselves as defined by the totality of the organization (the development of Lagerbewusstsein) was intensified by the relative isolation of the ethnic group.[178] At any rate, the tension between ethnic awareness and class consciousness across lines of language and nationality and, correspondingly, waves of anti-radicalism directed against aliens, continued to shape the character of the American labor and radical movements, until the Second World War and the ensuing period of Cold War and Mc-Carthyism -- along with decreases in the number of immigrants and their assimilation into the English-speaking world around them -- brought the era of the "Old Left" to a close.

With respect to the German-American socialists during and after the 1890's, changes in party leadership and organization did not necessarily entail changes on the relatively autonomous level of culture and community, at least until the twenties and the growth of the Communist Party. They had established secure institutions -- particularly their press -- which provided many facets of communication and a source of solidarity within their community, even as contact with English-speaking comrades increased, and these institutions had never been tightly integrated into party organizational structure. Therefore, while the following chapters will concentrate on the period up to 1890 when the Germans totally dominated socialism in the United States, they will also give at least some indication of cultural developments and continuity extending beyond this date. As long as the language group existed, German-American socialists perpetuated their cultural traditions as a means of shaping and asserting their identity and of processing and confronting their American experiences.

8. SOCIALISTS ASSESS THE OBSTACLES CONFRONTING THEIR MOVEMENT

But this should not be the end of our discussion of the aftermath of the events of 1886. After all, following the rise of the Knights of Labor, the spectacular emergence of violent class confrontation in the strike for the eight-hour day and the Haymarket Affair, and Henry George's second-place finish in New York City's mayoral election, many observers had predicted that the overthrow of capitalism was imminent and inevitable. The American labor movement, along with the German SPD (which continued to increase its share of the electorate in spite of the Anti-Socialist Laws), was regarded by many as the most advanced in the world. The comments of the French newspaper Le Socialiste in May of 1886 on the Haymarket bombing were typical: "The social revolution announces itself in the United States ... and is the tocsin for the social revolution in England, France, Germany, in a word, in all the civilized world."[179] And Friedrich Engels, in his preface to the American edition (1887) of The Condition of the Working Class in England, stated with great enthusiasm that

> during these ten months, a revolution has been accomplished in American society such as, in any other country, would have taken at least ten years. In February 1885, American public opinion was almost unanimous on this one point; that there was no working class, in the European sense of the word, in America; that consequently no class struggle between workmen and capitalists, such as tore European society to pieces, was possible in the American Republic; and that, therefore, socialism was a thing of foreign importation which could never take root on American soil. And yet, at that moment, the coming class struggle was casting its gigantic shadow before it in the strikes of the Pennsylvania coal miners, and of many other trades, and especially in the preparations, all over the country, for the great eight hours' movement which was to come off and did come off in the May following. ... No one could then foresee that in such a short time the movement would burst out with such irresistible force, would spread with the rapidity of a prairie fire, would shake American society to its very foundations. ...
> The spontaneous, instinctive movements of these vast masses of working people, over a vast extent of country, the simultaneous outburst of their common discontent with a miserable social condition, the same everywhere and due to the same causes, made them conscious of the fact, that they formed a new and distinct class of American society: a class of -- practically speaking -- more or less hereditary wage-workers, proletarians. And with true American instinct this consciousness led them at once to take the next step towards their deliverance: the formation of a political workingmen's party, with a platform of its own, and with the conquest of the Capitol and the White House for its goal. ...
> In European countries, it took the working class years and years before they fully realized the fact that they formed a distinct and, under

the existing social conditions, a permanent class of modern society; and it took years again until this class-consciousness led them to form themselves into a distinct political party, independent of, and opposed to, all the old political parties, formed by the various sections of the ruling classes. On the more favored soil of America, where no medieval ruins bar the way, where history begins with the elements of the modern bourgeois society as evolved in the seventeenth century, the working class passed through these two stages of its development within ten months.
Still, all this is but a beginning. (180)

This passage voices eloquently the optimism engendered in socialist circles throughout the world by the sudden upsurge of the United States labor movement and reflects the belief held by socialists in Europe and the United States that growing impoverishment would necessarily lead to the development of class consciousness and the formation of an independent proletarian political movement. But after 1886, this failed to materialize in America. The Knights of Labor dwindled back into obscurity as rapidly as they had risen to prominence. The execution of the leaders in the Haymarket Affair and the temporary collapse of the eight-hour movement proved beyond a doubt the repressive capabilities of American capitalism. The Henry George candidacy ceased to be an effective political force. And skilled workers seemed to be shifting gradually towards the "business" unionism of the AFL and away from linking the immediate goals of trade unionism with the broader political demands of an independent labor party.

After these unexpected developments, both European and German-American socialists began to reassess their views about the prospects for socialism in the United States and the reasons for its slow progress. A critical discussion of the endless debates on this issue would be an entire project in itself.[181] However, it is important to outline briefly the variety of explanations which were advanced by theoreticians and politicians in the German and German-American socialist press, in order to understand their own perception of the obstacles facing them and their concrete notions of how the spread of a socialist movement should proceed. With varying degrees of emphasis, the following factors were singled out:

1) The almost exclusively German leadership and membership of the SAP, and its lasting difficulty in adapting its strategies to particular American conditions.

2) The unique composition of the American working class, as a heterogeneous mixture of many different nationalities and language groups. It was not only the cultural and language differences among these groups which impeded labor solidarity and communication across ethnic lines -- though this was a crucial factor -- but also there was a division of labor which grew up along these lines, with certain nationalities dominating in particular trades or with the older, more established Northern and Western European groups controlling the better-paying, skilled trades and the Slavs, Southern Europeans and Asians providing a large, cheap supply of unskilled labor. Writing in 1893, Engels admitted that

> American conditions involve very great and peculiar difficulties for
> a steady development of a workers' party. ...
> Immigration ... divides the workers into two groups: the native-born
> and the foreigners, and the latter in turn into 1) the Irish, 2) the Ger-
> mans, 3) the many small groups, each of which understands only it-
> self: Czechs, Poles, Italians, Scandinavians, etc. And then the
> Negroes. To form a single party out of these requires quite unusually
> powerful incentives. Often there is a sudden violent élan, but the
> bourgeois need only wait passively, and the dissimilar elements of
> the working class fall apart again. (182)

This situation increased competition among different groups, made it easier for
employers to play off one against another, contributed to the strengthening of a
secure "labor aristocracy" within the AFL, and accordingly made union and socialist organizing more difficult.

3) Connected to the structure of the American immigrant working class and the
historical development of the country were the reality and ideology of social mobility. The commonly held belief in its possibility originated in the opportunities
for rising to the status of an independent craftsman in the antebellum period, and
in the actual contrast experienced by immigrants between living standards in the
United States and Europe. Some socialists also believed that the escape-valve
quality of the existence of an open frontier provided an alternative to the misery
of urban life and thus reduced worker militance. This "frontier thesis," which is
generally associated with Frederick Jackson Turner,[183] received the following
formulation from Engels in 1892:

> Only when the land -- the public lands -- is completely in the hands
> of the speculators, and settlement on the land thus becomes more
> and more difficult or falls victim to gouging -- only then, I think,
> will the time come, with peaceful development, for a third party.
> Land is the basis of speculation, and the American speculative mania
> and speculative opportunity are the chief levers that hold the native-
> born worker in bondage to the bourgeoisie. Only when there is a gen-
> eration of native-born workers that cannot expect anything from spec-
> ulation any more, will we have a solid foothold in America. (184)

Most European socialists, including Engels, thought that social mobility was
greater and that wages were higher in the United States than in Europe. This was
the impression of travelers to the United States such as Wilhelm Liebknecht, who
evaluated American working conditions positively in comparison to Europe,[185]
and, twenty years later, Franz Mehring, who wrote upon his return to Germany
in 1906 that "the most powerful bulwark of American capitalism ... is that, next
to the dark sides which are inseparable from capitalism, American life also pos-
sesses light sides."[186]

In contrast to this "roast beef and apple pie" thesis,[187] German-American socialists often editorialized about the miserable living and working conditions in the New World, and attempted to prove that the ideology of social mobility was just that, namely, an ideology. In 1883, New York Volkszeitung editor Adolf Douai was called to testify as a representative of the SAP before the United States Senate Committee on Education and Labor, which was conducting hearings on the "Relations between Labor and Capital,"[188] and in his statements there he voiced the opinion -- also typical of the party's analysis -- that upward mobility was a thing of the past but that it was still a powerful "superstition" which served to buttress capitalism. He testified:

> In former times it might truthfully be said that in the United States every person who was a real workingman and was industrious and diligent, and somewhat parsimonious, might ultimately come to a competency, and among thousands there might perhaps be one or two, or three at most, who might become rich; but the opportunities for this are past. ... Compare only the thirty last years of which I can bear witness, and it is now less possible than ever before to make savings, and still less possible, if you have some few savings, to employ them so as to make them useful, to make capital out of them. The chances are all now gone. ... Nowadays it is an impossibility, except under very favorable circumstances, to become a Vanderbilt or a rich man. And we know the means by which these men have become so rich. (189)

This analysis of the process of industrial development as resulting in increasing impoverishment, stratification, and stagnation corresponds to the way these socialists understood Marx's economic theory: as a demonstration of the inevitable, impending, even automatic collapse of capitalism. Douai's testimony continued:

> Marx' theory is this: that capital must ruin and must abolish itself, just as slavery has abolished itself. We cannot do anything against this natural action of economical and historical causes. It is a historical necessity that the kind of production which now prevails will ruin itself, and that, too, before this century is over. (190)

This increasing decay and the growing intensity of cyclical crises (like the depression just experienced from 1873-1878) should have unmasked the belief that social mobility and an improved standard of living were possible within the existing capitalist society and should have created more and more receptivity to socialist ideas and especially more willingness to vote for the SAP, in the opinion of Douai and other party leaders. When this failed to occur, the party was not prepared to reevaluate its analysis of the American situation or of the genesis of class consciousness, nor to pursue alternative strategies.

4) Related to the belief in the "land of opportunity" which, to despairing socialists, seemed to pervade the American working class thoroughly, was the difficulty of

creating a new third party which would be a serious challenge to the long-established, well-accepted two-party system. This contrasts to the situation in Germany, for example, where there was no tradition of democratic elections and a multi-party system which was constantly undergoing divisions and fusions. In the United States, the conviction that a vote for a third party was a wasted vote was validated by the strength of the Democratic and Republican Parties, their ability at times to incorporate partially into their platforms some of the most pressing demands raised by third parties, and their big-city machines which were able to assure candidates the necessary votes, often through stuffing ballot boxes and buying votes.[191] The pervasive extent of this control and power over public affairs and the country's political life was a grave impediment not only to the SAP, composed as it was mainly of German immigrants, but to other, larger, "native" third party movements as well -- such as the Greenback-Labor Party, the Populists, and later, the Socialist Party.

Already as early as 1881, in another period of crisis for the SAP when its votes and membership were declining, Adolf Douai delineated the hindrances to socialist propaganda and specifically socialist electoral success in America in an article written for the Jahrbuch für Sozialwissenschaft und Sozialpolitik:

> Die soziale Propaganda stösst ... auf eine vorherrschende Nationalität, welche andere Sprache redet; ... auf eine demokratische Staatsverfassung, welche ihre langjährige Parteigeschichte hat, in die man eingeweiht sein muss, um den Denkstandpunkt der hiesigen Arbeiterbevölkerung zu begreifen und zu wissen, wie man an ihn anknüpfen und ihn fortbilden soll; auf den Aberglauben an die Vorzüglichkeit dieser Verfassung gegen alle anderen und auf die Unbekanntschaft des Volkes mit der europäischen politischen Geschichte und die Unfähigkeit desselben, sich in die politischen Erkenntnisse der Europäer hineinzudenken. Sie stösst auf nationalen, religiösen und gesellschaftlichen Widerwillen und die damit verbundenen Vorurtheile gegen die Eingewanderten vom Festlande Europas. Sie stösst auf die Nothwendigkeit, sich auf die politische Kampfesweise der Eingebornen bis zu einem gewissen Grade einzulassen und sie sehr langsam und schrittweise in unsere Volkswirthschaftslehre einzuweihen. Sie stösst auf ganz abgefeimte politische Parteigauner, welche ... den Leuten einbilden, sie regierten sich selbst, während sie nur regiert werden. Sie stösst auf eine wahre Schafsgeduld der Stimmgeber, welche sich immer auf's Neue mit nicht ernstlich gemeinten Versprechungen hinhalten und betrügen lassen, und auf die unselige Gewohnheit der unabhängigeren Stimmgeber, von der einen der beiden alten, aber gleich nichtswürdigen Parteien zur anderen überzuspringen, wenn es die herrschende zuweit getrieben hat, weil jede neue dritte Partei beargwöhnt wird, dass sie im Dienste einer der beiden alten stehe und ausverkaufen wolle, wenn es zur Wahl geht. (192)

Including the overtones of arrogance and exasperation -- only fueled by the frustrations of life in exile -- this is a quite typical statement of how the Germans in the SAP viewed the American electorate.

5) Contained in this analysis of the American political system was the thesis that attempted to explain the attachment of large sectors of the American working class to the established parties by the lack of a feudal past in the United States, the resulting domination of politics by bourgeois parties, and the concomitant long-standing tradition of bourgeois freedoms such as universal male suffrage. That is, the American working class did not have to constitute itself as a class into an independent political party in order to secure even bourgeois freedoms, in contrast to a country such as Germany where, as the historian Vernon Lidtke states, "the working classes thrust themselves into the political arena before the bourgeoisie had succeeded in ordering the constitutional structure according to its own conceptions."[193] Thus, in a letter to Sorge written in 1892, Engels maintained that

> It is remarkable, but quite natural, how firmly rooted bourgeois prejudices are even in the working class in such a young country, which has never known feudalism and has grown up on a bourgeois basis from the beginning. Out of his very opposition to the mother country -- which is still clothed in its feudal disguise -- the American worker also imagines that the traditionally inherited bourgeois regime is something progressive and superior by nature and for all time, a non plus ultra. (194)

German-American socialists made similar judgments, often in the most condescending and patronizing tones. In an article "Ueber die Arbeiterbewegung in Amerika" (Die neue Zeit, 1889), SAP journalist Philipp Rappaport declared:

> Die amerikanische Verfassung ist für ihn der Inbegriff aller politischen Weisheit, aller politischen Freiheit, und dieser Dünkel wird von oben herab so genährt, dass, es ist kaum übertrieben, der ärmste Teufel sein Elend leichter trägt, weil es amerikanisches Elend ist. (195)

In a like vein, Adolf Hepner, accused along with Bebel and Liebknecht in the Leipzig Hochverratsprozess in 1872, wrote from St. Louis to bemoan the lack of class consciousness among American workers in Die neue Zeit (1893):

> Die grosse Masse der amerikanischen Proletarier ist geduldiger als Hiob, patriotischer als es die Konstitution verlangt, und lässt sich missbrauchen wie die Null, die man neben die Eins setzt, um eine Zehn aus ihr zu machen und die dabei immer eine Null bleibt.

It was not only the German members of the SAP who pointed their accusing fingers at "backward" American workers. Daniel DeLeon, the outstanding party figure in the 1890's, also complained about how difficult it was to "enlighten" workers who seemed to be satisfied with the American political process.[197] In turn, the response of the majority of the electorate when the SAP argued that America possessed only the _form_ of democracy was to dismiss them as cranks or visionaries.

6) Along similar lines, the SAP viewed non-socialist unions as one of the main barriers to the spread of socialism, for they also fostered the belief that redress of grievances was possible within the existing political and economic system.[198] Unlike the situation in Europe, American trade unionism emerged before and without the sponsorship of a socialist political movement, and therefore the socialists had to work their way into pre-existing economic organizations having only a partial comprehension of their joint interests. For their part, the unions thought they could avoid politics. The discontent which workers certainly felt with their economic status was reflected in a growth of union membership, but socialist organizers found that even unionized workers were not ready to overthrow management. In reports sent by local socialist organizers to the SLP party organ The People during the 1890's, three reasons for the unreceptivity of workers to the idea of joining a socialist party were most frequently cited: 1) the bread and butter issues which were their main concern seemed attainable through strikes, boycotts, etc. 2) the perception that their economic situation was always precarious and even more so if they were branded as socialists, 3) the socialist alternative of a revolutionary attack upon the whole social system was criticized as unrealistic. These factors, plus the "foreign" image of the SLP, clearly hindered its ability to gain many "native" union supporters.[199]

7) If bourgeois, capitalist interests dominated in the fields of politics and economics, they also asserted their hegemony in determining the "ruling ideas" of the society. The primary news medium of the time, print, overwhelmingly supported the status quo, and socialists viewed these newspapers and this mass literature as one of the main transmitters of an anti-socialist message.[200] As we have already seen in the two instances of the 1877 strike and the Haymarket Affair, the press either neglected or defamed socialist activity, thus being an accomplice to its repression. As far as other public institutions were concerned, religious revivalism was flourishing, schools were promoting uncritical thinking, and the gospel of Social Darwinism was being preached from pulpits, universities, and the press.

As well as indicating the difficulties and obstacles facing immigrant socialists in their attempts to organize a political movement, these factors are particularly significant for what they imply about how these socialists perceived the sources of class consciousness and solidarity within their ethnic group and in the working class as a whole, and how this shaped their concept of practice. As can be seen from the above points, these socialists stressed both economic explanations and broader social and cultural factors as impediments. However, upon closer scrutiny, it becomes clear that they placed their main emphasis on economic causes, and that even though they saw some of the ideological aspects of capitalist hegemony which impeded the growth of a class-conscious proletariat, they did not consider these as equally important or take them seriously on some levels. This can be seen from the two modes of argument which are characteristic of their editorials in the press and other statements. They tried to prove either that economic conditions in the United States were already as bad as in Europe or that they would soon become so, or, on the other hand, in an appeal to conscience, that even if American workers were enjoying a higher standard of living and greater social mobility than their European counterparts, they should resist integration into the political system which seemed to be providing for them and vote for the socialists as the only party which had their real interests at heart. They were unwilling to believe that "as long as reformist solutions seem practicable, the masses will opt for reformist parties," and that "here, the appeal to socialist ideals accomplishes nothing."[201] Thus, the complex problem here is that the continued existence of a political socialist movement among German immigrants in America does reflect class divisions which the socialists encountered here as well as in Europe, but in important respects the socialists denied or could not come to terms with the real experience of immigrant and native workers. They tended to dismiss perceptions of American reality such as social mobility, a better standard of living, the possibility of making desired changes through the established parties and the non-socialist unions as mere superstitions which could be overcome by force of will after those who held these beliefs were enlightened as to their "real" interests. The socialists' belief that the downfall of capitalism was imminent, their apocalyptic vision of the social revolution which they believed would be ushered in by devastating impoverishment, also led them to devalue and underestimate the integrative power of ideological factors. That is, the German-American socialist groups and parties were both an expression of societal conflicts and an expression of lack of rootedness in the working class and its real structure and concerns.

Here, in critically examining the practice of these socialists, it is helpful to distinguish among several levels of success and failure in order to locate the areas of life in which they were most successful at challenging capitalist hegemony. Many historians who pose the question "Why is there no socialism in the United States?"[202] and those who state that socialism failed in this country because it was "in but not of the world"[203] are concerned primarily with a political movement in the sense of a party strong enough to offer a serious challenge for governmental power. But who, after all, were the German-American socialists, and what was the real strength and influence of their movement? Were they only the few thousand adherents of the First International, the 1500 members of the SAP at its nadir in the early 1880's, or even the 7000 members and sympathizers of the Social-Revolutionaries? Such figures necessarily provoke grave doubts about whether such small political groups were important at all, and whether they are worth discussing any longer as anything of more than academic interest. On the level of electoral politics, then, and in their attempts to function officially as tightly knit, structured parties or associations, the German-American socialists had no appreciable success. However, even in this respect, it would be artificial to separate internal problems (such as divisiveness and inflexibility) from external causes, for the difficulties within these groups over political strategy were for the most part a result of their lack of success in the external realm of politics, and a consequence of the surrounding, pervasive capitalist institutions and values.[204] On the level of union organizing, the relationship of the socialists to the larger labor movement becomes more concrete and influential, as discussed above, reflecting their concern with economic issues, and their real activities in this area do not necessarily correspond to their stated theoretical differences of opinion over the efficacy of unionism.

However, if we consider only the levels of electoral politics and trade unionism, we are merely focusing on the areas which the German-American socialists themselves officially recognized in their party statements and editorials as important for creating class consciousness and spreading a socialist movement. Upon closer examination, there seems to be a fundamental disparity between this self-perception, on the one hand, and the reasons for the cohesion of the larger German socialist or working-class communities, on the other. The creation of class solidarity within an ethnic group may have as much to do with the creation of common cultural experiences, of a socialist subculture, of a shared perception of daily life in work and leisure, as with political activities in the narrow sense of membership in a party or union. Particularly in the situation of exile and immigration, where the German-language SAP could never exert any significant influence on the mainstream of American politics, much less entertain hopes of coming to power, these cultural and social factors assume crucial importance in unifying a class within the ethnic group. If we look beyond the official policy of the party (which, like the SPD, was to have no coherent policy at all regarding culture), we find that an extensive subculture in which thousands participated existed on the periphery of the party. Such activities as Arbeiterbildungsvereine, socialist schools for children, women's branches, producers' and consumers' cooperatives, workers' singing and dramatic groups, large, frequent festivals, workers' halls and labor lyceums, workers' gymnastic societies (Turners), insurance and benefit societies, and of course, the publication of socialist newspapers attempted to reshape life in a more cooperative way.[205] The lack of a theoretical formulation of socialist cultural aims means that it is necessary to proceed inductively, from the real cultural practice of these socialists, in order to understand their goals, what importance they attached to these activities, and the true extent and nature of their influence. That this aspect of German-American radicalism has been neglected and overlooked testifies to the widespread tendency of viewing history primarily in terms of political organizations and power struggles, and accordingly, of viewing these institutions as satisfying and expressing the totality of their members' interests, of making rigid divisions based on organizational affiliation between socialists and non-socialists, unionists and non-unionists, etc., under the assumption that these categories encompass the "whole" proletarian.[206] But, as Oskar Negt stated in an article directed precisely at these questions of organization:

> The "whole" person, whose characteristics, capabilities, interests, and needs are fragmented by capitalist production and consumption stands at the end of the revolutionary process, not at the beginning. (207)

The following chapters will analyze one aspect of the relationship between culture and the socialist political movement by focusing on the literature (poetry, drama, prose) produced and distributed by German-American socialist writers and the function this literature assumed (conceived as it was as operative) in the German-American ethnic and working class community. As a means of articulating their situation in the present and their visions of the future, this literature constituted a vital part of the socialist subculture. Since this literature was intended to create a certain political response or attitude in its audience -- unlike bourgeois conceptions of disinterested, unengaged l'art pour l'art -- and since its writers only viewed it as meaningful and worthwhile in this context, it will be necessary to include in the analysis of the literary form and content a critical discussion of both its intended effect and the sorts of channels through which it was transmitted to its working-class audience. Therefore, while this is not meant to be an empirical sociological investigation of German-American communities in various cities, the analysis will attempt to explicate and critique the interaction of literary forms and contents with the function this literature assumed within the community, thus necessitating, at times, more general observations on the experience of immigrant workers in the United States, and the interaction between socialist, working-class and ethnic subcultures.

III. GERMAN-AMERICAN SOCIALIST LITERATURE:
THE POLITICAL AND FUNCTIONAL CONTEXT

1. INTRODUCTION AND DEFINITION OF GERMAN-AMERICAN SOCIALIST LITERATURE

Just as the socialist movement described in Chapter II was both a continuation and modification of political strategies and theories developed in a European context, the literature written by the German-American socialists also must be analyzed in terms of carrying on certain traditions and of developing them further and adapting them to a new social situation. On the one hand, this early socialist literature -- whether written in Germany or America -- shows the influence of political poetry from the Vormärz period, in such features as the tendency towards rhetorical, moralizing argumentation, the use of allegory and the predominance of certain genres calculated to have immediate, direct effect. Also, many of these immigrant writers had already contributed poems, plays or prose works to SPD publications before coming to the United States. Having begun their activity as writers and journalists in Germany and in many cases immigrating only because they were forced to by the Anti-Socialist Laws, these writers naturally continued to produce the same sort of literary works they had written before their immigration. In addition, the language barrier prevented, at least for a time, their being directly influenced by American writers. On the other hand, however, this literature was not merely a tradition continued in a vacuum. Rather, it reacted to the new environment, and it was perceived by its writers as assuming particular meanings and functions within the German-American ethnic group and the American context. On the simplest level, this means that at times this literature interpreted or reacted to contemporary American political events or issues from a socialist perspective. For example, many of the events discussed in Chapter II became thematic material: the 1877 strike, the need for political unity among the various socialist factions, the Lehr- und Wehrvereine, the Haymarket bombing and executions, and so forth. More general problems encountered in America such as working-class poverty and material insecurity were also common topics for literary portrayal. However, on a more fundamental level, this literature was shaped throughout by the political functions it was intended to carry out within the ethnic group, and the effort to create alternative possibilities for cultural expression. With respect to its content and form, and to the conditions for its production and distribution, this literature was intended to serve a different function from that produced by the rest of the German-American ethnic group. At the same time, it was not only an alternative means of literary expression, but it was also part of a more general effort to separate the German-American working class from bourgeois or petty-bourgeois institutions in other areas of life as well -- education, the constitution of leisure time, festivals, etc. -- and to establish connections with the working class of other ethnic groups. Therefore, German-American socialist literature should be situated in the context of the socialist movement to which it was connected, and in the context of German-American literature as a whole.

Before proceeding any further, a few words of definition are in order as to the meaning of the term "German-American socialist literature." This is understood here as literature written by immigrants associated with the groups discussed in Chapter II which was intended to carry out particular functions within this socialist movement, thus standing in an oppositional tradition to bourgeois concepts of "l'art pour l'art."[1] In many cases, it was impossible to determine whether a writer was actually a member of a particular organization, but in these instances there was an indication of participation in activities such as socialist journalism, workers' theater groups or musical groups. The mere fact that a writer's works were published in the socialist press was not a criterion for selection, since these literary sections and supplements of socialist newspapers were extremely eclectic in their choice of material, ranging from popular literature to Zola and modern realistic works. Rather, the connection to the German-American socialist movement and the "functionality" of the literary works were the deciding factors. In this context, however, the term "socialist" is used very loosely, in order to include the most representative group of writers possible. Thus, no attempt has been made to narrow the topic to consideration of a particularly "Marxist," "Lassallean," "Social-Revolutionary" or "anarchist" literature.

One more qualifying remark is essential here. There is a fundamental methodological distinction to be made between the literature and culture of the working class as a whole and that of the (socialist) workers' movement, and this study is concerned with the latter, primarily with the aspect of literature. Just as historians with an interest in legitimating present-day political standpoints have often reduced the history of the working class to the political history of the socialist movement in various countries, so there has also been a tendency to focus on the cultural forms associated with the workers' movement to the neglect of working class culture in general. This problematic can only be indicated here, but it will be important for future research to devote more attention to the interrelationship between workers' culture and the culture of the workers' movement in different countries and historical settings. For example, in an article on "Arbeiterkultur als Forschungsthema," Jürgen Kocka contrasts Germany and England in this respect, hypothesizing that in Germany, where the working class developed almost simultaneously with the workers' movement, we can perhaps only speak of an "Arbeiterkultur" after the emergence of an "Arbeiterbewegungskultur."[2] In England, he then suggests, where absolutistic and bureaucratic forms of rule were much weaker than in Germany, a workers' culture was able to develop before the rise of the organized workers' movement which provided a basis for resistance to the capitalist economic system and to bourgeois forms of social control. Research by Herbert Gutman and others indicates that the American development is more similar to that of Britain. It will remain to be seen how the experience of the working class of various ethnic groups in the United States fits into these models, and to accomplish this task adequately would demand a cooperative research effort. Nevertheless, let it be emphasized here again that this study is dealing with the literature of the German-American socialist workers' movement, and that this affects its procedure and conclusions.

2. THE CONTEXT OF GERMAN-AMERICAN LITERATURE

German-American literature as a whole has generally been evaluated as esthetically second-rate, anachronistic, written in a vacuum, composed of no schools
or movements and thus lacking in continuity, possessing no outstanding writers
to boast of, and centering its content around the poetic areas of "deutsche Hei-
mat, Liebe, Sehnsucht, Traum"[3] -- that is, around a backwards-looking portrayal
of sentimentalized inner realms of the soul withdrawn as far as possible from any
social context. As Frank Trommler has pointed out, this poetic internalization
and avoidance of social issues was not due solely to the immigrant experience in
America, but was part of an intensely cultivated cultural trend in Germany at this
time which manifested itself in such things as a flood of poems in the style of Gei-
bel and national, romantic songs of unity. Referring to German-American poetry,
Trommler states:

> In ihrer "poetischen" Substanz, in ihrer Harmonisierung und Welt-
> flucht artikulierten sich gesellschaftliche Stellungnahmen, die von
> der "Beschwichtigungspoesie" in Deutschland oft nur wenig unter-
> schieden waren. (4)

Since these tendencies towards escapism and social pacification have always been
dominant in German-American literature, it was particularly likely that any works
which did not conform to this model of cultural internalization would soon lose their
receptive audience and have little chance to enter the pages of literary histories.
In his article, Trommler is concerned with contributing to a more differentiated
image of German-American literature through uncovering and analyzing the political poetry written by the revolutionary, democratic forty-eighters in the United
States, viewing this as an attempt to utilize literature in the service of progressive political goals (above all in support of the Republican Party, Lincoln and the
North in the Civil War) rather than as an expression of sentimental estrangement
from society.[5] The immigrant socialists in the period after the Civil War were the
next group of writers to continue this literary tradition of social and political involvement.

Perhaps the first writers to reflect on the miserable quality of German-American
literature and to try to get to the root of it were nineteenth century immigrant socialists. For example, in a polemical review published in 1888, New York Volkszeitung editor Sergius Schewitsch lambasted contemporary German-American
writers as follows:

> Der Geist, der sie einst in der Sturm- und Drang-Periode mit seinem
> göttlichen Odem berührt, hat sich längst ausgetobt, hat seine Flügel
> auf ewig gefaltet und auf sein kahl gewordenes Haupt die Zipfelmütze
> des Philisters gedrückt. Die alten Ideale sind entweder im Elend ver-
> trocknet, oder im Fett des Wohllebens vergangen. ... Verschont
> uns, ihr Herren, mit Eurer todtgeborener Poesie! ... Ein solches

Organ [the book he is reviewing] wird verhängnisvoll seine Bestim-
mung erfüllen: ein Asyl zu werden für verkrüppelte, selbstgefällige
Mittelmässigkeit. (6)

Here, the generation of forty-eighters is accused of having given up its revolutionary, democratic ideals to assume a pose of tired, indifferent, self-satisfied nar-
row-mindedness. By extension, this criticism would have been applied by socialists like Schewitsch to all those writers who had made their peace with the American political and economic system after the abolition of slavery and who no longer
expressed a concern for social justice in their writings. Unfortunately, it seemed
that the bulk of German-American literature was characterized by this avoidance
of involvement, by a withdrawal from contemporary problems, and by a nostalgia
for the past. Wilhelm Rosenberg, one-time National Secretary of the SAP, explained this attitude of internalization as follows:

> Durch die deutsch-amerikanische Literatur zieht sich, seit länger
> als einem Jahrhundert, wie ein rother Faden, das Heimweh. ...
> Das Heimweh ist eine Krankheit, die in der Unfähigkeit wurzelt,
> neue Verhältnisse zu verstehen. ... Und doch ist Nichts schlimmer
> als diese Illusionskrankheit, indem sie uns abzieht von der regen und
> tatkräftigen Anteilnahme an den socialen Kämpfen der Gegenwart. (7)

Here, Rosenberg explains the pervasive longing for Germany which is characteristic of much of German-American literature -- and implicitly also explains its tendency towards concentrating on personal, "private" thematic areas such as love,
nature, friendship and conviviality -- as due to an inability to come fully to grips
with life in America, to understand and draw consequences from social issues and
problems, and to find a way as a writer of participating or taking sides in these
conflicts. Rosenberg, Schewitsch and other socialists also clearly believed that
only a certain privileged group of writers could afford to adopt this sort of pose of
longing for what they had lost in the first place, namely, those who left their homeland of their own free will rather than because of persecution for their political
beliefs.

Therefore, as an initial, explicit reaction to the rest of German-American literature, these socialist writers produced works which transform or expose such in-
ward- or backward-looking attitudes, or which directly attack certain figures or
standpoints within the ethnic group, such as those who supported Bismarck and the
Kaiser and those like Carl Schurz who supported the established American parties.
Consequently, these works can be taken as conscious alternatives to the dominant
literature and ideology of the ethnic group, and as attempts to create a particular
oppositional consciousness. The unmasking of nostalgia is encountered especially
often, sometimes -- though not always -- culminating in a favorable comparison
of America with Germany. For example, in a group of poems entitled "Heimath
und Heimweh," Wilhelm Rosenberg wrote:

Warum wir aus der Heimath scheiden?
Warum wir in die Fremde geh'n?
Weil müd' der Drangsal und der Leiden
Die wir von Jugend auf geseh'n.
. . .
Was liegt daran, wo wir geboren?
Wo nur die Sklavenpeitsche droht,
Hat Noth und Elend sich verschworen
Von uns'rer Wiege bis zum Tod. (8)

And in a poem entitled "Falsches Heimweh" he continued in the same vein:

O nein, an falschem Heimweh krank' ich nicht,
Hab eine neue Heimath längst gefunden --
Der alten, was ich jetzt bin, dank' ich nicht,
Sie schlug mir stündlich neue Seelenwunden.
. . .
Wohl weiss ich, dass auch hier den Kampf es gilt
Um höh're gröss're Menschheitsideale,
Doch wie man auf Amerika auch schilt,
Eins fehlt ihm ganz: Der Zopf und das Feudale! (9)

Similarly, after emigrating to the United States, the former SPD <u>Reichstagsabge-</u>
<u>ordneter</u> Friedrich Wilhelm Fritzsche proclaimed in a poem entitled "Mein Vater-
land" that he was sent into exile,

Weil ich an Bruderlieb' und Gleichheit glaubte,
Den Kampf um Gleichheit, Recht und Freiheit pries,

and expressed his repudiation of Germany:

Zerrissen ist das Band, das mich gekettet
Mit treuer Liebe an das Vaterland,
Hab mir ein neues Vaterland gerettet,
Die weite Welt ist nun mein Vaterland.
Kein Völkerhass hat Raum in meinem Herzen,
Kein Rassenhass erfüllt die Brust,
Verwunden habe ich des Heimwehs Schmerzen
Und neu erwacht die alte Lebenslust. (10)

These poems are all marked by the realization that political persecution caused
these exiles to leave Germany, but they also express the belief that a new, active
involvement in social struggle is possible. Thus, they are a rejection of the nostalgia expressed in other works of German-American literature, an unveiling of
its class basis and a presentation of an alternative perspective.

Implicitly, two fundamentally different concepts of literature confront each other here, one which views literature primarily as a vehicle for individual, "subjective" expression unconnected to larger social issues, and one which strives to strengthen the ties between literature and society both by the selection of relevant material as content and by the intended function of these works. These socialists often expressed their contempt for the former group of writers (and scholars, too, for that matter), and viewed their own creative direction as a consciously chosen alternative. In this vein, Wilhelm Rosenberg expressed the choice to be made as follows:

> Auch ich hab' einst der Blumen Pracht besungen,
> Die Liebe und die Schönheit der Natur,
> Doch all' dies ist, wie Saitenspiel verklungen,
> Kaum blieb davon mir der Erinnrung Spur.
>
> Anstatt der Rosen, die ich einst geschwungen,
> Schwing' ich das Schwert jetzt in der Geisterschlacht ... (11)

However, such explicit statements represent only the most obvious level of criticism by socialist writers of prevalent attitudes towards what literature should properly express. In a more fundamental sense, the whole of German-American socialist literary production, distribution and reception should be understood as an effort to create an alternative to the rest of German-American literature. Whereas the latter confined itself to the private realm or to supporting the status quo, the literature produced by the socialists was closely connected to their political movement, and indeed only becomes meaningful when viewed in this context. That is, with respect to its content and form, and to the conditions for its production and circulation, this literature was decisively shaped by the political function it was intended to serve within the German-American socialist movement. Here, however, it seems essential methodologically to distinguish sharply among precisely these three areas: content, form and function. In the article referred to above, Jürgen Kocka recommends that these distinctions be made when raising the question of the relationship between the culture of the workers' movement and bourgeois or other middle or upper class cultures. He asserts that with respect to form, and even content, workers' culture is similar in many respects to (petty) bourgeois culture, but that a comparison of function brings important differences to light because of class conflicts and differing life styles. These distinctions can help to illuminate the contradictory makeup of early socialist literature, and German-American socialist literature in particular, and can be used as indicators of the extent to which it represented a qualitatively different alternative to literature which turned away from social involvement. For now, as a tentative conclusion, in the context of being a part of the development of a working class culture within the ethnic group, it could be maintained that this literature -- along with the political poetry of the forty-eighters written before the Civil War -- is really the only portion of German-American literature which went beyond internalization and affirmation to grasp and enter into the real social conflicts German working-class immigrants experienced in America. Therefore, before turning to an analysis of the literary works themselves, it is necessary to explicate how the particular political goals of these writers defined who could even become such a writer, led them to shy away from concentrating on the private sphere, influenced their choice of genres, determined where their works were published, and established the channels through which this literature reached its intended audience.

3. WRITERS

In Germany, the political persecution of writers and the history of literature written in exile constitute a particularly long-lasting and unpleasant tradition. From
the German Jacobins of the 18th century,[12] to the radical forty-eighters of the
19th, to all those diverse groups fleeing the Nazis and their book-burnings, progressive German authors have been forced again and again to seek asylum
abroad.[13] From some of the most prominent names in German literary history
(Heine, Brecht, Thomas Mann, Heinrich Mann) to scores of others less well-
known, German writers have been forcibly cut off from their audience and from
participation in public affairs and debate. The fate of SPD journalists and writers
under the Anti-Socialist Laws constitutes yet another link in this chain of censorship and repression. In this instance, while the party was not banned and its deputies were still allowed membership in the Reichstag, it was forbidden to circu-
late any publications or to carry out any public activities such as speeches, demonstrations or organizing avowedly political Vereine.[14] The party's immediate
reaction was to establish a headquarters abroad in Zürich, to issue its publications there and to form an elaborate network for smuggling them into Germany
(rote Feldpost). Many of the active socialists abroad had been expelled from various cities under the Kleiner Belagerungszustand, for with the stigma this carried,
their possibilities of finding employment in Germany to support themselves and
their families were effectively non-existent. Therefore, emigration to Switzerland, England or America was the only solution for many. However, once situated
in their new surroundings, they did not give up their political convictions. Rather,
they continued to attempt to influence politics in Germany from other European
countries, or to create a viable socialist movement in America. Writing in 1909,
August Bebel praised those socialist exiles and emigrés who had not given up in
resignation in the following letter addressed to German-American socialists:

> Die führenden Gewalthaber, die einst das Sozialistengesetz schufen,
> um auf Grund desselben so vielen wackeren und braven Genossen die
> Heimath zu verleiden, sind sämmtlich aller Menschen los verfallen,
> viele mit Schmach und Schande bedeckt. Kaum gedenken wir ihrer
> noch und dann nur mit einem Fluch. Aber dass ihre Gewaltmassregeln
> die Wirkung haben würden, den Geist des Socialismus in die neue Welt
> zu tragen und damit neue Gebiete der socialistischen Bewegung zu er-
> schliessen, hat keiner von ihnen geahnt. So schafften sie, die nur
> Böses wollten, wider ihren Willen Gutes. Das hat sich auch in Deutsch-
> land vielfach gezeigt. (15)

The antebellum generation of socially critical German-American writers, the forty-
eighters, had made peace overwhelmingly with the American governmental and economic system after the abolition of slavery. Only a few continued to be dissatisfied
with the representation of the established parties and took more radical directions,
affiliating themselves with socialist groups. Rather, a more recent group of immigrants, those with exposure to Lassalle's ADAV, the Eisenach Party or the uni-

fied SPD, set the tone for German-American socialist literature. The decades of the 1870's and 1880's, the period of the Anti-Socialist Laws and the establishment and consolidation of socialist groups within German-American communities, saw the greatest amount of original literary production by these writers, usually in connection with the socialist press. Only a very few of these writers chose to return to Germany (after the expiration of the Anti-Socialist Laws in 1890),[16] but most who remained gradually became less involved politically or dropped out of sight altogether. They were not replaced by a comparable generation of new writers, except to an extent in the largest and best-organized communities of New York, Chicago and later Milwaukee. Rather, socialist papers tended simply to print more works by SPD writers, and it was only with the formation of the German language federation within the Communist Party that a new impetus was given to revolutionary literature written in German.[17]

As far as can be determined from the incomplete biographical information available, these writers came from a wide variety of family backgrounds, ranging from middle-class intellectuals to artisans and proletarians. In principle, this literature was not the well-guarded province of a few highly talented and well-educated authors, but any reader could also potentially become a writer, and the press was open to contributions. For example, the Neue Arbeiter-Zeitung of New York featured a series called the "Fabrikantenspiegel" (1873), consisting of reports by workers, usually on working conditions in different factories.[18] However, no matter what the class origins of its writers were, this early socialist literature as a whole is part of an "antibürgerlicher Traditionszusammenhang" in which the connection to the socialist movement and the attempt to create political and cultural solidarity are the deciding factors.[19] These common political perspectives and common goals lead to a striking uniformity in the literary works by various writers with respect to both content and technique. Methodologically, this has the consequences that for the purposes of a survey, these works can be analyzed as a body, focusing on their shared features, and that it is unnecessary for the most part to discuss individual writers in detail since the similarity of their works would only lead to repetitiveness.

As was consistent with their commitment to political involvement and with their understanding of literary production as only one facet of the socialist movement, German-American socialist writers were without exception also active as journalists, party officials and/or trade unionists, often continuing occupations begun in Germany. That is, these writers never became independent authors (in contrast to Germany, where this type is encountered more frequently within the socialist movement after 1900). For these writers, there was no division of labor between journalists and Literaten, or between the producers of political and economic pamphlets and essays and the producers of poetry, plays and fiction. Thus, the majority also contributed to or edited socialist newspapers or journals, and many of them also wrote articles and pamphlets on non-literary topics. In addition, they also served in various capacities within the different socialist organizations, particularly in the SAP and the Chicago groups. These functions ranged from holding the post of National Executive Secretary of the SAP (Wilhelm Rosenberg, one of the most prolific writers), to running for local office, to serving as popular, influential speakers at socialist and trade union meetings, festivals and demonstrations.

As is true for all early socialist and workers' literature, almost all of these German-American works were written by and directed at men. As was the case in Germany (with Minna Kautsky as the most notable exception there),[20] only a miniscule number of German-American women writers were published in the socialist press.[21] However, in contrast to the majority of male writers, it is significant that these women sometimes at least mention problems of women's emancipation or alternative arrangements to marriage, or are tolerant towards the practice of "free love" which was a hotly debated topic within the women's movement at this time. They do not view these issues as contradictory to the goals of the workers' movement, but as a necessary expansion of them -- although there is still an emphasis on the necessity of solidarity between men and women and a tendency to subordinate women's particular needs to the tasks faced by the socialist movement. Although there were other women who wrote articles on subjects such as literary and art criticism for the socialist press, or who were active as speakers and organizers, in general the role of women within the German-American socialist movement was small and often limited to more traditional service roles such as planning social events or teaching in the socialist schools.[22] As part of the alternative socialist culture, this will be discussed in a following chapter. Also, it may be that the nature of the socialist movement as primarily concerned with male workers (in its own self-understanding) influenced the kind of literature which was written in connection with it and functioned to discourage women from writing along these lines.

Since none of the socialist organizations formulated a plan for cultural politics, these writers were left to their own initiative with respect to their journalistic and literary production.[23] However, despite the absence of a unified plan, the similarity of the works they produced suggests that they shared common, if unexpressed, views of literature and its place within their political activity. A following chapter will attempt to arrive at these underlying assumptions through analyzing the literary works.

4. GENRES

The literature produced by the German-American socialists within the framework of their political movement fits into the general rubric of "operative" literature, as works intended to fulfill quite specific functions. With whatever they wrote, these socialist writers wanted to have a direct, public, political effect on their readers, listeners or spectators. Through rational persuasion or emotional appeal, they sought to arouse outrage at social inequity and injustice, to create feelings of solidarity among the exploited, to enlighten them about the causes of misery and suffering, to move them to join the socialist movement, and to inspire their belief in a better future. Unlike much of German-American literature, these writers do not concentrate on individual, "private" experiences or personal, subjective impressions, but relegate these to a sphere separate from "political" involvement. Consequently, the preferred genres in this early socialist literature were those which could best be adapted to the goal of direct, immediate influence, often within the context of a political meeting, festival or demonstration. In the following discussion, it should be kept in mind that almost all of the varieties of literary expression utilized by these socialists were traditional forms in no way necessarily connected to specific working-class perspectives or interests. Rather, socialists were indiscriminate with regard to the forms they chose, selecting genres such as the fable, Festspiel or sonnet to convey their political message. In other words, while there are few formal innovations in this literature, its content and utilization are explicitly involved in the socialist movement.

Political poetry was by far the most well-represented and widely distributed genre. It often took the form of songs which expressed consciousness of the class struggle and were meant to be sung at party functions or by certain groups, such as the Lehr- und Wehrvereine. Frequently, poems took current events in America or Europe as their subject matter and assumed the function of Leitartikel in the papers where they were printed. Of special interest here are poems which reflect the experience of exile and which explicitly criticize or express disillusionment with American society. In addition, a large number of poems were written for specific occasions commemorating progressive or revolutionary events (the Paris Commune, Lassalle's birth and death, the execution of the Haymarket martyrs on November 11, etc.), thus fitting into the context of an oppositional view of history. We also find Kontrafakturen, songs written to be sung to familiar melodies -- often German ones like "Die Wacht am Rhein," but sometimes American melodies such as "The Star-Spangled Banner" -- and usually expressing a diametrically opposed content to the original text, thus implicitly calling it into question. On a more general level, another group of poems is concerned with elucidating certain doctrines or social messages, often through the use of allegory.[24] Running through all of these categories of poems is a particular view of the working class, of the process of socialist organization and of the future revolution and socialist society to be established thereafter, which shapes both the structure and content of the individual works in ways to be specified later. While the lines between these groups of poems are often not absolutely demarcated, they suffice as broad categorizations of German-American socialist poetry. Finally, some of these writers also produced "non-political" nature and love poetry. The significance of such "non-functional" works will be discussed in a following chapter.

The production of original plays was less important. A small number, almost all consisting of one act and a minimal number of characters, were written by German-American socialists, but more often their amateur workers' theater groups preferred simply to perform available plays by German SPD writers such as J.B. von Schweitzer or Max Kegel. However, two writers deserve special mention here. In the late 1870's and early 1880's, August Otto-Walster, delegate of the SPD to the final conference of the First International held in Philadelphia in 1876, traveled to New York, St. Louis and Cincinnati establishing workers' theaters and providing them with his own one-act plays. Also, Wilhelm Rosenberg wrote about a dozen short plays, some meant expressly for workers' theaters and situated in an American context. Rosenberg was also the only German-American socialist playwright who published a drama intended for performance by professional actors, his Crumbleton (1898), dealing with corruption in American business and city government. In addition to these short plays. Festspiele were written for special occasions, including Ludwig Geissler's Allegorisches Weihnachtsfestspiel (c. 1880) and the anonymous Die Nihilisten (1882), performed to commemorate the Paris Commune by groups of Social-Revolutionaries and members of the Lehr- und Wehrverein in Chicago. While the Festspiel itself was a form which could be traced back to the Middle Ages and earlier, and which was often used to serve patriotic, nationalistic purposes in the 19th century, socialists wrote their own Festspiele which reinterpreted traditional festivals such as Christmas or which celebrated historical events of significance to the working class.[24] Finally, lebende Bilder or tableaus often formed a popular and important part of festivals and celebrations. These tableaus were particularly well-suited to bring out blatant social contrasts or to provide a schematic representation of historical development. Thus, they most often illustrated themes such as "the life of the poor and the life of the rich," "the proletariat in the past, present and future," or representations of historical subjects such as scenes from the Paris Commune or the exploitation of black and white wage workers. Like the Festspiel, lebende Bilder had a history reaching back to the Middle Ages, where they were employed to portray religious subjects such as the manger scene, and in the 18th and 19th centuries, they enjoyed popularity within aristocratic circles, including the court of Friedrich Wilhelm III. Therefore, this is another example of how socialists took over traditional forms, in this instance from the aristocratic and bourgeois Laientheater. These forms could then be reutilized to suit their own purposes, here a black-and-white portrayal of social classes and antagonisms, and a representative image of identification for the audience being addressed (the Goddess of Freedom, the Paris Commune barricades, a vision of the future under socialism).

Whereas the largest portion of the poetry and dramatic works was meant to be sung, recited or performed in public, at occasions connected in some way with the socialist political movement, the prose written by these authors was of course intended for private reading. Nevertheless, their political goals also influenced their choice of forms even here. The novel, as a bourgeois genre focused on the development of individual characters rather than class situations, played no part in this literary production, though novels from every literary period and niveau -- with popular novels dominating -- were serialized in the socialist press.[26] Rather, the prose forms most often selected by these writers were short, argumentative, didactic, rhetorical, and could be employed to make succinct, direct political statements. The portion of German-American socialist literature which is perhaps still the most readable today is the reportage sketches and calendar stories of proletarian, immigrant urban life, such as, for example, those "New Yorker Geschichten" written by editors Sergius Schweitsch and Alexander Jonas for the New York Volkszeitung in the 1880's. A forerunner of such sketches were the reports workers were encouraged to submit to the socialist press on exploitative working conditions or impoverished living situations. For example, the series of "Fabrikantenspiegel" published in the New York Neue Arbeiter-Zeitung in 1873 consists of reports by workers on various factories and employers in the New York area who were taking particularly outrageous advantage of their employees. Aside from strengthening consciousness of the "Raubsucht und Habgier der Kapitalisten" which was driving towards an ever-lengthening working day, these reports had the concrete purpose of warning unaware immigrant workers away from especially unscrupulous establishments. In contrast, later reportage sketches by Schewitsch, Jonas and others, while claiming to make no "esthetic" pretensions but to be only "Photographien nach und aus dem Leben, ... nur den einen Anspruch erhebend, wahr zu sein,"[27] add economic interpretations of the events they recount, as well as sometimes cataclysmic invocations of future revolution and utopia. In addition to factual, journalistic techniques, these prose writers often make liberal use of the sentimentalized, black-and-white portrayals of popular literature to convey their political message, which becomes particularly evident in the calendar stories attempting to combine both socialist teachings and "Unterhaltung."

Other, shorter prose forms were also popular among the socialists. Essays, manifestoes and political pamphlets attempted to enlighten or call to action. Fables and Märchen, complete with concluding morals and interpretations, were refunctioned and conceived as analogies to social situations of conflict. Parodies and spoofs of traditional texts were popular, including the Ten Commandments, the catechism, the ABC, the United States Constitution, or the dictionary, which were rewritten into "Arbeiter-Katechismen," "Chicagoer Fibelverse," "Eine neue Constitution für die verunreinigten Staaten von Amerika," or an "Arbeiter-Wörterbuch" with a socialist message. Finally, Streitgespräche and dialogues meant primarily for reading were frequently printed in the socialist press. These usually commented -- often humorously or satirically -- on current events or issues, or they presented a debate on the social situation, economic or political issues, perhaps between a worker and a capitalist or between a socialist and a non-socialist worker. One of the most popular and successful political pamphlets put out by the SAP, Alexander Jonas' Reporter und Sozialist (1884), follows this format. All of these prose forms, while traditional in themselves, were refunctioned to serve the goals of enlightenment and persuasion within the context of the socialist movement.

The graphic art produced in connection with the German-American socialist movement was published in its press and either related to certain festive occasions or,
in the form of caricatures and political cartoons, satirized prominent figures or
events. The illustrations for festivals or commemorations are quite similar to
the popular lebende Bilder presented at public occasions with respect to the subject matter chosen, to their use of allegorical figures (the Goddess of Freedom,
Justice, etc.) and their tendency towards black-and-white portrayals. Like the
lebende Bilder, these drawings in the press functioned to present a schematic
view of history and of opposing social groups, to attack the opposition and strength-
en a positive self-image, and to invoke a utopian future.[28]

As well as can be determined from the few scores available,[29] the music composed
by German-American socialists remained within the tradition of songs for male
choruses, quartets, etc. with respect to its form. However, there was indeed a
recognition that the common practice of simply writing new words to old melodies
-- some with patriotic or religious associations -- was problematic. In an article
published in the Festzeitung des Arbeiter-Sängerbundes des Nordwestens in 1904,
entitled "Eine practische Aufgabe für die proletarischen Sänger," Wilhelm Rosenberg criticized the practice of putting "new wine in old jugs," asserting that some
of the old content would necessarily be brought to mind if the melodies of "Solda-
tenlieder, einseitige Vaterlandslieder, oder Heimath- und Heimwehlieder" were
reutilized.[30] Therefore, Rosenberg suggested that writers and composers should
place themselves in the service of workers' singing societies by creating new songs
and compositions. In one of the most sweeping statements mady by any of these socialist writers on the necessity of developing an alternative proletarian culture to
replace the bourgeois tradition, Rosenberg went on to say:

> Was heutzutage noch als gross in der Literatur dasteht, wird eines
> Tages der Vergangenheit überliefert sein, um erweiterten Mensch-
> lichkeitsideen Raum zu geben, und mit ihm daher werden auch alle
> Lieder verklungen sein, die einseitige Gefühle und falsche Anschau-
> ungen porträtiren. ... An Stelle der nationalen Beschränktheit wird
> das Weltbürgertum treten, an Stelle der Anbetung von Thron, Altar
> und Geldsack das ökonomisch befreite Menschenthum. ... Mein Vor-
> schlag ... kann und muss sogar noch erweitert werden, wenn die Auf-
> gabe erfüllt werden soll, die ganze bürgerliche Kunstmache im pro-
> letarischen Lager überflüssig zu machen und daraus zu verdrängen.
> (31)

Twenty years earlier, Rosenberg had begun to work to realize these suggestions.
Beginning in 1885, he and Emil Kirchner, a music engraver active in union circles and expelled from Leipzig under the Kleiner Belagerungszustand, operated a
publishing company in New York (Rosenberg & Kirchner) to issue new musical
compositions for workers' singing societies. They began by issuing a collection
entitled "Vorwärts. Liederschatz für Männer-Gesang-Vereine," and continued to
publish a significant number of works.[32] At this time there were several German
socialists living in New York whose compositions were regularly published by this

company and who were active as directors of workers' singing groups and mass choruses, or involved in the musicians' unions of New York City. Special mention should be made of one of these composers, Karl Sahm (1821-1883), a forty-eighter who worked as a music director to further the unification of workers' singing societies, and who composed over 500 choral works (many with texts written by himself or other socialists), thus rivaling Georg Uthmann's production in Germany.[33] At a memorial meeting of 3-4000 people held in New York after his death, a fellow socialist composer, Wilhelm Gundlach, evaluated the position taken by Sahm and artists like him within a class context as follows:

> So hat sich die Gesellschaft in zwei Klassen gespalten und nun blicken Sie um sich, zu welcher Klasse die Repräsentanten der Künste und Wissenschaft sich gesellen. Hier sehen Sie die Künstlerwelt in ganzen Schaaren vor dem König Mammon sich in den Staub werfen und dort hat sich die Zunft der Gelehrten demselben Götzen zugewandt. ... Und wenn nur ein Vertreter der Kunst, alle ihn lockenden Vorurtheile hintansetzend, sich zu der unterdrückten, also der Arbeiterklasse hält, dann ist es wohl zu begreifen, warum diese Klasse einem solchen Manne die höchste Verehrung zollt. (34)

That is, these composers viewed their activities as part of the general effort to create alternatives to art which affirmed the system of capitalism, rather than questioning or attacking it. And here, as with the literature, it is essential to make the distinction between the form, content and functional context of this music. With respect to musical form and technique, these works were no different from the standard 19th century repertoire for male choruses. However, new melodies were sometimes written, and the selection of texts corresponded to the political standpoint of the composers. Also, these compositions were meant to be sung at workers' social gatherings, festivals and demonstrations. Written primarily for men, and thus reflecting the consciousness and main political thrust of the socialist movement, many of these compositions were written for performance by mass choruses of hundreds of voices before large audiences. Aside from the individual Gesangverein, the mass chorus was the most popular form of musical performance, providing a vivid, palpable demonstration of unity and common resolve. Here again, art was situated in a working-class social and political context, and functioned as part of the attempt to create alternative cultural expressions.

5. PUBLICATION AND DISTRIBUTION OF GERMAN-AMERICAN SOCIALIST LITERATURE

The unremittant goal of political effectiveness not only led these writers to prefer certain genres, but it also shaped the way in which this literature was published and distributed. In contrast to bourgeois literature intended for individual, solitary perusal by those who could afford to purchase books, separately published works such as anthologies of poetry, plays or novels were of secondary importance. Rather, German-American socialist writers received their widest distribution through publication of their works in the socialist press. In this way, they could reach the largest possible audience, penetrate into the families of workers (feuilleton sections of these papers often stated explicitly that they were aimed at women and workers' families), and complement the news and editorial content · of the papers. The vast majority of the literature published in this press was reprinted nowhere else, and many of the poems in the small number of anthologies published first appeared in newspapers.

As the most important place of publication for this literature, therefore, the socialist press constitutes the essential source for any analysis. By far the most important papers of this period (in terms of their large circulation, prominent editors and content), and the ones which are relied upon most heavily in this study, were the New York Volkszeitung (1878-1933) and its Sunday edition, and the Chicago Arbeiter-Zeitung (1876-1919) with its Sunday (Fackel) and weekly (Vorbote) editions, the New York paper being connected with the SAP until the 1890's and the Chicago papers with the Social-Revolutionaries. In addition, the following papers, here arranged according to political affiliation, provided useful material:

1) the very earliest papers advocating the vaguely socialist doctrines of Schulze-Delitzsch:
   New York Arbeiter-Zeitung (1864-65)
   Der deutsche Arbeiter (Chicago, 1869-70)

2) the First International:
   New York Neue Arbeiter-Zeitung (1873-75)
   Milwaukee Socialist (1875-78)

3) the Sozial-Demokratische Arbeiter-Partei and the WPUSA:
   Arbeiter-Stimme (New York, 1874-76)

4) the SAP:
   Volksstimme des Westens (St. Louis, 1877-80)
   Social-Democrat (New York, 1876-78)
   Vorwärts (New York, 1892-94)
   Der Sozialist (New York, 1885-1892)
   Der Tramp (New York, 1888)

5) the Social-Revolutionary or anarchist press:
   Freiheit (New York, 1882-1910, edited by Johann Most)

Brandfackel (New York, 1893-95)
Sturmvogel (New York, 1897-99)
Parole (St. Louis, 1884-86)
Anarchist (St. Louis, 1889-95)

6) papers affiliated with unions but not with a socialist organization:
Arbeiter-Union (New York, 1868-70)
Philadelphia Tageblatt (1877-1944)
Der Hammer (Philadelphia, 1882-87)

7) the Socialist Party:
Wisconsin Vorwärts (1892-1932)
Neues Leben (Chicago, 1902-10)

Though these papers were the main channels for publication and distribution of German-American socialist literature, it must be admitted that -- as is also true for the SPD press in Germany -- this literature constituted by far the smallest portion of the feuilleton pages. Rather, the largest amount of literature published in these organs was selected from the sort of "Unterhaltungsliteratur" which might have been published in the Gartenlaube, or from the works of modern realists or naturalists such as Keller, Raabe, Fontane or Zola. Political poetry from the Vormärz period was often reprinted, and occasionally German SPD writers such as Minna Kautsky, Rudolf Lavant or Robert Schweichel were included, but in general there was little attempt to select literature for publication according to any consistent view of cultural politics, particularly with respect to the novels chosen for serialization. At the same time, however, these papers devoted a relatively large amount of space to their literary sections -- perhaps one-fourth or more in the earlier or smaller papers, and a whole feuilleton section in the New York and Chicago press. Several reasons may be advanced for the particular choice of works and the form these literary sections took. The above reference to the Gartenlaube was not arbitrary: these papers realized that they were competing with such non-socialist publications -- both those imported from Germany and those published by other German-American groups -- and therefore they attempted to offer their readers some of the same kinds of reading material. In this way, they sought to satisfy a need for entertainment and diversion. From various statements, it can be gathered that they thought women were the main readers of the literary section, and that if women bought the papers for this purpose, then they or their husbands might also read the political articles. That is, the literary sections were viewed as providing necessary entertainment and as an enticement to a working-class audience to buy the papers and perhaps become interested in socialism. They were not viewed as serving a political function in themselves, except in the general context of Bildung. For example, the Chicago Fackel is described on its masthead as an "unabhängiges Organ zur Belehrung, Unterhaltung und Erheiterung." These feuilleton sections or literary supplements did not contain only belletristic works, but also offered a selection of articles on scientific, historical, political, economic and social topics calculated to be of interest to a working class audience and to provide information which was not easily available elsewhere. Along with the Arbeiterbildungsvereine, this was an attempt to help raise the educational niveau of the readers of these papers, and a familiarity with recognized works of literature was part of this goal. That is, such literary works were viewed as necessary entertainment, as part of a well-rounded education, and as essentially harmless, or even non-political. Though German-American socialist writers did attempt to create an alternative body of literature, the attitude of socialist journalists and writers towards the literature of the bourgeois tradition was far from iconoclastic and continued to make the separation between the esthetic and the political realms.

Two more points are significant with respect to the selection of literature published in the socialist press. First of all, it is striking how few translations of works by American authors were published in these papers. With the exception of writers like Bret Harte or Mark Twain, whose works occasionally appeared, there seems to have been almost no effort to acquaint German-speaking readers with American literature. Rather, editors preferred to remain within the confines of the German literary tradition. Secondly, it seems to be the case that over the years, less and less socialist literature by German-American writers was published. It is during the 1870's and the period of the Anti-Socialist Laws that we find the most original literature by such writers, and this begins to decline in the late 1880's. In its place, the papers either reprint more literature by SPD writers or they decrease the space given to such literature altogether in favor of more popular literature or works from the non-socialist literary tradition. It could be that the earlier generation of writers, who were often active as SPD journalists before immigration and who were often forced unwillingly to emigrate, were more likely to carry on their literary activities in America than their children or than later groups of immigrants. It could also be that in the earlier period, German-American socialism was more militant, at least until 1886, and that this encouraged a more intense investment of energy, including the creation of an alternative literature and culture. Later, then, with the increasing assimilation of the German-speaking working class and ethnic group, there was not as much of an incentive to create a literature and culture based on a perspective of class confrontation.[35]

What other avenues of publication were open for German-American socialist writers? Aside from the newspapers, perhaps the most important socialist publication was the Pionier-Kalender, a yearly volume along the lines of similar calendars published by the SPD, put out by the New York Volkszeitung from 1882-1933 and usually consisting of well over 100 pages.[36] Like the socialist newspapers, the Pionier was intended as an alternative to publications issued by other interest groups, and the idea of publishing a socialist calendar was considered important because it might be one of the few book-length publications that a working-class family would be likely to buy every year. The announcement for the first volume stated: "In der unaufhörlichen Propaganda für unsere Ideen hat dieser 'Volks-Kalender' eine neue und gute Waffe zu sein,"[37] and the fiftieth volume affirmed these goals: "Der Pionier bot niemals den seichten Unterhaltungsstoff anderer Kalender, der den Geschmack verdirbt und dem Menschen das Denken verlernen lässt."[38] Like the feuilleton sections of the newspapers, the content of the Pionier should be viewed in the context of serving both an educational and an entertaining function, and as a vehicle for bringing socialist ideas into the family. Therefore, the following sorts of texts were included: fiction and poetry (with a much stronger emphasis on works by German or German-American socialist writers than on popular literature, in contrast to the newspapers); biographies of famous socialists or other important radicals; historical, theoretical and statistical articles on socialism and the workers' movement; articles on Arbeiterbildung; illustrations which were sometimes used as a starting point for social commentary; a political analysis of the events of the preceding year in Europe and America; various scientific and informative articles, humor, and cartoons; and, beginning in 1922, a section "für die Frau der Arbeit." The calendar section itself noted important dates from the history of the labor and socialist movement. German-American socialist writers, many of whom were associated with the Volkszeitung, contributed many of these articles and literary works. With respect to the literature, although quite a bit of poetry is included, this calendar contains more short stories and sketches by German-American socialists than any other source. Rather than simply reprinting any available "Unterhaltungsliteratur," as was the practice of the socialist press, the Pionier-Kalender provided an opportunity for these writers to offer to the public their attempts at creating a socialist "Unterhaltungsliteratur."

Aside from these channels, there were few opportunities for German-American socialist writers to publish their works. There were at least two short-lived ventures in publishing satirical weekly journals, Milwaukeer Leuchtkugeln (edited by Gustav Lyser in 1876),[39] and Der Tramp (edited by Wilhelm Rosenberg and Georg Biedenkapp in New York in 1888), but both of these undertakings lasted for less than a year due to lack of financial support. It was really only the largest papers which were able to survive over a long period of time, those enjoying solid support from the working-class community and organized labor.[40] After the mid-1880's, therefore, the number of German-American socialist papers with a small format and circulation dropped and only the largest ones survived and consolidated. Aside from the press, then, there were basically two possibilities for these writers, to publish their works in small editions on their own, "im Selbstverlag," or through the socialist cooperative publishing companies which put out the newspapers. As was pointed out earlier, the socialist newspapers were not published officially by the parties, but by private, "cooperative publishing associations." These associations also published a small number of works (more along the lines of political pamphlets than poetry or fiction) by German-American writers, and imported socialist books from Europe, combining these into special offers to the readers of their newspapers. For example, a wide selection was offered by the New York "Volkszeitungs-Bibliothek," and by the SAP's Labor News Company, and various collections of pamphlets were also published by different groups.[41] In general, however, the publication of individual works or collections remained of secondary importance, perhaps with the one exception of several collections of socialist songs,[42] which were meant in any case for use within the context of the political movement rather than for individual perusal. It should also be noted that a large amount of socialist literature was available from Germany, and that this certainly must have weakened the impetus of German-American writers to produce original works themselves, particularly after the 1880's. Works by SPD writers such as

Minna Kautsky, Schweichel and Lavant were often published in the press, plays by Kegel, Schweitzer and others were frequently performed, and SPD publications such as Die neue Welt, Der arme Konrad, Die neue Zeit and newspapers were readily available.[43]

As a final note on the channels through which this literature appeared in print, it should be emphasized that the mode of distributing most of this literature through periodical publications has led to difficulties in collecting and studying it. These publication forms are also tied to the goals of immediate political effect and the self-perception of these writers as being engaged in something other than artistic creation, in that they themselves made little effort to preserve these works after they had fulfilled their immediate purpose. Literary historians, concerned with masterpieces rather than with such ephemeral works, did not collect or anthologize them. Therefore, it is precisely some of the potentially most interesting sources, such as papers edited by Joseph Weydemeyer or August Otto-Walster and plays written by German-American socialists which have not been preserved. Archives contain few complete runs of papers, and often the special sections on Belletristik are lacking. This reflects a general neglect of labor and socialist history within academics in the United States which, accordingly, has consequences for the study of socialist literature and culture, since in this instance at least, research in all of these subject areas must refer to essentially the same sources. Therefore, the state of the most important source material means that any study of this literature will necessarily be incomplete and tentative in some respects.

6. ORGANIZED FORMS OF MEDIATION

In addition to being closely connected with the socialist movement through publication in its press, this literature also reached its intended audience through certain organizations and public activities which were also integrally related to socialist political groups, and which were part of the emerging socialist workers' culture within the ethnic group. An analysis of the functions these writers hoped this literature would fulfill would be incomplete without also discussing these ways through which it was disseminated. Found in many cities around the country were socialist workers' theaters which presented the available repertoire of Tendenzstücke as well as "non-political" comedies and farces. More important in terms of numbers were the workers' singing societies, which eventually united to form regional branches of the Arbeiter-Sängerbund von Nord-Amerika. These organizations attracted thousands to their festivals held around the country, and continued ongoing discussions of proletarian culture in their Festzeitungen. Finally, festivals, demonstrations, benefits and commemorations frequently provided the occasion for such groups to perform before a sizeable working class audience in a political setting, and for presentations involving large numbers of participants, such as festival plays, lebende Bilder or mass choruses. Thus, through conduits such as these, literature by socialist writers entered into a larger political context, and was intended to have specific functions.

A. Socialist Workers' Theaters

In the spring of 1877, in the first indication of amateur theatrical activity among German-American socialists, the New York Volkszeitung reported that the New York Arbeiter-Bühne, directed by August Otto-Walster, was just giving its successful first performances, including Max Kegel's Pressprozesse and Otto-Walster's Die Staatsretter.[44] Performances by local socialist theater groups soon became a popular feature of mass meetings and festivals in other large cities such as Brooklyn, Cincinnati, Louisville, Chicago, St. Louis, and in many smaller towns too numerous to mention.[45] These theater groups were affiliated with varying degrees of closeness to socialist political organizations. Some of them were actually local sections or groups within sections of a party, while others were composed of a politically more heterogeneous membership.

As can be seen from their repertoire and the occasions upon which they performed, these workers' theaters aimed at serving both entertaining and didactic functions. With respect to providing entertainment, the majority of plays in their repertoire were the same third-rate farces and comedies that could be seen any evening in petty-bourgeois clubrooms (Benedix, Körner, etc.), and these plays were performed within the circle of the dramatic group, for relatives and friends, in the context of a social evening. One dramatic group reported that in order to satisfy everyone's taste, it would perform two "Tendenzstücke," two "Volksstücke" and two "Possen" during the season, and this is a rather typical selection.[46] Thus, like the amateur theater activity which was a popular pastime in non-socialist circles, these theater groups served to provide entertainment of a compensatory nature in the small amount of leisure time remaining after work to both actors and audience. It should also be noted that American vaudeville and minstrel shows were advertised in German socialist newspapers and certainly drew from this audience. However, this compensatory function was not the main impetus behind the establishment of socialist workers' theaters. Rather, those involved intended to accomplish certain tasks within the context of the socialist movement, and it is this which sets these groups apart from other Laientheater of the time, as well as from established, professional German-American theater troupes. Through the performance of political plays at public meetings and festivals, these groups hoped to spread fundamental ideas of socialism in an entertaining way, to offer models for action and images of a better future, and thereby to reach an audience which would be less receptive to political lectures, which perhaps did not read the socialist press, and which would be difficult to approach in other ways. As an article on "Dilettanten-Bühnen" in the New York Sozialist stated:

> Wir sind ... der Ansicht, dass solche Tendenzstücke von allergrösstem Werth für die Verbreitung unserer Ideen in weiteren Schichten der Bevölkerung sind, welche aus leicht begreiflichen Gründen an wissenschaftlichen Vorträgen nicht den Antheil nehmen und dafür nicht das Verständnis haben und haben können, wie es vielleicht im Interesse der Sache zu wünschen wäre. (47)

Other reports also mention the desired agitational effect, and statements can be found that new members joined party sections after seeing such performances.

However, these workers' theaters were constantly faced with the problem that the repertoire of available "Tendenzstücke" was severely limited. Consequently, we find these groups performing the same plays over and over again by SPD writers such as Max Kegel and complaining about the lack of "tendenziöse Stücke."[48] Thus, in a review recommending Otto-Walster's play for workers' theater, In eigener Falle, a correspondent to Der Sozialist wrote:

> Auf dem Gebiete der Dramatik ist die sozialistische Literatur ... geradezu armselig. Ausser einem Dutzend kleiner Sachen, von denen wiederum nur ein paar bühnenfähig und bühnenwirksam sind, herrscht hier gähnende Oede, und wenn 'mal ein neues erscheint, so bleibt es unbeachtet, weil die Agitation von der (Arbeiter-) Bühne herab bis jetzt ziemlich stiefmütterlich behandelt wird und sich daher auch keine schriftstellerischen Talente entwickeln können. (49)

The socialist political organizations did not make it their concern to print and distribute copies of such plays to their local sections, although a few German and German-American plays could be ordered through the various newspapers or the Labor News Company of the SAP.[50] Therefore, it was left up to individual party members or members of workers' dramatic groups to write their own plays. It has been possible to identify approximately fifty such plays written before 1900, by writers who also fit the pattern discussed above of fulfilling other capacities within socialist organizations and of originating from varying class backgrounds, including the working class. Unfortunately, however, since many of these plays were circulated only in manuscript, for immediate performance, only the titles of many or very brief descriptions of their contents can be found. In a certain sense, this reflects the self-understanding of the writers: they did not view their works as esthetic creations meant to be preserved and to last for eternity, but as products meant to fulfill a specific political purpose at a particular time, which could be forgotten as soon as they had accomplished their task. As nearly as can be determined, by far the majority of these plays did not deal with a specifically American milieu. Instead, they continued to take their material from European situations, to portray generalized conflicts which could be applicable to any indus-trializing country, or to make use of allegory or abstract confrontations such as debates between a proletarian and a capitalist. However, a few plays dealt with significant issues in American society, including Gustav Lyser's Congress zur Verwirrung der Arbeiterfrage in New-York (1878) on governmental hearings after the 1877 railroad strike, and Wilhelm Rosenberg's Crumbleton (1898), on corrup-tion within business and industry. Also, at least one active SAP member, Chris-tian Pattberg of Brooklyn, wrote political plays meant especially to be performed by children at local party meetings and festivals.[51]

Several prominent German-American socialists took an interest in developing theater as a means of political agitation, including Rosenberg, Otto-Walster, and, perhaps surprisingly, Johann Most. Rosenberg, and particularly Otto-Walster, put their energies into writing short plays for workers' theaters, and Otto-Wal-ster supplied several of his own plays to dramatic groups that he organized in New York, St. Louis and Cincinnati in connection with the SAP. His plays were among the most popular selections for socialist workers' theaters, including Ein verunglückter Agitator, Die Staatsretter, and In eigener Falle, the latter one of the tiny number of plays by these writers to deal with police corruption and anti-socialism in an American milieu. A different approach to the development of ama-teur theater was taken by Johann Most.[52] Having always had an ambition to act, Most undertook to establish workers' theaters in his travels to New York, Chicago and San Francisco which he called "Freie Bühnen." The first play performed by these groups was always Die Weber, with Most himself playing the role of "der alte Baumert." In New York and Chicago, these amateur theaters were able to sustain themselves for several years, continuing to give performances of Die We-ber and other naturalist dramas. Most's reputation as a dangerous anarchist led to the only discoverable instance of police interference in German-American so-cialist theatrical activity, in connection with a performance of Die Weber by his New York "Freie Bühne." In an article captioned "Die Weber staatsgefährlich," the New York Volkszeitung reported on Oct. 29, 1894 that a performance had been forbidden by the Newark police. The police chief explained his motivation as fol-lows:

> Wir leben in einer Zeit grosser Aufregung. Im 4. Precinct sind
> 1000 Striker seit 9 Wochen ausser Arbeit, ihre Familien sind am
> Verhungern und ich halte es daher für gefährlich, einem Agitator wie
> John Most zu gestatten, sie noch weiter aufzuregen. Sollte er es da-
> her wagen, hier zu sprechen, werde ich ihn verhaften. (53)

Such performances were given by socialist workers' theaters as the high point or
featured attraction of political meetings or festivals such as those commemorating
the Paris Commune, or before smaller audiences in the course of the winter season, at New Year's or what might be termed "anti-Christmas" gatherings. In this
sense, they were part of the evolving German-American socialist workers' culture
and creation of alternative festival and social possibilities. Rather than simply
listing the various events at which such plays were performed, it seems more
informative to discuss one production in some detail, in order to bring out the
interconnections between socialist writers, journalists and political groups, and
to show what functions the production of such plays was meant to have. Of all the
plays produced by German-American socialists, the one which was reviewed most
extensively in their press was Die Nihilisten, a Festspiel written for the Commune
Festival of the Social-Revolutionaries in Chicago in 1882. In their list of proscribed
publications, German authorities enforcing the Anti-Socialist Laws attributed this
play to August Spies, but it seems more likely that two other socialists living in
Chicago, Wilhelm Rosenberg and Paul Grottkau, were the authors.[54] In any event,
the authors were active socialists, and the actors were also connected with Chicago
socialist groups, including the Haymarket martyrs August Spies and Oskar Neebe.
The play was the main event at the yearly Commune Festical sponsored by the Socialistic Publishing Company for the benefit of the party press, that is, the Chicago
Arbeiter-Zeitung, Fackel and Vorbote. This was a typical use of such festivals,
theatrical presentations or concerts -- to raise money for the party, the press,
SPD election funds or comrades in need.

The Chicago socialists had a special admiration for the Russian Nihilists, who
formed a nucleus of opposition to czardom and finally assassinated Alexander II
in 1881. The festival play Die Nihilisten, written and performed one year later,
deals with this group of revolutionaries. In the first act, which takes place in their
secret headquarters, the nihilists are printing and discussing their proclamations
to the people and their vision of Russia after its liberation from tyranny. In the
second act, members of the aristocracy and the military gather to plan the suppression of the nihilists. In the third act, the nihilists have been arrested and their
leaflets and press confiscated, and they are placed on trial. Accused of treason,
they give speeches to the court, accusing the accusers, and explaining how the perception of social injustice drove them to nihilism. Here it should be noted that since
the characters are modeled after real historical figures, two women have major
parts in this scene before court.[55] Finally, in the last act, the nihilists have been
condemned to exile and are on their way to Siberia through the desolate winter
landscape. But just when they are beginning to lose hope, their comrades find them,
kill the Cossack guards, and save them, announcing that Czar Alexander has been

killed according to the will of the people. Amid cheers to the nihilists, the play closes with the following appeal:

> Erhebt Euch, Brüder, aus dem Staube der Knechtschaft, schliesst fest die Reihen, und muthig und heldenhaft greift in den Busen der Entschliessung. Und wenn Ihr Alle an dem Unmuth Eurer Leiden das Schwert der Vergeltung schärft, wird die Stunde der sozialen Revolution und die kommende neue Zeit der Genius der Freiheit beschleunigen! (56)

As expressed in reports from the socialist press on the performance, which was described as enormously successful, this play was meant to serve several functions. The first was didactic, to transmit historical information and to educate the audience about the nihilistic movement:

> Die Nihilisten, dieses so trefflich gelungene Portrait russischer Autokratie, korrupter Beamtenwirthschaft und despotischer Herrschaft auf der einen, und die Noth und das Elend, sowie die heroische und edelmüthige Hingabe der Nihilisten für die Sache der Menschheit auf der anderen Seite, ist wohl am besten geeignet, dem Publikum einen annähernden Begriff über die Sachlage Russlands, sowie über die noch vielfach verkannten Bestrebungen des Nihilismus beizubringen. (57)

However, this was not meant to be the dramatic portrayal of a historical event for its own sake, but, presented within the context of a German-American socialist festival, the audience was also given an impetus to make connections between the goals of the revolutionaries portrayed on stage and their own situation. With respect to the production of the play, this connection between its content and the audience is shown most concretely by the fact that members of the armed socialist organization of Chicago, the Lehr- und Wehrverein, played the parts of the armed rescuers of the nihilists in the last act.[58] Thus, the appeal quoted above which immediately follows this rescue scene clearly takes on the character of a direct address to the actors and their sympathizers in the audience, and the call to raise the "Schwert der Vergeltung" takes on a (problematic) contemporary relevance. Also, the defense speeches of the nihilists in court, their attacks on tyranny and their program for the future were meant to be generalizable and could also be taken as statements of the Chicago socialists' goals. The hoped-for emotional reaction of the audience was described as follows in the Arbeiter-Zeitung:

> Die Vertheidigungsreden der Gefangenen sind durchaus objektiv und tragen trotzdem ein idealisiertes Gepräge, welches den Zuschauer zur Entrüstung gegen das herrschende Unrecht und zur Begeisterung für die Sache der Menschheit unwillkürlich hinreisst. (59)

Finally, the presentation of such a play was also seen as a conscious political statement in the context of the whole German ethnic group and the class divisions of

American society. As the announcement for this Commune festival stated, it was
extremely important that all friends of progress and freedom attend the festival
production,

> damit die herrschende Gesellschaft begreifen lerne, dass der Geist
> jener Märtyrer, die durch Henkershand einen leider nur zu frühzeiti-
> gen Tod fanden ..., immer mächtiger und gewaltiger die Menschheit
> durchdringt. (60)

That is, attendance at such a festival was viewed as a public, political statement
of commitment to revolutionary goals, as a continuation and further creation of
an alternative, progressive view of history, as a statement of self-identification
and self-definition of a group separating itself from ruling class power and ideology, and in this sense, as part of a growing socialist workers' culture. This function of socialist festivals will be discussed further below. For now it is worth
noting that the most important non-socialist German-American newspaper of Chicago, the Illinois Staats-Zeitung, totally ignored the performance of Die Nihilisten,
reflecting its typical lack of concern for working-class affairs.

Die Nihilisten continued to be performed occasionally at festivals in Chicago and
other cities, but the problematic nature of its content and the use to which it was
put is shown by the fact that the groups which performed it were all associated with
the IWPA, the Anarchist International, and that, coming under the increasing influence of Johann Most, they understood the message of the play to be a call to
carry out acts of terrorism, "die Propaganda der Tat." Thus, at a performance
for a Commune festival in St. Louis in 1885, reportedly attended by 3000 people,
the anarchist paper of this city, Die Parole, described the play as "agitational" in
the sense of having an educational function of historical enlightenment, awakening
feelings of solidarity, and encouraging the drawing of parallels to the audience's
own social situation. However, according to this article, the final lesson to be
learned from the play was "die Logik der Propaganda der Tat, wie sie uns in den
Nihilisten vorgeführt wird. Wir lernen, unsere Sklavenkette zu hassen, und dass
unsere 'Selbstregierung' durch den Stimmkasten eine Farce ist" (referring to the
more moderate strategy of the SAP).[61]

However, in spite of the fact that Die Nihilisten was eventually appropriated by
groups outside the mainstream of German-American socialism, the conditions of
its production were typical of socialist workers' theater. Both its authors and actors were active as journalists or party members and officials. As part of a political festival which was an anticipated yearly event and which attracted a working-
class audience of up to several thousand, it was used to spread ideas to people outside the narrow circle of party or union activists who might not be reached in other
ways. At the same time, participation in and attendance at the performance was a
public statement of self-identification with certain political goals, and thus part
of the creation of alternative possibilities for cultural expression within the ethnic
group. On the other hand, of course, this sort of use of dramatic productions also
has its quite problematic sides, including the understanding of "agitational" theater,

105

the desired effect of the plays as based on enlightenment and audience identification, the literary quality and technique of the plays and the quality of the acting, and even the conscious distinction made by these writers and actors between "disinterested" art and political theater in the service of a specific point of view. These questions should be kept in mind for further analysis.

German-American socialist workers' theater never went beyond the level of amateur performances, and, unlike the development in Germany after about 1900, no groups of socialist authors began to write plays which might have been performed by professional theaters. There were only scattered efforts by socialist groups to engage professional theater companies to perform plays such as Schiller's Die Räuber, or contemporary naturalist plays such as Hauptmann's Die Weber or Suderman's Die Ehre for a working-class audience. Amateur theaters continued to exist into the 1930's within the framework of the Socialist Party, performing almost solely the plays for workers' theaters which were being published in the meantime in Germany.[62] It was only with the formation of the Proletbühne, an agit-prop troupe associated with the Communist Party which performed in New York in the late twenties and early thirties, that a German-American workers' theater was formed which created its own material collectively and entered into productive contact with other troupes, including American ones.[63]

B. Workers' Singing Societies

Mass meetings would have been thought incomplete without the participation of one or more workers' singing societies (usually men, but occasionally women or even children). Although these groups were associated with the socialist movement from its beginnings in the 1860's and 1870's, it was in 1892 that the Arbeiter Sängerbund der Nordöstlichen Staaten was formed as a central federation of these societies, and it was followed in 1897 by the Arbeiter-Sängerbund des Nordwestens, centered in Chicago. Mid-northern (Detroit) and Pacific regional organizations also existed.[64] Approximately every three years, until the second World War, each region held a singers' festival which could attract 3-4000 participants and a much larger audience. The selection of pieces for these concerts, which consisted before World War I almost solely of the songs of German Social Democracy and songs by German-American socialist writers, drew more and more with time from the Liedertafelrepertoire (Heimatlieder, Jägerlieder, Trinklieder) which these societies had initially avoided. Referring to this growing trend, in 1928 the Communist paper Der Arbeiter criticized the "reformist" tendencies evident in the programs of the singing societies, and called for these groups to affiliate with the revolutionary workers' movement.[65]

However, in spite of this development, these singing societies were until the first World War the main channel through which socialist poetry reached its intended working class audience (aside from the socialist press). In this context, those involved in the societies viewed both their repertoire and their close connections to the socialist political movement as desired, necessary alternatives to what they saw as bourgeois or petty bourgeois culture and literature. The importance of these organizations as alternative possibilities for cultural participation is heightened when we note that, aside from unions and certain political demonstrations, the frequent festivals and concerts of these singing societies and the number of their participants and audience made them the largest German-American socialist organizations. How, then, did socialists perceive the difference between these worker's singing societies and others which were affiliated with the non-socialist Nordamerikanischer Sängerbund? Writing in a Festzeitung for a singers' festival in 1906, the socialist journalist Adolf Hepner of St. Louis (who was tried for high treason along with August Bebel and Wilhelm Liebknecht in Leipzig in 1872), divided German-American singing societies into three categories, consisting of the well-to-do in large cities, petty-bourgeois and non-socialist workers, and societies of socialist workers. The latter groups found it necessary to break away, he explained, because

> den Sozialisten das entsetzliche Philistertum der kleinbürgerlichen Sängerklubs unerträglich wurde: ich meine, ... die Gleichgültigkeit gegen weltbewegende Fragen,die Theilnahmslosigkeit fortschrittlichen Ideen gegenüber. ... Die Sozialisten wollten in den grossen Rahmen der Ausübung Freiheitslieder einfügen, welche dem Horizonte des Durchschnitts-Sangesbruders fernliegen. (66)

Writing in the same Festzeitung, Eduard Deuss explained more specifically what some of these differences were with respect to the songs performed by bourgeois and religious groups:

> Letztere verherrlichen in ihren Gesängen alles das, was wir als vernunftwidrig, nebensächlich und kriecherisch ansehen. Sie singen darin einer vernunftwidrigen Gottheit ihr Hosiannah; sie beweihräuchern darin ein königliches Gottesgnadenthum und ergeben sich in Bücklingen und Rückgratkrümmungen vor Dingen und Menschen, denen wir unsere Reverenz versagen müssen, während sie das Arbeiterlied in Acht und Bann thun. Dieses geschieht, wie die Anhänger dieser Gesangvereine behaupten, im Interesse der Kunst des Gesanges; der Realismus im Gesang wird verpönt, weil die Kunst darüber erhaben sein soll. (67)

Non-socialist singing societies were taken quite seriously by these socialists, then, (particularly because many of their members were from the working class) as effectively encouraging and strengthening attitudes of political indifference, Mordspatriotismus or religious belief.

As alternative cultural organizations, the workers' singing societies hoped to fulfill several purposes. First and foremost, they saw their function as political agitation, through the content of the songs they chose to perform, and with the goal of winning new participants to the socialist movement. Thus, the "Prinzipien-Er-klärung" of the Northwestern Federation declared:

> Der "Arbeiter-Sängerbund des Nordwestens" anerkennt die fortschritt-liche Bewegung der Lohnarbeiter in ökonomischer sowie politischer Beziehung und unterstützt das Proletariat im Klassenkampf gegen die Kapitalherrschaft.
> Zweck des Arbeiter-Sängerbundes soll sein: Durch Pflege von Ten-denzliedern im Besonderen und der Geselligkeit im Allgemeinen, sowie durch aktive Betheiligung an fortschrittlichen Arbeiterfestlich-keiten den Uebergang der Sänger von neutralen Vereinen in die fort-schrittliche Arbeiter-Bewegung zu erleichtern. (68)

Concretely, how were these groups connected to the organized socialist movement? There is very scattered evidence that a few singing societies required their mem-bers to join the SAP, but this generally does not seem to have been the case. How-ever, their membership certainly would have been sympathetic to socialist goals. With their active and passive members, the singing societies encompassed a wide variety of people beyond the narrow circles of party membership or activity, and drew them into socialist political events. This is shown most clearly by the parti-cipation of workers' singing societies in festivals or meetings which had the pur-pose of raising money for the socialist press or other party and political activities. Indeed, the impetus for forming city and regional federations of these societies arose from their joint performances at such events. For example, the New York City federation was created in 1883 after a concert in Madison Square Garden fea-turing a mass chorus of 500 voices, attended by 10,000 people, for the benefit of a SAP party organ in English.[69] After the first festival of this federation later in the year, the New York Volkszeitung wrote:

> Es ist den Arbeitern endlich gelungen, sich von der bisherigen phili-sterhaften Vereinsmeierei loszusagen und einen Bund zu gründen, welcher mehr als viele andere Vereinigungen geeignet ist, die Arbei-ter zusammenzuhalten und brüderliches Verfolgen gemeinnütziger In-teressen zu befördern. (70)

Similarly, after a concert held by 29 groups in New York in 1891 to benefit the SAP paper The People, the Northeastern Federation was formed and the practice of holding regular festivals adopted.[71] Additional examples could be cited, but the significant point here is that performances by these workers' singing societies were an integral part of socialist festivals and meetings, as well as being in their own right an alternative to other societies reflecting differing political orientations within the German-American ethnic group. More generally speaking, therefore, these societies did not represent merely an automatic continuation of a familiar aspect of the socialist subculture as it had already developed in Germany, or merely a transplanting of tradition. Rather, they were more fundamentally a re-sponse to needs and conflicts which their participants experienced as immigrants in the American situation, within the ethnic group.

But this participation of the Arbeitergesangvereine in socialist meetings is only the most obvious level of their involvement in politics. After all, it was from the particular character of the songs they performed that they promised themselves the desired effect. As has been noted before, there was no "official" theoretical discussion of literature or culture in German-American socialist circles. However, we do find numerous statements by socialists active in the political movement, referring to the repertoire and activities of the singing societies, on the function of the agitational Arbeiterlied. Indeed, this is really the only topic which stimulated these socialists to state their views explicitly on what function they believed this sort of "operative" literature should have. Therefore, these articles in Festzeitungen and newspapers on the Arbeiterlied are worth reviewing in some detail, because they have wider applications for how these socialists viewed the connection between literature and politics.

First of all, the workers' singing societies, like immigrant cultural groups and activities of every social class and station, served the function of preserving something "old": the German language and traditional habits of leisure activity and entertainment. (This can also be seen in the emphasis placed on teaching the German language, folk songs, and classical writers in the German-American socialist schools for children). In this context, one exiled socialist (Jakob Winnen) wrote:

> Der deutsche Arbeiter, in dem die Erinnerung an die liederreiche, alte Heimath ewig wach bleibt, müsste in der amerikanischen Frohne total versauern, geistig und physisch verkommen, bliebe ihm nicht die eine Zufluchtsstätte: der Gesangverein mit seinen heimathlichen Liedern und deutschem Frohsinn, die Gesang- und Musikfeste, wo er der belebenden Sprache des deutschen Volksliedes lauschen, am Freiheits-Sang sein Gemüth wieder stärken könnte für den alltäglichen Kampf mit den kulturfeindlichen Einflüssen des kapitalistischen Ausbeutungssystems. (72)

This passage clearly highlights two conflicting functions of organizations such as these singing societies, as the first part of it could apply to any petty-bourgeois Liedertafel! These contradictory aspects were reflected in the repertoire of the workers' singing societies, which -- like the dramatic groups discussed above -- was far from consisting of only explicitly political works. For example, the musical archives of two of the largest and most active groups in New York contain the following: about 375 scores of songs, including folk songs and about 50 humorous songs.[73] Of the total, about 20% are political songs. In addition, there are about 20 manuscripts of original political songs, some by German-American socialists, and several adaptations of German political poems to famous arias or marches from operas. From this, it can be seen that there was no guiding principle behind the selection of material for these societies (although their public performances before large audiences drew overwhelmingly from the political works).

But perhaps it is inaccurate to describe the functions of such cultural activity as totally contradictory on the basis of the above passage and a sampling of the repertoire, or at least this deserves to be made more precise. The workers' singing societies were an attempt to shape independently their members' leisure time, to provide opportunities for social contact among members of the same class, separated and removed from those with differing political points of view and from cheap entertainment which these socialists viewed as an immoral, decadent byproduct of capitalism.[74] Also, the above reference to "deutscher Frohsinn" is not totally stereotypical, but rather it is also important in the context of the running battle between immigrant social customs and the pervasive legacy of the Puritan heritage, which proscribed entertainment such as Sunday theater, concerts and outings, and was particularly oppressive on workers for whom Sunday was usually their only free day. As the head of the German section of the Socialist Party in Chicago, A. M. Simons, wrote in 1909 with regard to the importance of workers' singing societies in the social life of their members:

> Je mehr die Arbeiter in der Lage sind, in ihrer eigenen Gesellschaft zu leben, mit ihren eigenen Vergnügen, ihren eigenen Bildungseinrichtungen, unabhängig von der kapitalistischen Klasse, um so rascher werden sie von jenem Klassenbewusstsein und Solidaritätsgefühl erfasst, das zur Freiheit führt. Es war allezeit eine Schwäche der englischsprachigen sozialistischen Bewegung, dass sie sich wenig angelegen sein liess, auf das gesellige Leben des Arbeiters ausserhalb seiner politischen Bethätigung Einfluss zu gewinnen. (75)

The problem here, of course, which also has wider ramifications for the phenomenon of a "second culture," is that while these social pastimes carried on by workers outside the workplace were often indeed separate and occurred in a different political environment from those of other classes, they often consisted of similar activities. In this context, with respect to the repertoire and programs of the workers' singing societies, these groups were attempts to create independent opportunities for leisure and creative participation by people with a shared political persuasion, but, like the workers' theaters, they were also dependent to a large extent on traditional material. Also -- perhaps this is so obvious that it needs to be stated -- these groups did not want to politicize every minute of their members' lives. They placed a value on entertainment and humor which was not explicitly political in its content, but which had its place within a more cooperative life style. Does this indicate the compensatory nature of such entertainment, compensatory leisure as a refuge from unremitting labor? In any event, sociability and politics coexisted here, entertainment remained partly a reflex of the working day, and the political message was not always the supreme goal.

However, as explained above, it was the political message expressed in their songs which distinguished these groups from others representing different points of view. How did these socialists define the function of the Arbeiterlieder they performed? Fundamentally, as they explained in frequent articles on the singing societies and their festivals, they had two complementary purposes in view, the first being po-

litical influence and the second what might be called "die ästhetische Erziehung
des Menschen in der Arbeiterbewegung."[76] Thus, the first goal was that of enlightenment, to expose social contradictions and to invest the working class singers
and audience with a sense of their just rights. But although Aufklärung was of indisputable importance, the evocation of certain emotional responses was of equal,
if not greater significance to them. These songs were meant to create feelings of
solidarity, enthusiasm, and courage on the one hand, and anger towards the opposition and oppressors on the other. In addition, through their assurances or portrayals of a happy future, they were to strengthen belief in the eventual victory
of socialism. Accordingly, we find many statements such as the following:

1) Die Erweckung gemeinsamer Begeisterung, des Muthes und der
Ausdauer im gemeinsamen Ringen, muss Ziel und Zweck des Ar-
beitersanges sein. (77)

2) Arbeiter-Gesangvereine sind berufen, eine äusserst wichtige Mission in der modernen Arbeiterbewegung zu erfüllen. Sie sind gleichsam der Herold, der kampfesmuthig das Banner der Freiheit und
Aufklärung in dem heissen Kampfgewühl der nach Erlösung von den
fluchbeladenen Fesseln der Kapitalsherrschaft ringenden Arbeiter-
heere voranträgt. Ihr Gesang ... ist Kampfesweise, Sammelruf,
Waffenklang, Schlachtruf! Siegverheissung!
[Das Leitmotiv eines jeden Arbeiter-Sängers soll sein]: Wacht auf!
Wacht auf! Ihr habt zu lange schon geschlafen, es will endlich lich-
ter Morgen werden. Bald wird die Sonne am Himmel prangen über
ein Geschlecht von Freien und Gleichen die sich des Daseins freuen,
und Unrecht und Gier wird nicht mehr unter ihnen sein. (78)

A following chapter will analyze the literary techniques employed to serve these
purposes, but for now it should be noted that such statements postulate either an
attempt to persuade or a direct emotional identification of the recipient with the
attitudes expressed in the work.[79]

The second important goal which these socialists intended the workers' singing societies to realize, through the artistic experience of performing choral works and
through their content, was to create esthetic sensibility in their members and
audience, a sense for the "beautiful" and for "higher ideals." This was viewed as
a viable function of performing music, in particular, which would then lead to moral and social improvements over the former vices of those held at the lowest levels
of the social pyramid. A quote from Lassalle was sometimes cited in this connection of self-improvement: "Es ziemen Ihnen nicht mehr die Laster der Unterdrückten, noch die müssigen Zerstreuungen der Gedankenlosen, noch selbst der harm-
lose Leichtsinn der Unbedeutenden."[80] In this sense of appropriating the cultural
experience of music, both the routine-breaking experience of performing in the
singing societies and the large festivals, and the music and poetry themselves were
viewed as refining, transfiguring experiences which raised the participants to a
higher, more noble (i.e. respectable?) sphere beyond the misery and brutality of

everyday life. Let us look at some typical statements by these socialists on the task of music with respect to "ästhetische Erziehung:"

1) Der Sozialismus ist bestrebt, Kunstgeschmack und Sinn für das Schöne in der breiten Masse des Volkes zu wecken, die Kunst zu demokratisieren. ... Wo wäre wohl ein so mächtiger Faktor, dieses Sehnen nach edlerem Genuss, künstlerischem Geschmack zu fördern, als wie der Gesang, Sängervereinigungen und Sängerfeste?

   Die moderne Arbeiterbewegung sucht dem Arbeiter begreiflich zu machen, dass auch er ein Recht auf Antheil an den Errungenschaften des menschlichen Geistes, dass auch er ein Recht habe, sich zu erfreuen an den Schöpfungen gottbegnadeter Künstler! Gerade dieses Streben nach Vervollkommnung ihres Wissens, gerade dieses Sehnen nach edleren Genüssen zeichnet die Arbeiter aus, die unter dem Einfluss socialistischer Anschauungen stehen. (81)

2) [Die Aufgabe der Musik und des Gesanges ist]: den Menschen zu veredeln, ihn emporzuheben aus der Misere des alltäglichen Lebens nach idealeren Sphären, wenn auch nur für Augenblicke. (82)

3) Das Arbeiterlied erfüllt eine hohe Kulturmission in einem Zeitalter der unnatürlichsten Zustände. Es läutert die Herzen, veredelt die Gemüther, bringt uns einander nah und mildert unsere Leiden, zeigt uns im Rosenschein der Hoffnung das Licht der endlichen Befreiung. (83)

4) Poesie erleichtert den Kampf und das Leben, verklärt das Leben, erhebt und erweitert die Seele, und gewährt ihr einen Zufluchtsort, wo sie sich erholen kann vom Streite, wo sie die Kleinlichkeiten des Alltagsdaseins vergisst und ihres eigenen Daseins erst in vollem Masse froh wird.

   Arbeitergesangvereine sind nicht allein ästhetische Bildungsanstalten für die Arbeiter, sondern auch Mittel, dem höheren Streben der arbeitenden Klasse nach einem schöneren, menschlicheren Dasein Ausdruck zu geben. (84)

5) Wenn bei den bürgerlichen Gesangvereinen Musik und Gesang lediglich Selbstzweck ist, so sollen sie bei den Arbeiter-Gesangvereinen in der Hauptsache Mittel zum Zweck sein, -- sie sollen höheren Zwecken dienen. Sie sollen in erster Linie die Massen im Kampfe um ihre Befreiung begeistern zur Ausdauer, entflammen zur Hingabe für die hohe, gerechte Sache. Dieses ist jedoch nur ein Theil ihrer Aufgabe. Sie sollen die Liebe und den Sinn für Musik und Gesang in der Arbeiterklasse wecken und in die richtigen Bahnen lenken, so dass diese Kunst veredelnd auf sie einwirken kann. Wir brauchen ein neues Geschlecht, das frei ist von den Gebrechen der Unterdrückten, und den Lastern der gedankenlosen bürgerlichen Welt. (85)

These statements on the desirability of education to esthetic appreciation do not apply only to the Arbeiterlied. Rather, they can be extended to poetry and music in general as the sphere of art, of "gottbegnadete Künstler," to be distinguished from the sphere of everyday life. On the one hand, then, as is clearly expressed in (5), these songs were intended to have a certain politically didactic and emotional effect on the recipients, but they were also to create esthetic sensibility, an ability to appreciate beauty as an entity in itself. That is, on the one hand these socialists viewed art as a means to an end, a means of creating a desired political response, but on the other hand, they also deemed it essential to train the recipients to be able to assume a contemplative attitude of appreciation for art, for the beautiful. Indeed, this extension of esthetic sensibility to all members of society is presented as the main goal of socialism with respect to art: in the socialist society of the future artists will no longer be dependent on rich patrons for their existence, and the masses will be better educated and able to appreciate their works. Therefore, according to this view, socialism does not mean that artists would have to "cast their pearls before swine" (as Heine feared), but would enable a flowering of artistic, creative activity.[86]

In the final analysis, this goal of a democratization of art does not call into question the nature of this concept of the "beautiful" and art itself as a sphere removed from everyday life. The contemplative, appreciative attitude envisioned here is in no way different from bourgeois concepts of art emanating from the 18th century. However, this should be seen in the context of the particular stage of development of the working class at this time, and the prevalent concept of Arbeiterbildung.[87] This acceptance and propagation of a bourgeois concept of art and of educating the worker to fill his/her leisure time with ennobling pursuits was aimed in part against habits and traditions carried over from artisan times or acquired in the milieu of the poor quarters of large industrial cities. As Peter Brückner/Gabriele Ricke state,

> die ganze Kultivierung des Proletariats richtete sich auch gegen eine ältere Geschichte der Handwerker- und Bauernsolidarität. Verloren geht im 19. Jhdt. eine in Resten überlieferte jahrhundertealte Kampfestradition. ... Kultivierung, die zerstört hier Elemente der Klassen-Erinnerung. (88)

The contradiction between the political and the esthetic goals in the above passage is only too evident: it must imply that these socialists understood bourgeois art as neutral with respect to class if they could so praise the esthetic experience. Again Brückner/Ricke:

> ... die Absicht erst der Bildungsvereine, dann der SPD usw., den Arbeiter -- durch Befassung mit Kunst, mit Wissenschaft; durch moralische Erziehung und Disziplin -- 'auf eine höhere sittliche Stufe zu heben', [verweist] allerdings auch auf Probleme, denen pädagogisch zu begegnen nahe lag: etwa Alkoholismus, Elendsverwahrlosung, sexuelle Not. Gerade die Armen hatten nur die Wahl, das Objekt von

Wohlfahrt, oder das von Polizei, <u>oder</u> das Objekt dieser Erziehung (zum Deutschen, zum Staatsbürger ...) zu sein. Erziehung, das bedeutete jedoch die Arbeiter den bürgerlichen standards anzupassen. (89)

This passage is an excellent statement of the contradictory aspects of (esthetic) education within the socialist movement, emphasizing as it does both the real, serious deficiencies of contemporary working-class life and the affirmation of bourgeois cultural norms as antidotes. Thus, to return to the statements on the task of workers' singing societies, concern with art becomes a compensatory, contemplative activity, a way of filling leisure time which is in turn a refuge, a reflex of the working day, a time for the reproduction of labor power.

Now it begins to appear that the political and esthetic goals for the <u>Arbeiterlieder</u> and singing societies expressed in these statements are perhaps not as contradictory as they seemed at first. The tasks are the following: to enlighten the workers, to persuade them, to call forth certain emotional states through direct identification with what is being expressed, to mold their esthetic sensibility (and thus their emotions and needs) along the lines of certain preestablished standards which separate art and life. What all these goals have in common is that the recipient is perceived as an object to be shaped, enlightened and otherwise "improved" by literature and art, but not as a potentially active, creative social subject. As Brückner/Ricke state:

> Kunst wurde allerdings schon von der alten Sozialdemokratie vor dem 1. Weltkrieg als eine Art von Psychohygiene und seelischer Massage aufgefasst, die die Massen mit revolutionärem Kampfesmut erfüllen sollte. Bemerkenswerter Weise galt dieser Auffassung dann Kunst jedoch nur als Mittel politischer Erziehung, wenn sie selber nicht politisch war.
> Was soll denn die Kunst <u>wirklich</u> verändern? ... Es soll wohl nicht das Verhalten der Menschen durch Kunst verändert werden, sondern nur die Vorstellung in ihren Köpfen über die Realität. ...
> Die Leute müssen dem zustimmen, was mit ihnen geschieht. ... (90)

That is, art is not seen as having the function of exposing contradictions, of encouraging independent thought which would lead to changes in behavior, to praxis, but assumes either a commanding, hortatory posture (to which obedience is the desired response) or removes itself from the arena of social conflict altogether.[91]

It is important to ask whether the affirmation of these bourgeois views of art had the same meaning for the German-American working class as it had for its counterpart in Germany. There was never a figure in America like Mehring, whose advocacy of "bürgerliche Literatur" from within the "proletarische Partei" was a crucial influence on the future development of socialist literary criticism.[92] But with respect to the musical groups, the context in which these esthetic considerations were most often voiced, they did follow the same path as the <u>Deutscher Arbeiter-Sängerbund</u> in Germany, becoming progressively more similar to non-socialist groups. The sense of class identification dissipated as the ethnic group became more assimilated into the mainstream of American society, and undoubtedly the affirmation of bourgeois artistic standards and the separation of art from life contributed to this integration.

C. Festivals, Demonstrations, Commemorations

Up to now, the ongoing festival activity created within working class movements has been neglected, on the whole.[93] However, in the United States as well as in Germany, it was also part of the effort to create alternative opportunities for cultural expression. Specifically, festivals provided yet another avenue for socialist literature to reach a working-class audience. More generally speaking, socialists perceived the festivals themselves as important cultural events in their own right.

German-American socialists reached their greatest degree of public visibility through their participation in mass meetings, which were often connected with large labor organizations such as the Central Labor Unions of New York City and Chicago and which served several purposes. There were demonstrations in support of particular demands, especially the eight-hour day. Festivals were held to commemorate important events in the international working-class movement, such as the Paris Commune, Lassalle's birth and death (around which a real cult was created), the assassination of Czar Alexander II, and the execution of the Haymarket martyrs on November 11. (Of particular interest is the memorial meeting held after Marx's death in Cooper Union in New York on March 20, 1883, where speakers in German, English, Russian, Bohemian and French addressed an overflowing crowd of workers).[94] There were also festivals to counteract and provide alternatives to "bourgeois" religious and patriotic holidays such as Christmas, Thanksgiving and the Fourth of July. Finally, local sections of socialist organizations, together with unions, often sponsored smaller events such as benefits or fall and spring festivals and fairs, primarily for their German-speaking members.

Most of these mass activities shared common features. There were speeches by party or trade union officials in several languages, at least in German and English, but sometimes in others as well, depending on the makeup of the local population. These larger meetings thus provided a chance for workers from different ethnic groups to come into contact with each other, and for the strengthening of class ties across ethnic groups. Also, these meetings provided an occasion for socialist literature to be transmitted to a sizeable working class audience in a political setting. These gatherings usually featured declamations of poetry (from the Vormärz or by socialist writers), labor songs sung by mass choruses of workers or sometimes a play performed by a local socialist dramatic group or a lebendes Bild. Finally, after the speeches and literary and musical presentations, and after the audience had joined together in singing the "Marseillaise" or Audorf's "Arbeiter-Marseillaise," a dance would often follow which lasted far into the night.

The functions of these festivals were similar in some respects to the statements
discussed above on workers' theaters and singing societies, and can be related to
the socialists' understanding of the function of the literature they wrote and of art.
Here again, the distinction between form, content and context is methodologically
essential when discussing the possibilities for a developing workers' culture. In
the first place, the festivals were a source of entertainment, enjoyment, escape
from the rigors of the working day, a place for a renewal of strength (labor power)
and courage in the company of friends, family and comrades. The importance of
the creation of such opportunities for communal leisure time should not be mini-
malized or trivialized. As Gottfried Korff points out with reference to Germany,
even activities such as "Waldspaziergänge [the struggle to experience nature],
Kaffeekränzchen, Liederfeste" were sometimes punished as illegal refusals to
work, and therefore even what seems to be an <u>Abklatsch</u> of bourgeois festival customs also takes on a different meaning in the working-class context as an attempt
to build up an alternative culture and humanize work and life.[95] In the United States
the oppressive effect of the Puritan heritage on the leisure time of the working
class gave an added dimension to these efforts. Of course, this insistence on opportunities for enjoyment and leisure has a history as long as that of oppressed
classes themselves. Here, in particular, we may recall the discussion in Chapter I
on early workers' resistance to capitalist rationalization of their work habits and
their everyday lives, which took the form of simply refusing to work regular or
long hours, taking days off or insisting on long breaks for eating and drinking.
Later on, these vacation days became workers' festivals, gained through organized
struggle (and thus robbed of their spontaneous character), and retaining their importance as self-obtained leisure. In an article written for the <u>Pionier-Kalender</u>
on "Die amerikanischen Feiertage" (1896, p. 58ff), Friedrich Sorge pointed out
that workers did not necessarily have days off on "bourgeois" holidays such as New
Year's or Washington's birthday, and that Sunday was only a day of rest rather than
a holiday because of the strict closing laws. Here he emphasized the worker's need
for rest, social interaction and intellectual stimulation, and pointed out that the
designation of Labor Day as a legal holiday was the result of a protracted struggle.
The importance of workers' festivals as breaking monotony and providing an opportunity for escaping the rules and regulations of the factory, as offering an escape
from the misery of daily life, is well expressed in the following statement on a festival sponsored by the First International in New York in 1873:

> Die äusseren Eindrücke machen den inneren Menschen. Die Eintönig-
> keit unserer Lebensweise macht uns abgeschlossen und kleinmüthig;
> wie sehr aber hat der Arbeiter nöthig, seinen drückenden Verhältnis-
> sen gegenüber muthvoll und offenherzig zu sein. Dieser Muth, Mitar-
> beiter! erwächst uns erst, wenn wir uns in grosser Zahl sehen, haupt-
> sächlich aber dann, wenn uns nicht die Arbeitsregeln unserer Arbeits-
> geber in die Augen grinsen und die kleinlichen Chikanen derselben uns
> nicht erreichen können, also einmal einen heiteren Tag nach so vielen
> traurigen und qualvollen, um in gehobener Stimmung uns gegenseitig
> anzufeuern <u>zur</u> <u>tapferen Ausdauer</u> <u>in</u> <u>dem</u> <u>schweren,</u> unabweisbaren
> <u>Kampfe,</u> <u>den</u> <u>wir</u> <u>kämpfen.</u> (96)

A further function of these festivals, in addition to providing entertainment and leisure, is indicated in the last part of this passage and can be seen from the typical activities described above. Like the early socialist literature, these festivals were intended to enlighten the participants, to endow them with a certain oppositional sense of history, and to create feelings of solidarity. As one journalist wrote,

> Diese Feste verfolgen den Zweck, das Volk an seine Grossthaten zu erinnern, sie zu neuen erfolgreicheren Thaten anzufeuern und das Gefühl der Solidarität, der Interessengemeinschaft aller Enterbten und Geknechteten zu erwecken und lebendig zu erhalten. (97)

That is, the socialist workers' festivals contributed to the consciousness of progressive historical traditions and constituted alternative cultural expressions in which the transmission of socialist literature was situated. On the one hand, workers' festivals were often conceived as direct, political alternatives to customarily celebrated "bourgeois" festivals. Examples of this include patriotic holidays such as the Fourth of July (socialists proclaimed American independence to be invalid for workers), and religious holidays such as Christmas (when socialism would be invoked as the new Messiah or religious overtones omitted altogether) or Thanksgiving (notable here is a parade of the poor and unemployed organized by socialists in Chicago in 1884). On the other hand, a specific succession of festivals evolved which reflected events of historical importance to the international working-class movement. Also, May Day and Labor Day were established as holidays on which to voice demands for the future, at this time primarily the eight-hour day. Thus, these festivals and other large demonstrations were both statements of concrete political goals and expressions of cultural self-realization and self-determination. In the context of the ethnic group in America, they take on added significance for the following reason: these festivals and demonstrations were the main arena (aside from trade union activity) in which German-American socialists were really able to enter into public political debate and to gain attention outside of their own ethnic group. After all, German-American socialist literature, workers' theaters, singing societies and the press were all confined almost exclusively to the language group. Controversies raged within it, to be sure, particularly among newspapers of differing persuasions, but these were effectively insulated from the English-speaking world outside. Therefore, these large, public events assume a particular importance with respect to the consolidation of the working class within the ethnic group and its self-perception in the face of the rest of American society. Parallels may even be drawn to the German situation. As Gottfried Korff explains, the festival of May Day was often the only opportunity for workers' culture to become public (öffentlich), as a day of "demonstrative Selbstdarstellung."[98] We can find this consciousness of the crucial importance of taking a positive public stand in descriptions by German-American socialists themselves of their festivals, such as the following from 1878:

> Sie [die sozialistische Weltanschauung] wird verachtet, verspottet, entstellt. Daher ist es die Pflicht eines jeden ihrer Anhänger, jede

Gelegenheit zu ergreifen, um seine Ueberzeugung zu bekunden und in den Reihen seiner Gesinnungsgenossen Muth und Kraft zu neuem Kampfe zu schöpfen. ...

Für die Parteigenossen sind solche Feste eine Heerschau. Nach der mehr oder minder bedeutenden Anzahl der Theilnehmer wird die Kraftentwicklung der Partei, die Lebensfähigkeit der Idee bemessen.

Für die Gegner ist es eine ernste Mahnung, eine gewichtige, würdevolle Antwort auf alle Verleumdungen, Lügen und Spöttereien.

Für die Indifferenten ist es eine günstige, manchmal die einzige Gelegenheit, jene vielgeschmähten Sozialisten und "Umsturzmänner" zu sehen und ihre Lehren zu hören. Es ist ein wirksames Mittel für Propaganda und für Selbsterkennung seiner Kräfte. ...

Es gilt, den frechen Lügnern, die unsere Sache beschimpfen, eine imposante Antwort in's Gesicht zu schleudern. Es gilt, den Spöttereien dieser selbstsüchtigen Schurken gegenüber zu zeigen, dass Tausende und Abertausende der besten, tüchtigsten Arbeiter der Fahne des Sozialismus folgen. Wer sich da nicht auf seinem Posten einfindet -- der ist ein Deserteur, ein Verräther an seinem Gewissen, an seiner Ueberzeugung. (99)

Along these lines of self-definition and self-expression, socialist literature also took its place on the festival programs. Thus, quite a number of poems were written expressly as prologues or recitations for particular celebrations, thematizing the historical events noted above. In addition, although the workers' singing societies held their own independent festivals, they and the workers' theaters were also featured participants at most socialist festivals and mass meetings. At such gatherings, then, this literature was able to reach large numbers of the people it was intended for, and this occurred in conjunction with more explicit statements (in speeches, for example) of the political goals with which the authors sympathized. Here the literature entered into collective, public forms of self-expression although, to be sure, it retained its posture of enlightenment and command.

7. SUMMARY

In summation, then, while this German-American socialist literature is often
characterized by the use of traditional forms, its content and the circumstances
of its production and distribution set it apart from the rest of German-American
literature. Its authors were party officials, members or sympathizers, and theoretically any reader of this literature could also become a writer. The intent of
these authors that their literary productions should contribute to enlightenment
and the growth of class consciousness led them to prefer certain genres and shaped
the ways in which this literature reached its intended audience -- through the socialist press, singing societies and dramatic groups, and workers' festivals. At
the same time, they upheld the distinction between this "agitational" literature
geared towards evoking a desired political response on the one hand, and "high
art" on the other, believing that an important part of socialist Arbeiterbildung
was for workers to be educated to be able to appreciate (i.e. assume a contemplative, passive attitude towards) this portion of the cultural heritage. Nevertheless,
with all its problems and contradictory tendencies, this socialist literature was
part of the self-definition and consolidation of the German-American working class
within the ethnic group. Seen in this light, and keeping the historical development
described in Chapter II in mind, it becomes evident that this literature is not
merely an unthinking continuation or reproduction of traditions learned in Germany.
Rather, it is also a response to American situations and experiences, and an attempt to understand and influence them within a class context. It is a response to
the class oppression immigrants encountered in a rapidly industrializing America, an attempt to overcome disillusionment by utilizing familiar cultural forms
geared towards maintaining and strenghtening identity. The following chapters will
analyze how these goals shaped the form and content of the literature itself.

IV. EXCURSUS ON GERMAN WORKERS' LITERATURE:

A "FORSCHUNGSBERICHT"

In contrast to the past and present state of research on early workers' or social-ist literature in the United States, there has indeed been a debate over this topic (carried on with interruptions) within German literary criticism. A brief survey of the central issues here is relevant to the analysis of German-American social-ist literature because these writers continued literary activity begun in Germany and therefore this criticism can often be applied to their writings. As Bernd Wit-te points out, until recently the literature written within the framework of the or-ganized workers' movement in Germany before 1914 was almost totally forgot-ten.[1] On the one hand, this was due to the unwillingness of the SPD during the Weimar Republic to validate its more oppositional, revolutionary past. With re-spect to literature, this means that the conceptually and formally different "Ar-beiterdichtung" of writers such as Max Barthel, Karl Bröger and Heinrich Lersch came to be associated with the SPD.[2] Also, with its literary orientation around Soviet practice (Arbeiterkorrespondentenbewegung) and its propagation of the "So-zialfaschismus" theory, the KPD was certainly not inclined to preserve or call attention to the literary production of pre-war writers who supported its political rival. On the other hand, even where socialists recognized the existence of this literature, they maintained a perspective rooted in 18th-century concepts of es-thetics and did not include it in their theoretical reflections on art.[3] Its writers themselves only viewed it as "Gebrauchsliteratur" meant to carry out a particular function and then be put aside. And SPD theoreticians, most influentially Franz Mehring, held notions of art grounded in idealism which excluded such works as lacking in artistic value and too closely bound to pragmatic goals. As Mehring wrote in his essay on "Kunst und Proletariat" in 1898:

> Seit den zahlreichen Klageliedern, die um Lassalles frühen Tod er-schollen, schlang sich ein Kranz schlichter und schmuckloser Weisen durch die Geschichte der deutschen Sozialdemokratie, 'manch rund, manch rauh gestammelt, manch still, manch wild Gedicht': Audorf, Hasenclever, Frohme, Geib und wie viele noch schmiedeten ihren wackeren Reim in den Mussestunden des politischen Tageskampfs; andere, wie Max Kegel, Leopold Jacoby, Rudolf Lavant, standen der Politik ferner und der Dichtung näher, aber auch sie beanspruchten keine neue Aera der Kunst zu eröffnen. Sie wollten nur, wie sich der formvollendetste von ihnen einmal ausdrückte, allem Zorn, aller Trauer, allem Jubel Luft machen, womit sie der proletarische Be-freiungskampf in seinen wechselnden Phasen erfüllte. (4)

This separation according to esthetic principle between politics and high literature, between life and art, was typical of SPD attitudes and contributed to the neglect of literature written within the context of the workers' movement.

The literary criticism emanating from more "bourgeois" circles tended to arrive
at similar evaluations. It is unnecessary to unroll here the whole hair-splitting
debate over the definition of the term "Arbeiterdichtung" itself.[5] What is relevant
is that a certain concept was established in the twenties which continued to be accepted by literary historians until the sixties. In 1924 the Berlin theater critic
Julius Bab published a short study on "Arbeiterdichtung" which was the first attempt to comprehend this as a well-defined literary area. Specifically, Bab formulates two requirements that literature had to satisfy in order to qualify as
"Arbeiterdichtung:" it had to express proletarian class consciousness and do this
through formal innovations:

> Einmal muss die <u>Dichtung in ihrem inneren Wesen</u> wirklich vom Geist
> der Arbeiterklasse berührt und umgewandelt sein: d. h. es genügt
> durchaus nicht, wenn der Arbeiter und seine Welt als Stoff, als The-
> ma, als Idee in solchen Gedichten vorkommen, dies Thema aber ganz
> in der herkömmlichen Art irgendwelcher berühmter bürgerlicher
> Künstler behandelt wird. Das Entscheidende im Bereich der Kunst
> ist immer die <u>Formkraft,</u> und erst dann wird es irgendeinen Sinn ha-
> ben, von "Arbeiterdichtung" zu sprechen, wenn auch die eigentliche
> dichterische Form: die Wahl der Worte, ihre rhythmische und geisti-
> ge Anordnung, die Bilder der Sprache, die ganze Art der Phantasie
> deutliche Kennzeichen einer neuen Menschenart zeigen.
> Und zweitens müssen diese Dichtungen wirklich von einem <u>Arbeiter</u>
> in dem uns heute lebendigen Sinne des Wortes sein. ... Der heutige
> Arbeiter ist ein <u>Grosstadtmensch,</u> in innerster Berührung mit In-
> dustrie und Weltwirtschaft, und er ist vor allem ganz innerlich ge-
> zeichnet durch die Tatsache seines Klassenbewusstseins. (6)

In the succeeding discussion, then, Bab proceeds to place most of the weight on
the first criterion of formal refinement, and as a result dismisses early socialist
poetry from consideration as part of "Arbeiterdichtung" because in his opinion,
"künstlerisch betrachtet," it is "nicht mehr als ein warmherziger Gesinnungsaus-
druck, der seine rednerischen Mittel berühmten Vorbildern der bürgerlichen
Poesie entlehnt."[7] The place where he does find the formal skill he demands is in
the writings of such authors as Barthel, Bröger, Lersch, Alfons Petzold and Ger-
rit Engelke, who make use of forms and language taken over from Expressionism,
and who convey more of a subjective, individualized, emotional attitude and less
direct political engagement than the early socialist poetry. It is these writers of
poetry whom Bab designates as "erste wirkliche Arbeiterdichter deutscher Sprache."[8] Bab's emphasis on formal standards of evaluation and his postulation of a
"klassische Arbeiterdichtung" including only the above writers had the effect of
concealing its connections to the earlier socialist literature and also of glossing
over the connection between "Arbeiterdichtung" and the organized workers' movement.

After 1949 Bab's narrow definition of workers' literature was at first accepted
uncritically by West German literary historians. Here, as Bernd Witte has pointed

out, it is noteworthy that the early socialist literature which Bab dismisses for esthetic reasons is not even mentioned as existing by these later Germanists.[9] Also, the conception of a "non-political" workers' literature unconnected to political movements was most convenient for literary historians operating under the slogans of "Ideologieverdacht" or even "Ideologielosigkeit." Thus, standard literary histories and handbooks from these years echo Bab's definition and his selection of writers of workers' literature, as the following examples illustrate:

1) Martin Greiner (1957): Die Arbeiterdichtung als Versuch der literarischen Selbstdarstellung des Arbeiters wird, als sie im zweiten Jahrzehnt des 20. Jahrhunderts erstmals als literarisches Gesamtphänomen in Erscheinung tritt, wesentlich durch drei Faktoren bestimmt: 1. künstlerisch durch den Expressionismus, 2. sozial durch die Jugendbewegung, sie ist eher reformistisch als revolutionär, 3. politisch durch die nationale Erschütterung des ersten Weltkrieges, eher versöhnlich als kämpferisch. (10)

2. Fritz Martini (1958): Als Arbeiterdichtung wird eine literarische Bewegung bezeichnet, die in den ersten drei Jahrzehnten des 20. Jahrhunderts sich thematisch der technisch-industriellen Arbeitswelt zuwandte und von dichtenden Arbeitern getragen wurde. ... Die Entwicklung der Arbeiterdichtung im präzisen Sinne vollzog sich in Berührung mit dem Expressionismus und mit dem Erlebnis des Weltkrieges. ... [Martini names Lersch, Bröger, Petzold and Engelke as "Arbeiterdichter"]. (11)

3. Jürgen Rühle (1962): In den Jahren vor dem Weltkrieg traten die ersten Arbeiterdichter in die Literatur ein, K. Bröger, Heinrich Lersch, Max Barthel und andere. ... Sie gelangten nie über sozialdemokratische Erbauungslyrik, republikanische Feiertagspoesie hinaus. (12)

4. Gero von Wilpert (1964): In soziologischer Hinsicht [ist Arbeiterdichtung] die aus den Reihen der Arbeiter (bes. Fabrikarbeiter) selbst geschaffene und auf ihre Thematik beschränkte Dichtung. Sie entsteht erst mit Beginn des 20. Jahrhunderts und empfängt starke Impulse durch A. Holz und G. Hauptmann sowie den Expressionismus. Durch einzelne Stimmen vor und im 1. Weltkrieg vertreten, erfährt sie starke Förderung durch die folgende soziale Umschichtung wie durch die Hebung des Standes[sic!]-bewusstseins arbeitender Klassen. (13)

These continuing attempts by literary historians to uphold the distinction between political engagement and artistic quality, to depoliticize their topic of "Arbeiterdichtung," to avoid discussing its connection with the organized workers' movement and even to explain its origins as rooted in the "bis in letzte Tiefen greifenden völkischen Gemeinschaftserlebnis im Kriege" (Martini)[14] were typical of West German literary criticism until the mid-sixties.

It is only within the last fifteen years or so, in the context of a new interest in "operative" forms of art, that groups of literary historians in both the GDR and the FRG have begun to revise this image of "Arbeiterdichtung" by bringing to light again the essential connection between this literature and the organized workers' movement and by applying standards of evaluation in which artistic quality does not automatically exclude political engagement. One consequence of these methodological procedures was that in both the GDR and the FRG a new interest arose in pre-1914 workers' literature associated with the SPD, which, however, reflected differing intents and perspectives. Germanists in the GDR were the first to call attention to this neglected body of literary productions and to include these works in their theoretical discussions, from the perspective of unearthing and fostering the reception of the progressive German literary heritage. This sort of research was encouraged in a state which understood itself as the legitimate heir of both bourgeois humanism and the German socialist movement. Therefore, studies in this area belong within the context of a particular concept of the appropriation of the progressive cultural heritage as a whole. This in turn affects the evaluation made of these early socialist writers, who are judged according to their assimilation of the "realistic tradition." The best of them are placed in a direct line of literary development to "socialist national literature," as in the following assessment of the socialist writer Leopold Jacoby (1840-1895) by Manfred Häckel:

> Stellt man Jacoby in die literarische Entwicklungslinie, die von Weerth bis zur sozialistischen Nationalliteratur unserer Zeit reicht, so heisst das zugleich, ihn als einen Fortsetzer der Linie zu begreifen, die von Lessing über Goethe und Schiller hin zu Heine, den Weerth als seinen Lehrer bezeichnete, reicht, eben der deutschen Literatur, die die Selbstverwirklichung des Menschen in den Mittelpunkt ihrer Gestaltung rückte. Jacobys These, dass die Schönheit das Ziel des Werdens sei, besitzt nicht nur enge Beziehungen zum klassischen Schönheitsbegriff des 18. Jahrhunderts, sondern auch zu Marx' Prognose vom befreiten Menschen, der beginnt, "seine Umwelt nach den Gesetzen der Schönheit zu gestalten und damit das Bild des Menschen und seiner Beziehungen nach den Gesetzen der Schönheit zu formen." Gerade durch diese Bindung an die besten Traditionen deutscher Literaturentwicklung und marxistischer Gesellschaftsprognose wurde Leopold Jacoby zu einem unmittelbaren Vorläufer der sozialistischen Nationalliteratur. (15)

In view of the systematic, persistent neglect of this literature by literary historians, the first task necessary was to collect, select and reprint the existing material. In the GDR, the most extensive research in this area has been published in the series of Textausgaben zur frühen sozialistischen Literatur in Deutschland (Berlin: Akademie-Verlag, 1964ff), presently encompassing fifteen volumes. These include collections of works by individual authors (Friedrich Bosse, Leopold Jacoby, Minna Kautsky, Max Kegel, Rudolf Lavant, Adolf Lepp, Werner Möller, August Otto-Walster), women socialist writers, and new editions of socialist plays, calendar stories, workers' songbooks and poetry. The texts are always preceded by lengthy introductions which provide biographical information and literary and historical analysis. In addition to this series, the Lexikon sozialistischer deutscher Literatur. Von den Anfängen bis 1945 (1963, Raubdruck 1973) is indispensable and still the most comprehensive source on many aspects of this topic, particularly on early socialist prose, which has hardly been treated in other secondary literature. Furthermore, this literature also came to be regarded at this time in the GDR as an acceptable topic for discussion at the university, and has been treated in a number of dissertations and "Habilitationsschriften," beginning with those by Cäcilia Friedrich on Minna Kautsky (Halle, 1963), Wolfgang Friedrich on socialist literature up to 1878 (Halle, 1964), and Gustav Schröder on socialist drama up to 1914 (Potsdam, 1965). In general, then, here there has been a systematic and serious discussion of this literature, which has not taken place to such an extent in the West.

Broadly speaking, these literary historians view the merits of this literature as rooted in its opening up of certain thematic areas and problems (working class conditions, milieu and resistance), its "Parteinahme" for the interests of the working class, and its intended operative functions. As Silvia Schlenstedt states in the introductory survey to the Lexikon:

> Das Gedicht spielt in der proletarischen Bewegung eine grosse Rolle, es hat propagandistische Funktion bei der Verbreitung der sozialistischen Ideen unter den Massen. Es ist charakteristisch, dass diese Lyrik in der Regel direkt auf ihr Publikum gerichtet ist, ... und zur Bewusstseinsentwicklung und Kollektivbildung unmittelbar beitrug. ... Die Parteinahme des Schriftstellers, die Bejahung des Kampfes, die Siegesgewissheit trotz Verfolgungen wird unmittelbar ausgedruckt ... (16)

That is, the concept of an operative literature which is affirmed here entails the functions of enlightenment and creating solidarity. Also, it would seem to postulate an identity between the literary work and the recipient: presumedly the recipient is to reproduce or reflect the attitudes of "Parteinahme," "Bejahung des Kampfes," and "Siegesgewissheit" if this literature is to have the desired effect.

On the other hand, while these Germanists concede that this literature is of historical importance and that, as agitational, operative literature, it aimed at having a certain effect on its audience, they still criticize many works as both politically erroneous and as esthetically inadequate. That is, they do not advocate an unmitigatedly positive evaluation of this literature, but criticize it on several levels according to the standards of the progressive literary heritage voiced in the above quotation from Häckel. First of all, following in Mehring's footsteps, they see it as due to the undeveloped stage of the class struggle and the repression under the Sozialistengesetz that these writers had difficulty in assimilating the "realistic traditions." On the one hand, according to Manfred Häckel, this means that "[diese Schriftsteller] zunächst nur eine geringe Bindung zu den ästhetisch reifsten Epochen der deutschen Literatur -- zur Klassik z. B. -- fanden."[17] On the other hand, with respect to content, these Germanists emphasize the simultaneous prevalence of "petty-bourgeois" conceptions of democracy carried over from the Vormärz and of Lassallean ideas, maintaining that "diese Lyrik deutlich in der Vormärz-Tradition, kaum aber in der Heine- und Weerth-Tradition steht."[18] This assessment recalls Heine's ironic poetic characterization of the "Tendenzpoeten" whose strong social engagement ran the danger of degenerating into abstract, generalized, rhetorical phrases. Also, it is oriented around Engels' assessment of Weerth as "der erste und bedeutendste Dichter des Proletariats,"[19] as well as his insistence on the esthetic necessity of a connection between "Tendenz" and "Handlung" in his letters to the Social Democratic writer Minna Kautsky. Furthermore, a consequence of the failure to assimilate realistic literary tradition, according to these GDR critics, was an insufficient or inaccurate reflection of historial reality which manifested itself in marked tendencies towards generalities or abstractness. (LSDL: "Vielen Gedichten mangelt es ... an historisch konkreter Spiegelung des Kampfes; die Problematik der Zeitenwende ... tritt oft nur allgemein-deklarativ auf").[20] Finally, this typical use of rhetorical generalization is also seen as spontaneous emotional expression, reflecting a lack of understanding and incorporation of scientific Marxist theory on the part of socialist writers from the working class who were often autodidacts. Thus, Schlenstedt writes in the LSDL:

> Diese Allgemeinheit wurde wesentiich durch ein noch nicht überwundenes spontanes Element in der Weltanschauung der sozialdemokratischen Dichter, durch eine noch ungenügende Aneignung der marxistischen Ideen bedingt. ... [Hier finden wir] die Hinwendung zum lyrischen Erfassen der Wirklichkeit, zum Aussprechen der spontanen Erfahrungen im sozialen und politischen Kampf gegen Unterdrückung und Ausbeutung. Es findet sich jedoch zugleich das Unvermögen zu gegenständlicher Gestaltung, die Tendenz zum Bekenntnishaften, zu unvermitteltem Aussprechen eines subjektiven Optimismus, eines postulierten moralischen Muss. (21)

These four elements, then, make up the essential GDR critique of this early socialist literature: its lack of connection to the humanistic and realistic literary traditions, its influence by the "Tendenzdichtung" of the Vormärz, its failure to incorporate scientific Marxist theory and the resulting echoes of "Lassallean" concepts, and its "spontaneous" character. All of these features, then, are taken as accounting for the strong tendencies towards generalization, abstractness, and the use of rhetorical devices.

If we turn now to the situation in the FRG, the picture is somewhat different. On the whole, we find that there is less interest among literary historians in the topic of pre-1914 workers' literature, and that there is no emphasis put on integrating it into a progressive national heritage, in contrast to the GDR. Rather, literary historians deal with this literature from differing motives and perspectives. The first short surveys of "Arbeiterdichtung" were published in the FRG in 1966 -- that is, slightly later than the beginnings of research in this area in the GDR. Of these, one direction was represented by those associated with the Dortmund Gruppe 61, a group of authors turning their attention towards thematizing the world of work, which had heretofore been neglected in West German literature. Though not primarily concerned with theoretical reflection on the historial stages of "Arbeiterdichtung," Fritz Hüser, in a statement representative of this group, assessed that written before 1914 as subjectively well-intended, but as fundamentally lacking in artistic value, as "in Verse gepresste Tagesparolen."[22] Pointing out the fact that this "Arbeiterdichtung" came to an end with the end of the older workers' movement in 1933, Hüser very rightly states that it can no longer be a model for authors in an age of highly developed capitalism, "im Zeitalter der Mitbestimmung und der Automation, der Kybernetik und Atomkräfte, der Volksaktie und der 40-Stunden-Woche."[23] His suggested alternative, particularly as it has manifested itself in the literary practice of the Gruppe 61, is problematic, however, for it maintains the traditional dichotomy between high art and political concerns and effectiveness.

The second direction taken by those concerning themselves with early workers' literature was that which grew in connection with the student movement and which sought to critique previous "bürgerliche Literaturwissenschaft" for its preoccupation with "intrinsic" formal analysis and its neglect of the progressive literary tradition to the detriment of the reception of "operative" forms of literature. (This new interest by Germanists in "operativity" and "functionality" corresponds on the level of literary production to those who turned towards agitational poetry, slogans and songs, plays and street theater in the late sixties in an attempt to have a greater political effect on a larger, less elite audience).[24] Writing from this perspective, Helmut Lethen and Helga Gallas published their article on "Arbeiterdichtung -- Proletarische Literatur. Eine historische Skizze" in Alternative (December 1966). However, perhaps the most explicit criticism of the attitude taken by bourgeois literary scholars to early socialist literature was given by Michael Pehlke in his article on the Leipzig SPD dramatist Friedrich Bosse, which appeared in 1971.[25] Beginning with an introductory statement on "das geteilte Erbe," Pehlke points out that the study of proletarian literature in the West had been unsystematic, but that it was beginning to profit from the boom in studies of Trivialliteratur and the efforts by individual publishing companies to fill gaps in the market. He then asks why (bourgeois) Germanistik had been so unwilling to deal with proletarian literature, and postulates the following reasons: a lack of knowledge about social and economic history, the inherent arrogance of the bourgeois perspective, the assumption of a "wertfrei" stance which cannot deal with the "Parteilichkeit" of this literature as a central esthetic category, and the upholding of traditional esthetic norms, whether from the old "l'art pour l'art" perspective or from the perspective of the Frankfurt School which did not view art as having the task of indicating social alternatives.[26] Pehlke's critique was typical of that directed by some representatives of progressive tendencies in Germanistik against the preoccupations of established literary scholarship. However, among those who have worked at rescuing socialist literary traditions from obscurity, there has continued to be a much stronger interest in the period of the Weimar Republic than in pre-1914 workers' literature. And even with respect to the Weimar Republic, recent research has focused much less on the so-called "klassische Arbeiterdichtung" (Barthel, Bröger, Lersch, Engelke, etc.) than on the <u>Bund</u> <u>proletarisch-revolutionärer</u> <u>Schriftsteller</u> (BPRS). This is due in large part to the differences in literary quality and to the exposition here of central problems of esthetic theory which are still relevant today for the development of a materialist theory of art and literature -- in contrast to the lack of theoretical impulses in pre-1914 workers' literature.

Aside from these more programmatic approaches, several longer surveys of early workers' literature have been published in the West. All of these conceive of themselves as alternatives to bourgeois methods of literary analysis which deny the validity of any connection between art and politics. As Gerald Stieg states:

> Die bürgerliche Literaturwissenschaft [he gives Martini and Pongs as examples] hat sich nur mit der klassischen Arbeiterdichtung befasst, nur in ihr sah sie die Kriterien von Dichtung verwirklicht. Dichtung als Motor politischer Emanzipation, die die frühe Arbeiterdichtung ist, bleibt ausserhalb des bürgerlichen Literaturbegriffs, der selbst von Marxisten wie Mehring übernommen wird. (27)

This criticism of bourgeois methodology means specifically that those who concern themselves with early workers' literature do not attempt to evaluate it in a vacuum according to some pre-established esthetic standards of formal complexity. Bernd Witte formulates this issue as follows:

> Haben wir es also mit den Produkten einer sterilen, als Dokument der Arbeiterkultur zwar interessanten, aber für den Literaturwissenschaftler unerheblichen Propandaliteratur zu tun? Diese Frage ist nur zu bejahen, wenn man die vorgelegten Texte ausschliesslich an den Massstäben der hohen, kanonischen Literatur misst. (28)

That is, these literary historians view this body of material as standing in an "antibürgerlicher Traditionszusammenhang," "als Gegenentwurf zur Literatur des 'schönen Scheins,'"[29] and therefore they are especially concerned with working out its connection to the organized workers' movement. Accordingly, they attempt to define this literature, and to analyze its form and content, with respect to its function within the framework of the socialist movement. Thus, Martin Ludwig, for example, in his <u>Sammlung Metzler</u> handbook on <u>Arbeiterliteratur in Deutschland</u> (1976), defines the object of his survey as "Dichtung im Gefolge der Arbeiterbewegung," and states:

> Arbeiterliteratur sollte sinnvollerweise im historischen Kontext der Arbeiterbewegung und der Sozialgeschichte sowie im Vergleich zu sozialwissenschaftlichen Beschreibungen der betrieblichen und der Lebenssituation der Arbeiter untersucht werden. (30)

The small number of additional surveys attempt to follow this methodological procedure, with varying degrees of success. The first representative anthology of early socialist theater was a collaboration between Ursula Münchow of the GDR and Friedrich Knilli of the FRG, Frühes deutsches Arbeitertheater 1847-1918 (1970). Under a motto taken from Béla Balázs, "Sie wollten nicht Bühnenstile ändern, sondern die Welt!" these two Germanists assembled an extensive, coherent group of plays, reviews and theoretical statements arranged -- at times too deterministically, it must be admitted -- according to the stages of development of the SPD. In 1973, based on some of this material, Peter von Rüden published his Sozialdemokratisches Arbeitertheater 1848-1914, the first overall history of early German workers' theater. Rüden was concerned with viewing this theater as a medium for political communication and therefore intended to explicate the effect that it had and the uses to which it was put within the context of the Social Democratic Party. He discusses in detail the twofold purposes of political enlightenment and agitation, and entertainment in the sense of compensatory leisure activity, tending to assume Engels' evaluative perspective on the necessity of an esthetic realization of socialist "Tendenz."[31]

Aside from these more detailed and specific studies on early socialist workers' theater, it has been Gerald Stieg and Bernd Witte who have written the most extensive survey of workers' literature. Here, their goal is a general characterization of the "functionality" of this literature and an outline of the main features of all the genres. (Gerald Stieg/Bernd Witte, Abriss einer Geschichte der deutschen Arbeiterliteratur, 1973; Gerald Stieg, "Thesen zur Arbeiterlyrik von 1863 bis 1933" in: Oesterreichische Gesellschaft für Kulturpolitik (ed.), Arbeiterdichtung, 1973; Bernd Witte (ed.), Deutsche Arbeiterliteratur von den Anfängen bis 1914, 1977; and Bernd Witte, "Literatur der Opposition. Ueber Geschichte, Funktion und Wirkmittel der frühen Arbeiterliteratur" in: Heinz Arnold (ed.), Handbuch zur deutschen Arbeiterliteratur, 1977). It is these studies which have arrived at the most promising results and which contain stimulating, provocative theses urging towards response and further research. Therefore, it is in order to summarize their arguments in some detail here, including their definition of "Arbeiterliteratur," their concept of operativity, and what they stress as the essential features of this literature. Specifically, many of the conclusions they reach will be valid for an interpretation of German-American socialist literature in so far as it is a continuation of literary activity begun in Germany.

In their Abriss Stieg and Witte trace the relationship between certain fictional texts and the development of the German workers' movement, covering the period before World War I (SPD), the Weimar Republic (SPD and KPD), the connections between "klassische Arbeiterdichtung" and National Socialism, and workers' literature in the FRG and the GDR. Specifically, they define the object of their study as literature written within the context of the organized workers' movement which has the twofold function of political organization, enlightening workers about their real situation and organizing them in the class struggle, and of serving as an instrument of creating cultural identity against the dominance of the bourgeoisie in this sphere.[32] That is, in contrast to some earlier definitions, workers' literature is not defined more generally as a literature by or for workers -- nor is it a requirement that authors belong to a party or consciously strive for political effect --

129

but rather it is defined as functional literature within the context of an anti-bourgeois tradition, as a "Gegenentwurf zur Literatur des 'schönen Scheins.'" (And indeed, this is why traditional Germanistics has taken no notice of it).[33] As the differences are specifically formulated, while the latter aims at cultivating the individual personality, workers' literature intends to organize a class, and while the latter is based on a model of inspired author/receptive reader, implicitly every reader can become a writer of workers' literature ("So fallen bei dieser literarischen Praxis Autor, Leser und Gegenstand im Idealfall in eins zusammen.")[34] Maintaining that it is meaningless to judge these texts according to the standards of "hohe, kanonische Literatur," Stieg/Witte place the overriding emphasis on their "operative" intent and point out that the literary techniques (Technik) used here must be understood as a function of the "politische Wirkabsichten" of the writers. As they state:

> Damit wird die Arbeiterliteratur als funktionale Literatur interpretiert, deren "literarische Technik" auf Grund ihrer Funktion, ihres Beitrags zur Emanzipation und "Selbstverständigung" des Proletariats, zu beurteilen ist. Das ist so zu verstehen, dass es den Autoren dieser Literatur nicht mehr in erster Linie um eine symbolische Darstellung individueller, sozialer oder kosmischer Zusammenhänge geht, sondern dass sie gesellschaftliche Antagonismen bewusstmachen wollen, um dadurch zu einer Veränderung der herrschenden Zustände beizutragen. (35)

Bernd Witte follows the organizing principle of functionality in the arrangement of his anthology of Deutsche Arbeiterliteratur, classifying the poetry according to the "literarisch-technische Mittel" used for the purpose of enlightening and uniting the recipients.[36] Using the model of the "Weberlied," the earliest example of German workers' literature, he deduces the following general characteristics of this functional genus: it proceeds from the concrete social situation of the addressees to arrive at political conclusions, using a traditional form and a familiar melody which is easily learned and remembered, in order to fulfill an organizing function in demonstrations and protest marches.[37] Witte then proposes seven categories of this workers' poetry, which all manifest one or more of these characteristics of operativity. First are the "Lieder, Partei- und Kampfgesänge" meant to serve an official organizing function at meetings or demonstrations. Similarly, the "Prologe" also perform a direct function within the organization, serving to open festivals, theater performances and party conferences. The next two categories are circumscribed as "Weltanschauungs- und Lehrdichtung" and "Allegorien," which are aimed at the individual reader in an effort to convince, with the goal of demonstrating a political fact or state of affairs. In particular, the manifold use of allegories taken from nature, mythology, Christianity and even abstract concepts is stressed here as one of the main features of this workers' poetry.[38] Witte (and Stieg also) likens this use of allegory to that found in medieval or Baroque poetry and hypothesizes that a comparable philosophical and social consciousness must be the explanation for this similarity: "Steht doch hinter all diesen Formen der Allegorie ein umgreifendes politisches Heilswissen, das die Phänomene dieser

Welt zu blossen Zeichen abwertet und seiner ausschliesslichen Ausdrucksintention unterordnet."[39] However, there are also "Lehrgedichte" such as those by Leopold Jacoby which employ a more "rational" argumentation. The fifth category encompasses a special kind of "Lehrgedicht," the "Zeitgedichte" which react directly to historical or political events and may assume the function of "Leitartikel" in the press. The sixth group, "Satiren und Karikaturen," and the seventh, "Kontrafakturen," are the poems which demonstrate most clearly for Witte the countercultural characteristics of this early workers' poetry. Whereas the former attack and ridicule the political opposition (the National Liberals, Bismarck, the church, industrialists), the latter feature new (and often diametrically opposed) contents for old or familiar forms and melodies, taking over religious hymns, Volkslieder, poems from the literary canon, military, patriotic and student songs and rewriting them with new words reflecting the socialist world view. Although these seven categories overlap in some instances, they are nevertheless useful as an indication of the particular function each poem was intended to fulfill within the organized workers' movement, and thus stress the specific "operative" character of this literature.

The same basic characteristics are also applied by Witte to early workers' theater and, in a more limited way, to socialist prose literature. The plays were performed by workers and had the political, agitational goals of familiarizing their working-class audiences with basic tenets of socialism and of creating solidarity and activating towards particular ends. Various forms and techniques were utilized. The "ökonomische Gespräche" of J. B. von Schweitzer presented economic theory in the form of dramatic dialogue, the "Kampfdrama" and the "Maifestspiel" thematized strikes or other situations of class confrontation, and, as was the case for the poetry, all these forms made frequent use of allegory. As for the prose produced by these writers, Witte points out that it has thus far received the least attention of any genre, and attributes this to its similarities to "Trivialliteratur." With its "Mischung von Elementen des niederen Unterhaltungsromans und sozialistischer Bekehrungsschriften" it appears to be "ein besonders abstossendes Beispiel ideologisch gefärbter Trivialliteratur."[40] However, Witte is able to interpret even this phenomenon as a consciously utilized technique meant to fulfill a particular function within the context of "enlightenment." For these novels and their serialized publication in the party press were aimed at enticing an audience of women and young people away from "Kolportageromane" and the Gartenlaube. To be sure, Witte makes the necessary qualifying statement that a more in-depth investigation is needed of the utilization of elements from "Trivialliteratur" to communicate socialist theories and messages, but he ascertains that techniques such as montage, the documentary report, and a combination of levels of style were also employed.

In summation, then, Witte's analysis is informed throughout by an understanding of the literary techniques employed in early socialist poetry, drama and prose as a function of their intended political effect.[41] This is certainly the only sound methodological procedure for dealing with literature which made the claim of influencing "sowohl ... das allgemeine soziale wie auch ... das literarische Verhalten ihrer

Leser."[42] However, Witte/Stieg's evaluation of this sort of "functional," "operative" literature as a positive alternative to the bourgeois separation between "pure" art and tacked-on political ideology (Tendenz) leads them in some instances to adopt an uncritical attitude toward the workers' literature which is the object of their study. Thus, not only is there a tendency here to overlook the problematic disparity between (progressive) content and (traditional) form, but this body of literature tends to be taken at face value, without critiquing the intent of its writers, as fulfilling an unqualifiedly emancipatory function. Witte states flatly that these texts "wirkten als Instrument der Emanzipation für ihre Leser wie für ihre Produzenten."[43] Furthermore, the supposedly exclusive concentration on class issues rather than individual, "subjective" thematic areas by these writers, which Witte/Stieg work out as one of the most typical characteristics of this literature, is not problematized by them. Rather, Witte evaluates positively the absence of a "Darstellung des Subjektiven, der Empfindungen und Erlebnisse des Einzelnen," stating:

> Durch diese Beschränkung gewinnt die frühe Arbeiterliteratur jedoch eine soziale Kommunikationsfunktion zurück, die die bürgerliche Literatur seit der Zeit der Aufklärung immer mehr eingebüsst hat. Sie vermag ihre Leser zum Verständnis der eigenen gesellschaftlichen Rolle und deren geschichtlicher Bedingtheit zu führen, weil sie stets auf deren gesellschaftliche Erfahrungen eingeht und explizit ihre alltäglichen Probleme und Sorgen thematisiert. (44)

While this assessment of the increasingly asocial character of bourgeois literature is certainly on the mark, it seems that by upholding the dichotomy between individual expression, experience and development on the one hand and class issues on the other, the concept of operativity becomes somewhat undifferentiated. Stieg writes:

> Die frühe Lyrik des Proletariats spricht nie die individuelle Sprache des Proletariers, sondern eine kollektive, politische, bewusst operative Klassensprache, die sich alle verwertbaren Formen zu eigen macht. Ihre Uniformität ist bemerkenswert. Das neue politische Bewusstsein entwickelt keine neuen künstlerischen Formen, sondern verkleidet sich in alten, ja uralten. (45)

Here, it seems that instead of looking for signs of dialectical interaction between individual and society, they are simply turning over the coin of bourgeois "l'art pour l'art" and associating operativity or political effect with literature which expresses solely and exclusively the "objective" interests of a class rather than integrating these with individually perceived needs and experiences. But after all, can "objective" class interests be totally separated from the individuals who constitute the class?

Therefore, an analysis of early socialist workers' literature which attempted to differentiate and critique the conclusions reached by Witte/Stieg (while accepting their basic premise that the literary techniques used here were developed in connection with the intended political effect) would have to come to grips with the following problems:

1) Perhaps most importantly, to make more precise just what the intended political effect of these writers was. It is not enough simply to accept the goals of dispensing enlightenment and creating solidarity as having been fulfilled here or even as unqualifiedly positive goals in the first place, just as the additional goal of "ästhetische Erziehung" mentioned by Witte is also ambivalent.[46] That is, to what extent do elements of bourgeois ideology pervade this literature?

2) An analysis of the political effect entails both an evaluation of the forms and contents employed to these ends and also a discussion of the channels through which this literature reached its intended audience, its concrete utilization in working-class contexts.

3) If in fact it is the case that individual, "subjective" (this itself needs to be defined more precisely) thematic areas or points of view are not typical of this literature, the reasons for this exclusion need to be examined more closely, as well as its implications for possible trends towards literary ritualization. It is simply not true, as Witte maintains in the above quote, that this literature explicitly thematizes everyday problems and concerns of workers.[47]

4) All of this aims at a critical discussion of the concept of operativity, at critiquing the social functions this literature was intended to have and how it was used in fact, and at analyzing its potential as a means for creating cultural identity in opposition to the cultural hegemony of dominant social groups. In this way, the analysis of literature written by German socialist immigrants to the United States fits into larger literary, theoretical and hopefully political debates, and, while of course it is concerned here with working out specific characteristics of this literature, it also should attempt to arrive at conclusions applicable to early socialist literature in general.

V. GERMAN-AMERICAN SOCIALIST LITERATURE: THE WORKS

1. INTRODUCTION

A preceding chapter discussed the functional and political context of German-American socialist literature and began to work out some of its operative goals. The present chapter will discuss the works themselves, analyzing their content and form with an eye towards discovering more precisely what their writers intended these "functional" literary works to accomplish. (In general, since much of this literature follows similar patterns of content and imagery, the works will be discussed as a body, though significant examples will also be cited. Here, it is important to keep in mind the implications of such similarity and repetitiousness for the ritualization of literature, as it was read, performed or received). It seems that one of the fundamental characteristics of early socialist literature (written by Germans) or workers' literature connected with unions and other groups (written by English-speaking Americans), is a quality of abstractness which means that only a minority of these works actually deal with specific, identifiable historical experiences. While in Germany the lack of concreteness could possibly be partially explained by the strict censorship under the Anti-Socialist Laws and the resulting necessity to veil directly political references, such immediate repression obviously could not be the deciding factor in the United States. Rather, the particular themes and techniques chosen by these writers must have been selected with certain desired responses from the recipients in view. Therefore, rather than arranging and critiquing the following material according to a division along the lines of the traditional genres -- a method used by previous criticism to arrive at valuable insights which can be integrated and developed further here -- it has seemed more appropriate to follow an organization based on three thematic areas which makes it possible to elucidate and critique the functions this literature sought to carry out. Running throughout most of these works is a preoccupation with the stages in the coming of socialism, and the portrayal of these stages, in turn, is geared towards eliciting particular responses. In brief, these three thematic areas consist of 1) the portrayal of the proletarian situation in the present, before attempts at socialist organization 2) the necessity and nature of socialist organization, to be brought about through both appeals and enlightenment, 3) the vision of revolution and the future under socialism, of a socialist society brought about through organization. An analysis of these three areas with respect to content and literary technique will not only clarify certain facets of how these writers viewed the political movement of socialism, but it will also lead into a critique of the "operative" character of this literature which its writers never explicitly formulated theoretically. Through this method of analysis, it will hopefully be possible to avoid simply repeating for German-American socialist literature what has already been written on the corresponding literature in Germany, and to arrive at some new insights into early socialist literature in general.[1]

2. THE WORKING CLASS BEFORE ORGANIZATION

> Die Unabhängigkeits-Erklärung, die nun 100 Jahre alt, verkündete die
> Menschenrechte und heute sind dieselben vom Ausbeuterpack, das sei-
> ne Unabhängigkeit feiert, mit Füssen getreten. Sollen wir Arbeiter
> der Ausbeuter Unabhängigkeit feiern? Sollen wir gleich Dummköpfen
> uns vom Unabhängigkeitsdusel begeistern lassen, während wir Arbei-
> tenden doch in Ketten gehen und furchtbar unter den Wirkungen des
> bald 100-jährigen Ausbeutungssystems der modernen Raubritter lei-
> den? Nein, das sei ferne von uns, die Ausbeuter sollen sehen, dass
> wir unsere Lage und unsere Feinde erkannt. Wir haben keine Ursache
> beim hundertjährigen Feste der Mastbürger-Republik aufzujubeln,
> denn uns war es keine Republik, kein Vaterland, uns war sie nur die
> Handlangerin des Geldsacks gegen uns, der mächtige Arm zur Unter-
> stützung der Ausbeuter in ihrem verdammungswürdigen Volksaus-
> plünderungswerke! (2)

When German socialists immigrated to the United States, they left behind a bureaucratic state, well-preserved remnants of feudal hierarchy and the Anti-Socialist
Laws, but they also entered into a society in which class contradictions and conflicts were continually increasing in intensity. Most of the writers discussed here
immigrated during the "Gilded Age" of the 1870's and 1880's, a time of hitherto
unparalleled growth of personal fortunes and industrial empires, and also of increasing impoverishment and labor violence. Therefore, if any of these writers
left their homeland with hopes for encountering more justice and freedom in the
New World, it seems that the rediscovery of class antagonisms led them to re-
nounce these hopes and to voice an often bitter disillusionment at what they actually found, as, for example, in the above statement made on the occasion of an anti-
centennial celebration (July 4, 1876) sponsored by German socialists in Chicago.
In their works which refer directly to America, these writers often express this
disillusionment in terms of encountering corruption in politics and government,
social conditions as bad as those they left behind, and the hegemony of capital in
every area of life. In short, they decry the hypocrisy of a country which held out
the promise of freedom and individual self-realization, but which, upon closer
contact, proved to be built on class structures and oppression. As one anonymous
writer proclaimed in a poem entitled "The Journey to America" (1886, available
to me only in English translation):

> That is the republic with the greatest freedom
> For fraud, for robbery and murder;
> And every born scoundrel so far
> Has become a cabinet minister.
>
> They say that in "free" America
> Justice is in full bloom;
> What a pity that it's always administered
> Only by moneybags! (3)

Or, in a poem written to welcome Wilhelm Liebknecht upon his arrival in New York in 1886, Emil Friedrich wrote:

> Willkommen uns hier im "gelobten Lande",
> Nach dem die Völker ohne Beispiel wallen --
> Als stünden offen hier des Glückes Hallen
> Fraglos für Jeden, den die Heimath sandte.
>
> Und die enttäuscht nun deinen Lehren lauschen --
> Die Du, des Volkes allertreuster Sohn,
> Verkündet hast ein Menschenalter schon --
> Und unsre Herzen hoffnungskühn durchrauschen! (4)

In addition to these more general accusations, writers also thematized specific events such as strikes and instances of police brutality to expose what they saw as the reality behind the ideology of freedom and opportunity. For example, after the bloody strike of 1877, Gustav Lyser asked who had destroyed the proud image of America, and answered as follows:

> Columbia, was ist aus Dir geworden?
> Wer trat Dich Stolze schmählich in den Staub?
> Wer lässt die braven Arbeitsmänner morden
> Und schützt mit blut'ger Faust den frechen Raub?
> Der Geldsack ist es, der allmächt'ge König,
> Er unterjochte dieses reiche Land,
> Die letzte Spur von Recht und Freiheit schwand
> Und die Gewalt nur rühmt man tausendtönig. (5)

Or, after the murder of striking workers in Hazleton, Pennsylvania in the fall of 1897, Wilhelm Rosenberg wrote:

> Schweigt mir auf immer von dem Lande
> Der Freien, auf Columbia's Flur!
> Seit jener Hazeltoner Schande
> Ist es ein Land von Mördern nur. (6)

The above-mentioned Gustav Lyser frequently denounced the "false promises" held out by America in his poems. Born in 1841, Lyser immigrated to New York in 1874 and edited socialist papers in several cities in the 1870's.[7] He printed his poetry, much of it satirical or in support of the Chicago Lehr- und Wehrverein, in all of the papers he edited. However, it is a dramatic sketch published in the Chicago Vorbote in 1878 which expresses most vividly the disillusionment with American society and which attempts to expose the economic foundations of the social structure.[8] Lyser's satire, Congress zur Verwirrung der Arbeiterfrage in New-York. Eine Comödie auf Kosten des Proletariats, is based on the hearings of the Hewitt committee, which had been appointed by Congress after the strikes of 1877 in order to investigate "the causes of the general depression in labor and business."[9] The committee called several representatives of the SAP to testify, including Adolf Douai, New York <u>Volkszeitung</u> editor. Lyser's dramatic sketch takes the form of a confrontation and debate between Hewitt, the chairman of the committee, and Leuthold Wahr, the spokesman of the people and as his name indicates, the representative of truth. From the beginning stage directions ("Ort der Handlung: Is nich, da nicht gehandelt, sondern nur geschwätzt wird") to the final, concluding prophecy of apocalyptic revolution, Lyser makes the point that the investigative committee is not really concerned at all with discovering the truth behind the present critical situation. In a prologue (where <u>Knittelvers</u> undermines the idealistic sentiments), Hewitt greets the committee, proclaiming that its purpose is to determine the truth of the charges brought before it:

> Ob's Menschen gibt, die niemals schaffen
> Und Schätze doch zusammenraffen?
> Ob hier im Lande Menschenschinder,
> Die selbst nicht schonen Weib und Kinder?
> Ob fleiss'ge Arbeitsmänner darben,
> Und manche schon vor Hunger starben?
> Ob neben Kirchenheuchelei
> Prostitution und Gaunerei?
> Ob durch die Bank die Tagespresse
> Nur wahrt das Bourgeois-Interesse?

The first person who asks to speak in answer to these charges is the labor leader Leuthold Wahr. Speaking in blank verse and quoting Goethe, Schiller and Heine, he first invokes an image of the richness of America, which has been spoiled through greed and violence:

> Steigst Du auf eines Berges Gipfel,
> Und überschaust die Fluren und die Auen,
> Wird ob des Anblicks, den Du dann geniessest,
> Das Herz Dir laut in Himmelswonne schlagen;
> Und mit dem deutschen Riesengeiste Faust,
> Den Bayard Taylor herrlich Euch erschlossen,
> Rufst vom Gefühl Du überwältigt aus,
> "Ein Paradies liegt mir zu Füssen!"
> Ja, ja ein Paradies! -- Wie selig könnten sein
> Die Ebenbilder Gottes, die's bewohnen,
> Wenn von der <u>Habsucht</u> nicht, wenn nicht von <u>Neid</u> und <u>Zorn</u>
> Vergiftet würden schon der Kinder Herzen!
> Doch ach, zu einer Hölle haben
> Dämonen dieses Paradies gestaltet,
> Dass von Zehntausenden oft Einer kaum
> Vermag des Lebens wirklich froh zu werden!

Upon this, Hewitt, not really interested in discovering the truth of the charges, enjoins the labor leader to refrain from painting such a black picture, but also

asks him what the source of the present crisis could be. Leuthold Wahr replies
in a long, didactic speech, that speculation and overproduction have brought about
the long working day, implying that if workers were in control of the situation, their
solution would be to shorten the hours of work. Hewitt counters that in a free country, the "Congress" has no power to set a limit on working hours, whereupon Wahr
replies that the state indeed has the power to do other things:

> Nun sagt: Habt Ihr denn nicht die Macht,
> Wenn Eurer Geldsack jemals scheint bedroht,
> Die Hungernden wie Hunde zu erschiessen?
> Habt Ihr nicht oft schon das Versammlungsrecht,
> Das uns durch die Verfassung längst gewährt,
> Missachtet und das Volk,
> Das unbewaffnet auf dem Platz erschien,
> Mit blut'gen Köpfen wieder heimgeschickt?
> Werft Ihr den Armen, der aus Hunger stiehlt,
> In's Zuchthaus nicht und lasst den reichen Schuft,
> Der um Millionen Tausende betrügt
> Als Volksvertreter im Congress sich brüsten?

After this statement of how the government disregards its own constitution and laws
whenever the interests of the propertied classes seem threatened, Wahr accuses
Hewitt and the Committee of hypocritically staging a farce, and predicts that one
day justice will be done and revenge accomplished. This short play contains in a
nutshell most of the accusations German-American socialists directed against
American society: its riches held out false promises for they were controlled exclusively by the few, corrupt politicians uninterested in the people's welfare were
in power, and the owners' interests were defended and promoted on all levels by
institutions such as the church, the press, the army and militia, and the legal
system.

Accordingly, even though these writers do not look back with longing, with "falsches Heimweh," on the Germany they left behind, they still cannot affirm the new
social system where they have resettled (in contrast to the vast portion of the rest
of German-American literature). The foregoing works were concrete examples of
disillusionment with and specific accusations against the United States as a class
society based on economic exploitation. Here, it is unquestionably clear that this
literature represents a response to particular immigrant experience. However,
the criticizing, oppositional attitude which emerges here is not confined only to
those works which make direct reference to America. Rather, the entire body of
this literature, in its depiction of the unorganized proletariat, the necessity of
organization, and the socialist future also relates to the encounter of these writers
with a rapidly industrializing society and the corresponding class antagonisms.
That is, this literature was not merely an unthinking continuation of familiar German traditions which had little meaning in the new immigrant context. Rather, even
in all its abstractness, it was also a response to the working class situation and an
attempt to carry out certain functions within it. In spite of the abstractness which

will become more evident in the following discussion, then, it should always be kept in mind that this was a literature which sought to expose class conflict in a country which has sometimes been smugly thought to have escaped this "European" social phenomenon.

An oppositional attitude towards the American economic system is the foundation for how these socialist writers portray the proletarian situation in the present, before attempts at socialist organization. Seen against this background, their treatment of the unorganized working class circumscribes the following areas: the misery of proletarian life, the image of the capitalists and the repressive forces in general, the work process itself (as both degrading and productive), workers' complicity in their own exploitation, and private life, including all those areas outside the spheres of work and politics, particularly women and the family. (It will be important to discern at a later point what the significant differences are in the portrayal of the working class in general versus workers organized in unions or socialist groups). For now, the following discussion will treat the thematic areas listed above.

The misery of proletarian life is depicted most graphically and concretely in series of prose sketches (reportage, Christmas stories, etc.) published in the socialist press, for example, those "New Yorker Geschichten" written by editors Sergius Schewitsch and Alexander Jonas for the New York Volkszeitung. These short sketches, frequently occasioned by current events of interest, most often revolve around the impoverished living conditions in New York tenement districts, the deleterious effects of a long working day and low wages or unemployment, the abuse of alcohol and the fact that poverty drove many women to prostitution. In other sketches, unemployment and the death of family members leave men with nothing to do but take to the road as tramps, reflecting the situation in which hundreds of thousands of people found themselves as a result of the depression of the 1870's.[10] A frequently employed device used by Schewitsch and other writers is to situate their depictions of misery and poverty around Christmastime, in order to expose the hypocrisy of a religion which promised a better afterlife to those who patiently endured their lot on earth, and also to bring out more strongly the material and moral contrast between the comfortable life of the well-to-do and that of the poor.

Written partly in the factual style of journalistic reporting, these sketches are concerned with actual situations encountered by immigrant workers in the United States, and as such, they would certainly have caught the attention of contemporary readers of the Volkszeitung. But although Schewitsch states that he intended these sketches to be merely "Photographien nach und aus dem Leben, ... mit dem einen Anspruch, wahr zu sein,"[11] they almost never exhaust themselves solely in depictions of proletarian misery. There are only infrequent instances of prose sketches tending towards Mitleidsdichtung and Elendsmalerei. Rather, when portraying the so-called "brutal" or "immoral" sides of proletarian life, these writers generally also attempt to convince the reader that poverty and material insecurity are at the root of this degradation (thus challenging prevalent theories of Social Darwinism), to place the blame on the appropriate agents, to make an emotional appeal against this state of affairs, perhaps calling for rebellion, or at least to urge the reader to reflect on who might be guilty for creating these conditions. Combining elements of the documentary, factual news story and fictional, often even sentimentalized dialogues and descriptions of persons, milieus and social contrasts, these sketches were designed to provide information and enlightenment, as well as entertaining, feuilletonistic reading material, and to provoke further reflection from readers on "Wer die Schuld trägt" (Schewitsch).

Turning to the portrayal of proletarian life in poetry and plays, we find that it immediately assumes a high degree of abstractness and that almost always, except in certain Gelegenheitsgedichte, it takes the form of a highly schematized contrast with the figure of the capitalist and his allies or the life of the rich. And when confronted with the figure of the capitalist, the worker being characterized or addressed is then invested with or urged to assume characteristics other than merely the passive acceptance and endurance of poverty. That is, the portrayal of the individual proletarian and proletarian life becomes intertwined with a particular image and understanding -- not only of the individual capitalist -- but also of the causes of proletarian suffering, of the repressive forces in society, of the opposition. Although individual capitalists such as Jay Gould or Rockefeller were sometimes the object of diatribes and satires, and although some of the prose sketches described above were concerned with exposing their opulent, wasteful life styles or particularly odious examples of their exploitation, in this literature the figure of the employer or the industrialist is rapidly associated with other repressive forces in society, and quickly takes on allegorical and even mythic dimensions, to which the figure of the worker is then opposed. Arrayed against wage workers is a formidable block of capitalists and their allies, who conspire together to control all spheres of life. Above all, this literature connects the interests of capital with the activity of the church, which hypocritically propagates a false ideology designed for social pacification, but the powers of money are also shown as able to buy and corrupt the services of politicians, the army, militia and police, the legal system, the bourgeois press, the educational establishment, and even union leaders. The following text to a lebendes Bild entitled "Die Gegenwart" presented at the 25th anniversary celebration of Johann Most's paper Freiheit in 1904 described how the allies of capital were to be shown on stage:

> Der Kapitalist spart unser Geld!
> Der Politikant regiert die Welt!
> Milizer schiesst die Striker tot!
> Fakir [i.e. union boss] verrät uns auf des Boss' Gebot!
> Richter spricht für Geldsack Recht!
> Pressbengel schreibt als Mammonsknecht!
> Polizist erfaulenst sich sein Brod
> Und schlägt mit Lust die Armen tot!
> Pfaff preist den Himmel mit salbendem Schwall
> Und Arbeiter, du ernährst sie All'! (12)

The conjunction of interests of all these groups is presented in these poems as an accomplished fact, with little, if any indication of how it came about or why these various groups should be acting in league with each other. The hegemony of capital in all areas of society, in the base as well as in the superstructure, thus takes on the character of an all-pervasive, omnipotent conspiracy of undifferentiated interests, in some instances even of a thus far eternal structure of power unchanged through history.

Upon evoking these seemingly invulnerable, overwhelming forces, these writers then turn to a historically familiar tactic, accusing the opposition of immorality and investing the suffering working class with attributes of virtue. On the most concrete level, the capitalists (or the "rich") are denounced as gluttons, drinkers, sloths, hypocrites, "Wüstlinge" who seduce proletarian daughters and wives, and robbers who have no feelings of brotherly love but who are only concerned with wringing out as much profit as possible. It is only a small step here to the frequently encountered images of the "faule Drohnen" who are nourished by the "fleissige Arbeitsbienen" or the "Vampiren" and "Blutsauger" who drain the life's blood of the poor. In this literature, these moral accusations do not remain on the level of associating such qualities with a particular human, individual figure. Rather, the qualities which characterize the opposition typically become disassociated from persons or real social forces and assume a life of their own, appearing as demonic, almost mythological powers. Such threatening and oppressive forces include Habgier, Heuchelei, Lüge, Betrug, List, Unvernunft, Tyrannei, and culminate in the figures of Moloch and Mammon, or in the allegorical battle of the powers of darkness and light (Finsternis/Licht, Nacht/Morgen). Certainly the most well-known example would be the opening lines of Jakob Audorf's "Arbeiter-Marseillaise": "Wenn auch die Lüg' uns noch umnachtet,/ Bald steigt der Morgen hell herauf!" But this was also a typical perception in German-American socialist poetry. For example, Wilhelm Rosenberg abstracted the "Weltenherrscher" to a level of bestial egotism in the following poem:

> Ich stehe auf Säcken, gefüllt mit Gold,
> Der Frucht der Menschenbienen,
> Ich schwinge die Peitsche über sie,
> Und zwinge sie, mir zu dienen.
>
> Ich werfe die Saat der Verderbnis aus
> Ueber alle Meere und Lande,
> Ich lösche die Fackel der Hoffnung aus,
> Füll' den Sorgenbecher zum Rande.
>
> Ich bin das verkörperte, selbstische Ich,
> Die Bestie im Menschenkleide,
> Sie erwürgt wie ein unersättlicher Wolf
> Die Lämmer auf blühender Weide. (13)

The world view which emerges here is that of a beleaguered group surrounded by irrational, inhuman, almost supernatural powers unconnected to any historical context and thus of a quasi-eternal nature. Indeed, there are references to the oppression which has lasted for "hundreds" or even "thousands" of years.

On the level of literary technique, the more concrete portrayals of capitalists and their allies utilize stereotypical images based on moral accusations rather than attempting to expose more fundamental levels of societal contradiction. In other words, through the use of these negative stereotypes, exploitation is made to seem a result of moral corruption alone, and capitalists are shown as exploiters due to their evil nature rather than to their role within the economic system. The transition from portraying the opposition as individual capitalist figures to portraying it as personified, timeless qualities (Habgier, etc.) or even more vague forces (Mammon) entails a transition from stereotyping individuals to allegorizing and mythologizing the evil, opposing forces. These negative attributes or qualities are not only reminiscent of the cardinal sins of religious tradition, but they also call to mind the portrayal of the villainous nobility found earlier in the literature of the rising bourgeoisie. That is, as soon as these writers abandon the level of somewhat realistic imagery, there is little sense of historical change or the changeability of the world, little sense that the enemy might be different now than in the past or that the enemy might be located not only outside the working class. In short, there is little sense of historical progression or of a dialectical view of history -- surprising at first thought when we consider who these writers were.

How are the workers and the poor depicted in this confrontation with the evil powers of money and greed? How have they been subjugated by the powers of darkness, and why do they remain in bondage? First of all, the allies of capital described above conspire to maintain control over all those who own nothing but their labor power. Thus, in keeping with the moral condemnation of exploitation, we sometimes encounter the figure of a worker or allegorical representations of poverty being cruelly abused by a figure representing an employer. These depictions generally have a passive, helpless quality, and women, defenseless children or child workers are often chosen to create a more extreme and even sentimentalized situation. For example, in a lebendes Bild presented at an anti-centennial celebration in Chicago, "Armut" and "Elend" were portrayed by two women, the first "eine abgehärmte Frau mit Kind" and the second "ein vor einem Ausbeuter flehendes Weib," and the exploiter is setting a dog after the two women.[14] It is within the context of this confrontation that the depiction of the work process itself occurs, a subject which occupies a relatively small place in this body of literature. Perhaps this is because these writers assumed their readers to be familiar with specific working conditions and not lacking in this experience -- though certainly conflicts and problems at the workplace would have provided a rich source of literary material -- or perhaps they were aiming at different goals. On one level, as in the prose sketches, work is portrayed as sheer, unmitigated misery and torture: the reference is often to "Knechtschaft," "Frondienst" or "Qual." The work itself is physically exhausting, mentally deadening, dangerous and never-ending. The workers themselves are degraded to the status of "Waren," and may be described as extensions of machines or even as having become machine-like themselves. Throughout, there is a sense of the dehumanization of work due to its transformation into a commodity, and indeed, of the penetration of capitalist economic relations into all areas of life. For example, in one of Sergius Schewitsch's "New Yorker Lebensbilder," the twelve-hour working day of a young cashier's helper in a large department store is described as repetitious and overtaxing:

> Wie eine Maschine, wie eine jener Puppen, die man aufzieht und die dann im Kreis herumlaufen, deren so viele in den letzten Tagen durch des Mädchens Hände gegangen waren, lief sie von und zu der Kasse, das Geld und die Pakete in der krampfhaft geballten kleinen Faust festhaltend. (15)

Although the work is exhausting, the girl must keep on because she is the sole support of her sick mother. But finally she falls asleep on the job (the store is open longer and longer as the Christmas season approaches -- here is an indirect indictment of religious hypocrisy), is falsely accused of stealing and fired without pay. In this literature, if a worker in such a situation is unfortunate enough to become unemployed because of unfathomable economic crises or an employer's whim, life on the road as a tramp for the men, prostitution for the women, or even death may be the result. In this unequal confrontation, the only choice for some seems to be between working themselves literally to death or facing unemployment and death through starvation.

However, this totally helpless, passive, vulnerable, machinelike depiction of the worker is typical of only a small part of this literature. In other works, coupled with descriptions of the work process as dangerous and exhausting, and of the worker as a commodity and appendage to the machinery, is also the realization that this is productive work and that the worker is therefore the producer of society's wealth. It is the wage worker who is taking all these risks, exposing him- or herself (usually him!) to danger, supporting families through honest toil, and creating all the things which society needs to continue operating. The employers, in contrast, like the lazy drones they are, appropriate and feast off the products of the hard-working proletarians.[16] For example, SAP member Carl Derossi enumerated the productive work of miners, factory workers, sailors on unsafe ships and farmers, all working for low wages and little reward, in this poem:

> Tief in der Erde dunklem Schooss
> Wühlst hastig Du nach ihren Schätzen.
> Zum Dank ist Elend nur Dein Loos,
> Dank Derer, die hinab Dich hetzen.
> Du darbst und hungerst mit Weib und Kind,
> Indessen sie am Prassen sind.
> $\qquad$ Erwach' o Volk, erwache!
>
> Bei Regen und im Sonnenbrand
> Musst Du das Feld des Herrn bebauen.
> Wo einst der schwarze Sklave stand,
> Bist Du als "freier" Mann zu schauen:

Frei, <u>wo</u> Du Dich schinden lassen willst,
Frei, <u>wo</u> Du Deinen Hunger stillst.
Erwach' o Volk, erwache! (17)

In addition to literary treatment, this division of society into producers and consumers, the industrious and the lazy, the virtuous and the corrupt, oppressed and
oppressors, is also demonstrated quite graphically in the "socialist iconography"
appearing on front pages of newspapers, in feuilleton sections, and in <u>lebende Bil-</u>
<u>der</u> performed at festivals. Thus we find <u>lebende Bilder</u> contrasting "the life of
the poor" and "the life of the rich," or, even more vividly, we find pyramidal constructions of society reminiscent of those used to illustrate the estates in feudalism
and the Baroque. On the upper levels are the capitalists and their allies (judges,
politicians, the military, the church), sometimes represented by allegorical figures,
consuming and draining off the riches which flow to them from below, and conspir-
ing to keep the workers in their place on the bottom of the social pyramid.[18] However, unlike Baroque or feudal illustrations which were intended to elucidate the
place of each individual within a God-given, eternal order, these representations,
situated in a different historical context, are meant to demonstrate the injustice
of the social hierarchy they expose. Nevertheless, because of the strict separation of society into these levels and the black-and-white contrasts (strengthened
by the use of allegory), the conflict between the lower and upper levels tends to
assume a static, eternal quality. Here, as in the literary works just referred to,
there seems to be no way out, no escape from grinding oppression, though to be
sure workers can enjoy the comfort of <u>moral</u> superiority.

However, the situation workers find themselves in is not always portrayed as solely
due to the actions of the ruling class or repressive forces, or as an eternal condition. In another group of writings, workers themselves are faulted for the fact that
they have been so cruelly exploited. For example, in the series of "Zeit- und
Streitfragen" dialogues published in the New York <u>Volkszeitung</u>,[19] the socialist
worker Helle undertakes to enlighten the non-socialist worker Doefe about the
real nature of the capitalist system and why he should become a socialist. Doefe,
as his name indicates, is portrayed as stupid, only concerned with his own advancement, falsely satisfied with things as they are, and irrationally suspicious
of the socialists -- in short, badly in need of enlightenment. As Helle explains in
exasperation, "Warum <u>Du</u> eigentlich ausgewandert bist, weiss ich wirklich nicht.
Einer, der so mit jedem Knochen zufrieden ist, den man ihm zuwirft, wie Du, der
passte doch herrlich für ein Land, in dem es heisst: 's Maul halten, Steuer zahlen,
Soldat werden!" But in the course of the conversation, Doefe learns the errors in
his previous thought and actions and finally agrees to subscribe to the <u>Volkszeitung</u>,
which will teach him to think correctly and thus to become a truly free man. In
general, then, workers who allow themselves to be totally dominated by their employers or the capitalist system as a whole are characterized as stupid, uncom-
prehending, lazy or indifferent, and religious. Though these qualities are understood as caused by the dominant system to an extent, particularly through the stul-
tifying agents of religion, schools and the bourgeois press, it is also suggested
that they can be overcome or transformed through rational persuasion and an act

of will on the part of those who are oppressed. (It will be important to determine what characteristics are to be their replacements, and whether these works attempt to suggest how they could be developed).

Only a small portion of this literature deals with the experience of workers in areas of life other than work and immediate class conflict. These writers characteristically relegate to the periphery thematic areas such as the cultural shocks and problems of adjustment of immigration, love and family relationships, or the experience of nature.[20] However, it is not entirely accurate to maintain as Stieg and Witte do that there is, for example, no "Liebeslyrik" in this early socialist literature.[21] If we look at collections of poetry published by these writers, we indeed find a number of poems dealing with the above areas of love, nature, etc., but by and large they are extremely conventional and sentimental.[22] That is, in their works dealing with the "private" realm, these socialists are virtually indistinguishable from the rest of German-American writers, with all their inwardness, passivity, and upholding of traditional values. The realm of love, family, friendship and nature is presented as a "whole world," as a haven from the conflicts of the workplace or politics, and thus as fundamentally unconnected with processes of social change. This split between private and political life is paradigmatically shown by the treatment of women in this literature, which reflects, in a more general sense, the role women played in German-American socialism. In this period, feminism and women's rights were growing movements in the United States, but the German-American socialists remained untouched -- or, as they might have said, "uncontaminated" by these ideas.[23] Relegating such considerations to the "unimportant" private sphere or to the status of "secondary" contradictions,[24] these writers either neglected interpersonal relationships or problems of particular interest to women, or dealt with these areas in thoroughly conventional ways, as in their love poetry addressed to the innocent, bashful girl or the virtuous, decent housewife.

With respect to literary technique, this separation between works dealing with the public, "political" realm and those concerned with the private, "non-political" sphere means that the former were operative, aiming towards political influence, whereas the latter were not written with a view towards carrying out any particular function. In the former group of works writers adopt rhetorical, appellatory, argumentative techniques designed to inform, persuade and arouse, whereas in the latter group these techniques directed at influencing the recipient are no longer evident. In poems dealing with the political or economic situation of the working class, two optics are employed: 1) the writer makes a direct address or appeal, speaking to the workers as "Ihr" or "Du," 2) "Wir" is used as the collective subject, emphasizing that individuals can only change their situation by uniting as a group. However, in poems by the same writers dealing with "private" experiences, the lyric "ich" is employed, and the standpoint is no longer one of appeal or defiant statement, but of an individual undergoing a particular experience in a sphere removed from political significance. In turn, the fact that these writers apply operative forms only in their overtly political works implies that they viewed the "non-political" private sphere as an inessential, non-influential adjunct to the real arena of conflict, the class struggle. Holding for the most part quite traditional attitudes towards the constitution of private life, they wrote contemplative poetry mirroring it, and had no urge to write literature directed at transforming it.

To summarize, upon their immigration to the United States, German socialists experienced disillusionment and anger at rediscovering a society based on class divisions and exploitation. Therefore, they set about writing literature directed at exposing the injustice they found. Their depictions of urban proletarian life and of the unorganized working class expose the misery and ugliness behind the facade of the Gilded Age, sometimes from the perspective of helpless, passive suffering, but sometimes also recognizing the contribution made by the productive worker to society as a thing of pride, worth and virtue. Over and against the whole working class, individual capitalists and the opposing interests in general are portrayed abstractly, either as stereotypical figures who act as they do because of their evil, greedy nature, or as allegorical, mythological forces which are omnipotent and unchanged through history. As a tentative conclusion, then, in this literature, class conflict is portrayed as fundamentally a matter of morality, with the evil forces having temporary control over humanity, and this moral interpretation of history is strengthened through the literary techniques of stereotyping and allegory. Thus, though the literature constantly refers to class differences and conflicts, it rarely goes beyond the surface level of accusations to penetrate to the basic economic forces at work. Finally, because of these writers' narrow understanding of politics, they exclude certain areas of life from their "functional" literature and treat these in thoroughly conventional ways in works (mostly poems) written as individual, subjective expression and not aimed at having an extra-literary effect. The private areas of love, the family, friendship and nature are treated in this way, as a contemplative sphere of leisure which, as a reflex of the working day, serves as a "whole" world in which to reproduce labor power. In addition, important aspects of the immigrant experience are neglected altogether. Perhaps the most glaring omission here is the paucity of works thematizing specific problems and adjustments faced by immigrants, most particularly those experiences discussed at the end of Chapter II which built up obstacles to the spread of socialism in the United States. For example, these would include conflicts at the workplace and outside it among different immigrant groups, the belief in and real experience of an improved standard of living and upward mobility, and the promise of the democratic traditions of America. Thus, not only does the portrayal of the unorganized working class tend to remain on the level of moral statement and accusation, but it also fails to reflect significant aspects of the immigrant experience.

3. CALLS TO ACTION: THE ORGANIZED PROLETARIAT

The portrayal of the proletarian situation in the present, before attempts at organization, made use of stereotypes, allegory, and an interpretation of history based
on moral categories, and operated on the assumption that the reader, performer
or spectator would identify with these oppositional attitudes toward social injustice.
Similarly, the part of this literature which is concerned primarily with the need
for proletarian organization, with unified action as a response to social inequality,
also depends for its effect on the premise that the recipient will identify with and
model his actions after the positive images expressed in the work. Again, the
techniques employed include the use of stereotypes (this time positively expressed)
and allegory, but new here are the appeals, exhortations and commands, often
also based on moral argument, which attempt to achieve certain effects through
their nature as rhetorical devices. That is, these writers sought to create unity
in their recipients on the level of content, by creating a positive image of the organized worker as a model for identification, and also on the level of the literary
techniques employed to urge workers towards solidarity.

How are proletarians depicted who unite to secure their rights? (It should be noted
at the beginning that the precise nature of this unity is almost always vague in the
literature and receives most of its meaning from the context in which the literature
reached its public. Sometimes workers are urged to unite to secure particular objectives, such as the eight-hour day or the election of socialist candidates, but
more often the call "Unite!" remains abstract). The attributes of the organized
workers -- always contrasted with the unorganized -- may be circumscribed by
three interwoven categories: a certain type of masculinity, a tendency towards
militaristic qualities, and a certain type of virtue or ethics.

With rare exceptions this literature was written by men, for men and about men.
Through organization, workers are described as becoming "männlich," "bewusste
Männer." Unorganized, they are "unmündige Kinder," impotent, at the mercy of
capital interests. Organized in solidarity, they regain their manhood and their collective strength. Those who before would have been characterized as "feig,"
"dumm," "unbewusst," "Knechte," or even "weibisch" now become "tapfer," "be-
wusst," "männlich." These associations of men organized in solidarity around
political and economic goals are frequently described as armies, well-organized
and disciplined, not to be diverted from their goal, which they pursue singlemind-
edly:

> Zusammen geschmiedet mit geistigem Band,
> Nicht wankend und beugend, gleich ehener Wand,
> So stehet im Kampfe das kernige Heer. (25)

In addition, the military analogy is furthered by the constant use of military meta-
phors and allegories. The class struggle is always a matter of "Kampf," "Schlacht,"

"Krieg," "Schwerter," "Fahnen," "Schläge," "Sieg und Verlust," or of allegorical battles between "Vernunft und Unvernunft," the powers of light and darkness, etc.

The call to "be a man," the appeal to male pride and ego, with all its "Requisiten," is both a reflection and an interpretation of the contemporary historical situation, and also should be viewed in connection with the attitudes of German-American socialists toward women's emancipation and sex roles in general. Thus, the emphasis on the masculine qualities noted above logically gives rise to the question whether women are ever directly addressed or portrayed in this literature, aside from the creatures of misery and helplessness or the allegorical representations referred to earlier. More precisely, the question is how women are portrayed in relation to the male socialists, the "starke Genossen."[26] Aside from some rare exceptions -- and most of this small number of poems and short stories are by women writers -- women workers and issues of women's equality are never specifically addressed. Rather, when women are referred to at all, they are shown either as submissive and happily protected by their husbands and fathers, or as hindrances to organized struggle, as fearful creatures who try to hold back their men from following their real political convictions: It is the man who enters into political debate and conflict, while the woman is concerned primarily with the narrow interests of home and children. A painting by the German-American artist Robert Koehler, entitled "The Strike" (1886), illustrates this configuration. Here, a group of angry male workers has left the smoky, dingy factory buildings to confront the well-dressed owner on the steps of his mansion. One worker is reaching down to pick up a stone, as a woman holds up her hand in a calming, warning gesture to another man, and to the side stands another woman with two small children, watching the unfolding of events. Other examples could be cited where women are shown as passive, as adjuncts to active men, or as brakes on their action. However, all in all, even these negative portrayals of women are infrequent -- it is more typical of this literature that women are neither specifically addressed nor portrayed at all.

That this was a selective interpretation of historical reality must certainly be evident. Not only were large numbers of women (and children) employed at factory work at this time and thus presumably valid "objects for organization" (one of the goals of this literature), but also the German-American socialist press often reported on the participation of women in demonstrations and even as speakers at socialist meetings.[27] Admittedly, women also tended to fulfill traditional roles within the socialist movement, teaching small children or arranging social events. Nevertheless, seen from the perspective of giving impetus to learning processes, this literature does not do justice to the complexity of the historical situation and does not express the contradictions experienced by women taking part in a workers' movement or between feminist and socialist goals. In general, therefore, the image of women which emerges with respect to the active male proletarian figure embodies that proletarian "anti-feminism" of which Thönnessen speaks.[28] As a response to the truly oppressive conditions of female and child labor, woman's rightful place was seen as the home, the politically unimportant sphere outside the labor market. Her entry into the labor force was never shown as also potentially having positive aspects, such as increased independence and self-determination. Thus, the depiction of positive masculine roles and the neglect of female figures expresses the perception that men were both the significant workers and political activists of the present and future, and that the role of women as workers outside the home was both undesirable and temporary.

Even in their portrayal of the unorganized working class as a whole, these writers began to contrast the figure of the industrious, productive, morally upright worker with the lazy, parasitical, evil owner, with a view towards strengthening proletarian self-esteem. If such qualities were sometimes used to characterize the working class in general, they were applied much more strongly to the organized socialist workers. Conscious of their self-image and the image that they present to the hostile outside world, this group is depicted as virtuous in the sense of being hard-working, industrious, orderly, frugal, sober, dependable friends and comrades, and reliable providers for wives and children. By creating this positive image of the organized proletariat, these writers attempt to transmit a sense of self-esteem and fraternal solidarity to the male comrades who identified themselves with these images and goals. This represents the historically recurring phenomenon of a rising class or group claiming moral superiority over its opponents, and as such, the appropriation of these qualities was a crucial moment in the development of class consciousness and a sense of self-worth in the socialist movement. However, keeping this in mind, it is also in order to take a closer look at the precise nature of these qualities: industry, orderliness, frugality, moderation, dependability, a sense of duty and of discipline. Fundamentally, these are exactly the qualities demanded of the worker by an increasingly rationalized capitalist economic system. Frequently, both in the literature and in reports on actual socialist demonstrations and festivals, this orderliness of the organized workers is emphasized, as a legitimation of their demands and activities. Characteristically (except for a few anarchist writers), it is contrasted with spontaneous activity and rebellion, as in this poem by Gustav Lyser:

> Lasst nur die Feinde spotten,
> Bald wird ihr Spott vergeh'n,
> Wenn sie, statt wilder Rotten,
> Bewusste Männer seh'n. (29)

Here, stress is placed on the importance of rational understanding of the task at hand ("Nur Mangel an Erkenntnis-Licht/Hielt fern sie noch von uns'ren Kreisen"), including the disavowal of acts of "Maschinenstürmerei" typical of the response to an earlier period of capitalist industrialization. However, this assumption of what are fundamentally the qualities of a work ethic necessary to the development of capitalist rationality[30] is also a denial of spontaneous activity based on the needs of daily life, and implies that there is a basic divergence of interests between the members of such a "straffe" organization and those outside it who are "unbewusst" but perform the same sort of work. Or, that it is primarily the "false consciousness" of the latter which keeps them outside the socialist organization. That is, this emphasis on discipline, order and the use of militaristic imagery could imply unconscious acceptance of the discipline imposed by developing capitalism on the formerly unruly work force in the course of the 19th century. As these values become internalized they are appropriated by the workers' movement as its own values, and enter into this literature. That is, the assumption of these qualities not only strengthens self-esteem and legitimates socialist organization, but paradoxically also has the function of actually integrating socialist values (and potentially those recipients who identify with them) into the capitalist work process. These qualities are also used to characterize the positive worker figures in American workers' literature of the time, and thus would seem to reflect a common stage of historical development of the working class rather than merely a specific German literary tradition. At this stage, the workers' movement accepts these values as its own, viewing them as a step upwards from brutality, ignorance and blind violence.[31]

If these writers attempted to encourage solidarity in their audience through creating positive images of the organized worker as models for identification and fraternity, the literary techniques they utilized also aimed at urging their working-class audience towards unity. First of all, it becomes evident from the kind of contrasts drawn between unorganized and organized workers that in this literature solidarity is presented as fundamentally a matter of <u>will</u>. We have already mentioned the portrayal of unorganized workers as "feig," "unvernünftig," "unbewusst," "weibisch," and often it is a question of the "Unverstand der Massen" or "der Schafe." But then, it is typical in this literature for unorganized workers to be addressed in the following ways:

> 1) Warum gehst du [i.e. die Welt] zornig nicht
>   Mit den Peinigern ins Gericht?
>   Warum brachst du nicht entzwei
>   Längst schon die Lohnsklaverei?
>
>   Bist an Männern du so arm,
>   Fürchtest du der Schergen Schwarm?
>   Regt in deiner Söhne Blut
>   Sich kein Funke heiliger Wut? (32)
>
> 2) So lang nur <u>klagend</u> Ihr den Frevel rächet,
>   Den frecher Uebermuth an Euch begeht;
>   So lang Ihr noch von <u>Eurer</u> Freiheit sprechet,
>   Die Ihr doch in den schwersten Ketten geht;
>   So lang Ihr nicht die volle Wahrheit kennet
>   Und einseht, dass der Reiche Euch betrügt,
>   So lang Euch niemals freie Männer nennt,
>   Denn <u>freie</u> Männer <u>kämpfen</u>, klagen nicht. (33)

These rhetorical accusations and questions ("<u>Wollt</u> Ihr nicht frei sein?" "<u>Wollt</u> Ihr ewig darben?") are aimed at appealing to a sense of guilt and shame among workers who are allowing themselves and their families to be exploited and thus not behaving like "men." In turn, these workers are assured that if they only have virile courage and a strong will, they can break their chains through rational, unified action ("Was dich erlöst ist nur der <u>Wille</u>,/ Gezeugt aus der <u>Erkenntnis</u> Blick"). Thus, after placing the blame for exploitation on the short-sightedness, cowardice and unmanliness of the unorganized workers, the solution is given in calls to join together in brotherly solidarity:

> 1) Und dieser Geist [i.e. der Freiheit], mög er auch ferner walten
> Und über allen Brüdern sich entfalten,
> Die jetzt noch zweifelnd müssig steh'n,
> Die ihre heil'ge Pflicht noch nicht erkannten
> Und blindlings sich auf Feindes Seite wandten,
> Statt mannhaft ihm zu wiedersteh'n.
> ...
> Lasst ringen uns um uns're Menschenrechte,
> Wie tapf're Männer handeln, nicht wie Knechte,
> Die feig sich beugen vor der Macht. (34)

> 2) Genug der Schmach! Jetzt heisst es männlich ringen
> Mit voller Kraft für unser Menschenrecht!
> ...
> So reicht Euch Alle denn die Hand zum Bunde,
> Als <u>Männer</u>, <u>Väter</u> denket Eurer Pflicht! (35)

> 3) O, schütt'le ab Verblendung, falschen Wahn,
> Den dir der Mammon knechtend eingepflanzt,
> Und schleud're Demut ab, und sei ein Mann!
> Du hast das Recht ja, dass du fragen kannst:
> Was wird aus mir? (36)

The posing of these contrasts between unorganized and united workers, the moral appeals to manly and fatherly sense of duty, the exhortations and commands, are among the most typical techniques used in this literature. Through argumentation, contrasts and appeals, the conclusion is explicitly drawn that unity is the only rational, manly response, the only effective tactic. Thus, this literature is already familiar with the model figure of the enlightened socialist worker, who has a ready, patient answer for all the objections of his less "progressive" colleagues, and whose belief in the eventual victory of his cause is firm and unshakeable in spite of all obstacles. However, on a more general level, the use of these techniques of persuasion and command demonstrates that the goal here was to "awaken" what these writers perceived as an essentially passive recipient. The intent was for the recipient to identify with and carry out the demands voiced in the literature. That is, the model here is that the writer tells the recipients what to do, though abstractly, and presumably they obey.

Since these writers so clearly and fervently intended their literature to have an organizing effect on workers in the particular situation of living as immigrants in

America, it would not be unfair to take them seriously enough to situate these works within this historical situation. The concluding section of Chapter II presented some of the most crucial material and ideological obstacles to the growth of a unified socialist movement in the United States. But typically, this literature which calls for proletarian unity does not bring out these contradictions: the conflicts among various immigrant groups in the community and at the workplace, the perception of America as the land of opportunity and the difficulty of socialist organizing in the face of this ideology of individual initiative, and so forth. To be sure, these works do set up oppositions: the ruling classes are lambasted and unorganized workers are criticized. However, as discussed above, in both cases the confrontations remain on an abstract level of moral accusation or appeal. To be sure, it is also the case that writers advocate certain specific tactics in their calls for unity, such as voting for the socialists, joining a union, or joining an armed organization (in the case of the Social-Revolutionaries). However, in general these calls to unity remain abstract appeals to the conscience, and the desired solidarity of the recipients is made to seem more a matter of moral choice rather than an outgrowth of their daily life and experience. That is, through its techniques of appeal, accusation and exhortation, and its failure to ground its calls for unity in working-class experience, this literature seems based on the assumption that changes in attitude, daily life and practice are brought about by argument and appeals rather than by learning from experience. Thus, even though this literature constantly appeals directly to the recipient, it does not address him as a subject capable of arriving at independent conclusions based on experience, but rather as an object to be enlightened, disciplined, shaped, improved -- that is, organized. This literature utilized statements, appeals and commands rather than attempting to stimulate learning processes which might lead the addressees really to be convinced of the necessity for (socialist) unity. Instead, this necessity is made a matter of a moral response to an abstract appeal. Thus, the operative goal of drawing workers into the socialist movement appears rather problematic. Indeed, it would perhaps be more accurate to assess this literature as an expression of self-affirmation for those who were already convinced, as an affirmative literature for the initiated.

4. IT WILL SURELY COME! REVOLUTION AND SOCIALIST SOCIETY

While this early socialist literature develops no detailed images of a utopian future, nevertheless its references to rebellion, revolution and a better society to come occur frequently and follow certain patterns. This invocation of social change constitutes the final link in the depiction here of the development of socialism: from the misery of the unorganized working class (calculated to arouse pity and a will to change these conditions), to exhortations to unity and the creation of positive models, to the final result of this unified struggle.

Relatively speaking, images of revolution itself occupy a rather small place in this literature compared to invocations of the future cooperative society, socialist society or Volksstaat. However, when the process of transformation from capitalism to socialism does become literary material, it is described as inevitable, as a day for revenge, but also as lasting a short time, as an apocalyptic social upheaval.[37] Even in the prose works which might be expected to develop a fuller concept, this apocalyptic, abstract image of revolution prevails, as in the concluding paragraphs of the following sketch by Alexander Jonas:

> Und nun erhob sich ein ungeheurer Kampfesschrei zum Himmel, wie eine gewaltige Lohe, und es schien als ob das Weltall in Flammen stände. Und die Reichen und Mächtigen, die Völkertreiber und Länderverwüster -- sie sahen mit kreideweissen Gesichtern und schlotternden Knieen die Stunde des Gerichts hereinbrechen.
> Der Kampf war furchtbar, aber kurz. Und als die Sonne aufgegangen war, beschien sie ein wunderbares Schauspiel. Millionen und aber Millionen von Menschen waren beschäftigt, die Trümmer des Kampfes fortzuschaffen und die Erde zu bereiten für eine neue, bessere Zukunft. (38)

In addition to the millenialism, another striking feature here is that revolution, the coming of socialism, or whatever name this process may be called, often seems "disembodied" in these works. "It" will "certainly" come, but the "it" is frequently unconnected to the actions of human subjects. The common use of allegory intensifies this abstractness and lack of mediation: the revolution is a "storm," it will come as surely as day follows night, as inevitably as spring follows winter.

The socialist society to arise after this cataclysm is portrayed somewhat more fully -- although allegory is still employed -- in poems, drawings, and in the tableaus or lebende Bilder presented at festivals which contrast the present conditions of exploitation with the future state of liberation. Basically, there are two elements which are stressed, the liberation of labor and family happiness. Implied in the first is equality and justice, that everyone works and is cared for and provided with time for leisure, education and cultural pursuits.[39] However, there is no reflection on a possible transformation in the nature of work itself. As we saw earlier, these writers generally accept the discipline necessary to industrial work, and so they only go as far as advocating that toil be distributed more evenly. But even this concrete suggestion is atypical. Fundamentally, the concept of the liberation of labor remains abstract in this literature. After social transformation there will be no more "vampires" or "parasites," but it is not clear what will replace them. Carl Derossi wrote:

> Drum Heil dem Tage, wo zerbrochen
> Das Joch der letzten Knechtschaft ward,
> Seitdem nicht mehr an unserm Marke
> Die Schaar der Parasiten nagt. (40)

The goals mentioned are always in the form of rallying demands taken over from the vocabulary of bourgeois revolutions: freedom, humanity, equality, fraternity, justice. However, these generally remain abstract slogans and would only receive more concrete content from the context in which they reached their audience -- say, for example, a union demonstration or socialist meeting. Consequently, these slogans and the occasional mention of an equal distribution of work make these images of the future seem more like a simple reaction to or reflex of the long working day and the misery of daily life, rather than an attempt to create a truly utopian statement.

Similarly, the image of the family under socialism also represents a reaction to the disintegration of the working-class family under developing capitalism and the necessity for women and children to perform factory work, as in the following examples:

> 1) Der Tag des Sieges ist nicht fern.
>   . . .
> Dann werden unsre Kinder nimmer
> Des Siechthums rasche Beute sein,
> Nein, angehaucht von ros'gem Schimmer
> Sich ihres jungen Daseins freun.
> Im Kohlenstaube der Fabriken
> Weilt keine Mutter mehr, kein Kind,
> Sie mögen froh zum Himmel blicken
> Indess die Spule läuft und spinnt. (41)

> 2) O schöner Tag, an dem das Recht
> Trotz Niedertracht zum Siege wird gelangen;
> Kein Mensch, wie jetzt, des andern Menschen Knecht,
> Wo Lieb' und Eintracht alle Welt umfangen.
> Zurückgekehrt das Weib an ihren Herd.
> Die Kindheit darf sich ihrer Spiele freuen
> Dem Manne wird nunmehr die Heimath werth,
> Und keinen Kampf braucht er dafür zu scheuen. (42)

155

In these poems, and perhaps even more clearly in the socialists' drawings and lebende Bilder, the vision of family happiness under socialism is contrasted with the depictions of present family misery and the exploitation and suffering of poverty-stricken women.[43] In the secure family of the future, the husband is shown as strong, muscular and outfitted with all the discipline and virtues enumerated above. He is reminiscent of the skilled craftsmen from an earlier period of industrial development -- perhaps he is shown standing over an anvil -- and has reached the point of being able to take care of his family independently through his own labor. It is no longer necessary for the wife (or children) to work. Women happily return to the home, their "proper sphere," occupy themselves with traditionally female duties, and enjoy the protection of their strong husbands.

The picture which emerges here of the self-sufficient family and a rigid division of sexual roles suggests a resurrection of the model of the independent artisan, an attempt to turn back the clock to what was felt to be a simpler, happier time, before the development of industry and technology. Thus, this image of the future society under socialism, while certainly containing oppositional elements to prevailing social conditions, must also be characterized as backwards-looking and nostalgic in the alternative it presents. Seeking to represent the future, these images were to a large extent reflexes and expressions of the misery and brutality of their own time. As such, they tended to seize upon the not-so-distant historical memory of artisan life, rather than to express concrete utopian goals with respect to a transformation in the nature of work or in the nature of human relationships and interaction.[44]

As these writers themselves stated, they had two basic goals in mind in presenting these images of revolution and the future, and in turn, they employed certain literary techniques to accomplish these goals. First of all, they wanted to provide certainty and thus a will to carry on, to instill the unshakeable belief that the revolution and a better society were sure to come in the near future. As explained above, these writers presented revolution abstractly, often unconnected to human subjects. To specify more clearly the nature of this abstractness, when these writers speak of the "certainty" of imminent revolution, they do this either through simple statements and assertions or through allegory. Thus, there are often direct statements such as "Es wird sicher kommen" or "Die Massen regen sich," or longer assertions of historical inevitability, such as this characterization of organized socialists:

> Sie schreiten in's Feld mit erhobenem Blick.
> Sie wissen das End' ja des heiligen Kriegs,
> Sie sind sich bewusst ja des endlichen Siegs.
> Den der Geschichte gebietendes Muss
> Verkündet als unbedingt geltenden Schluss. (45)

These assertions of certainty are coupled with the technique of presenting revolution and a happier future as nature allegories. Indeed, the use of these allegories as a way of expressing the process of social change is one of the most typical features of this literature, as in the following examples:

> 1) Es kann nicht immerfort so bleiben,
>   Schon lichtet sich die Finsternis,
>   Die neue Welt will Knospen treiben
>   Und Sieger bleibt das Licht gewiss. (46)

> 2) Ja, Menschheitsfrühling, sei gegrüsst,
>   Du <u>kommst</u>! Ja, wir hören Dein Wehen
>   Im Wettersturm, oh sei gegrüsst,
>   Du brichst des Winters starre Nacht
>   Du kommst und zerstörst uns're Bande
>   Es weicht des Stillstands kalte Nacht
>   Es tagt, ja es tagt jedem Lande. (47)

That is, revolution will come as surely as day follows night, as surely as spring follows and conquers winter. Revolution as a natural event independent of human initiative? Of course these allegories should not be taken absolutely literally, but on the other hand, credence is lent to this interpretation through the statements by many of these socialists on the unavoidable, imminent downfall of capitalism and coming of socialism, and on the natural, inevitable development of history.[48]

The second function which these writers intended their images of revolution and the future to fulfill was to serve as compensation in the face of everyday travail, as promises of a better future to be kept in mind through difficult times. We read, for example:

> 1) Das ist der Zukunft Bild, wie wir es hegen
>   Im treuen Herzen, wir der Bruderbund,
>   Das ist des Glaubens Saat, die treu wir pflegen
>   Bis hin zur Ernte, über's Erdenrund.
>   Das sei Ersatz für alle heut'ge Noth.
>   Das sei der Lohn für Dulden, Streben, Darben! (49)

> 2) Doch sicher wird kommen der herrliche Tag,
>   Der endet das Leiden, die Sorge, die Plag'!
>   Das stärkt sie im Kampfe, das hält sie zuhauf,
>   Das spornet sie stetig im siegenden Lauf. (50)

Such examples bring to mind the earlier discussion of the function of socialist festivals and of the statements on the compensatory quality of art as providing escapes from the misery of everyday life. Here, the goal of compensation becomes explicitly formulated in the literature itself.

Bernd Witte and Gerald Stieg compare such poetic expressions to Baroque emblems and medieval religious allegories, and assert that they are rooted in a similar philosophical and social consciousness. That is, Baroque poetry presents the whole

157

of earthly reality as mere <u>Schein</u>, to be overcome and transcended in the life to come, and similarly, Stieg/Witte maintain, these socialist writers possessed an ideology which led them to aim at transforming reality, though of course in the here and now.[51] It is certainly true that both the literary works and, to expand the focus somewhat, the socialist festivals, had a strong affective impact in their invocations of cataclysmic revolutionary upheaval, their statements of certainty, their promises of a better future to arrive like a natural event, and their attempts to provide compensation. As Gottfried Korff points out in an article on socialist May Day celebrations, the festivals, including songs performed at them, are often reminiscent of "chiliastische Heilserwartungen."[52] In addition, these writers sometimes even choose to refer to socialism in religious terms, as "der ewig wahre Volksmessias," or "die Erlösung." Also, the allegorical references to the triumph of light over darkness, of good over evil, and the abstract concepts or images used to designate good and evil forces ("Gott Mammon") would seem to have a religious affective content. We read, for example:

> Noch trieb kein neuer Heiland aus dem Tempel
> Die Wechsler und stiess ihre Tische um;
>
> . . .
>
> Hurrah, du neues Jahr, sei du die Pforte
> Zum Vorhof unsres neuen Tempelbaus!
> Der Stufenweg zu unserm Wallfahrtsorte,
> Die elfte Stunde vor dem Hochzeitsschmaus!
>
> . . .
>
> Bring liebes achtzehnhundert sechsundsiebzig,
> Der Völker endlichen Erlösungstag! (53)

However, it seems to me that the religious elements and images are not the crucial point here, or at least they should not be taken at face value. First of all, these writers chose material for allegories arbitrarily, from the spheres of Christian religion, mythology, nature and abstract concepts. Secondly, as discussed earlier with reference to the pyramidal constructions of society and "socialist iconography," while traditional forms and images may appear, the context in which they are used affects the meaning attached to them. Thus, if the representations of revolution and the future are taken as a whole, they are not directly comparable to religious images of salvation.[54] However, what does emerge in the final analysis is a mechanistic view of historical development which does not take into account the role of the human subject in bringing about social change and which, particularly evidenced through the technique of allegory, envisions progress as a quasi-"natural," inevitable unfolding of events.

5. SUMMARY

Upon arriving in the America of the Gilded Age, these German socialist immigrant writers experienced disillusionment with the class society they encountered. In works referring to specific conditions, events and persons, they expressed this disillusionment directly, but more generally speaking, their whole literary production was directed against exploitation, aiming at exposing and transforming it. In this sense, the literature they produced can be termed "operative" or "functional:" they sought to accomplish broader social objectives through their literary works rather than intending them as purely individual, subjective expression meant for individual reception and contemplation. That is, these works are "operative" in that they sought to move their audience to assume certain political standpoints and to act in accordance with certain political beliefs. However, a closer analysis of the content and literary technique of these works brings out problematic, contradictory aspects of these operative goals. The constant use of stereotyping and allegory means that the level of social perception tends to remain on the surface. Social conflicts are de-historicized and absolutized to become a matter of eternal conflicts between good and evil forces, of individual virtue, courage and manhood, and of individual rational understanding and strength of will.[55] At the same time, appeals, exhortations and commands are used to address the recipient's conscience or sense of justice. Solidarity is made a matter of will rather than a conscious choice resulting from experience. Finally, the images of apocalyptic revolution and socialist society, in their certainty and inevitability, seem strangely unconnected to the actions of those who have joined together in fraternity.

Fundamentally, the abstract nature of this optimistic perspective on history, that is, these assertions based on a belief in the unfolding of history as a quasi-natural development, has the effect of obscuring the role of human subjects acting to bring about these desired changes. First of all, in the literary works themselves there is a constant preoccupation with stating and restating the three thematic areas indicated in this chapter. Thus, rather than exposing or grappling with concrete conflicts and experience, these works reiterate again and again the stages in the development of socialism, ending with promises of certain improvement. Secondly, the characteristic utilization of rhetorical figures of assertion, castigation and command is based on the presumption that the recipient is to be instructed in the proper course of action and that he should then follow it for this literature to achieve the desired effect. There is little room for interpretation, little attempt to present experienced contradictions and conflicts in a way which might go beyond the surface manifestations of society. That is, there is little attempt to proceed from experiences common in the daily life of the recipients with a view towards activating and changing consciousness.[56]

Several social historians have pointed out the ritual-like nature of socialist festivals, in that these gatherings followed a prescribed, fixed order of events (always containing a song, a speech, etc.), and that they served to strengthen solidarity and draw sharp boundaries between insiders and outsiders.[57] The repetitive depiction of the stages in the development of socialism and the avoidance of subjective experience makes it plausible to extend this characterization of ritual to the literary works themselves. However, as these historians also point out, the simple designation of these festivals as following stereotypical forms and patterns neglects the question of the political context. Similarly, these early socialist literary works (and here this means primarily poetry and plays) were above all meant for group performance and collective reception in the context of the workers' movement. Therefore, the following concluding remarks will reintegrate the literary works discussed here into the historical context of the German-American socialist movement discussed earlier.

VI. CONCLUSION

Chapter II indicated the areas of activity of German-American socialists and suggested that they met with varying degrees of effectiveness and success in these areas. Only minimally successful in electoral politics, these socialists played a much more significant role in the establishment and provision of leadership to trade unions of various branches of skilled workers in major industrial centers, thus reaching out beyond the limits of their own language group. Also, they established and maintained a thriving press which, as part of their search for alternative means of communication and cultural models, served as an alternative and corrective to the non-socialist German-American press and other publications. These three areas of involvement were the ones which the socialists themselves viewed as essential parts of their political movement. That is, in the proceedings of their party conventions and in newspaper editorials we find explicit statements on the necessity of concentrating their activity on the areas of elections, unions and the press. We also find unequivocal statements on the necessity of maintaining doctrinal purity and the inadvisability of cooperating with other third parties, as explained in Chapter II. Indeed, it is these efforts to demarcate their own small, exclusive party and this failure to "Americanize" which have led historians from Engels to the present to characterize the German-American socialists as doctrinaire, as "in but not of the world." However, it seems to me that such a one-sided evaluation places too much weight on official statements by the socialists themselves, their failures as an organization at electoral politics, and on simply repeating the judgments of previous historians, whereas a closer perusal of the socialist press contributes to revealing the broad range of socialist participation both within the German-American working class community and with other ethnic groups. This is obviously true with respect to union activity, but it also holds for a whole range of cultural activities, as well. The various socialist parties composed primarily of Germans did not reach only the small inner circle of their actual membership. Rather, through their press and participation in cultural activities within the community, they reached far beyond these small groups of members to a much larger group of sympathizers. In the larger cities, it is probably accurate to say that the socialist newspapers were the institutions which did most to hold the working-class community together, furnishing information, supporting strikes, encouraging contributions from workers, intellectuals, and all members of the community, and sponsoring benefits, festivals and demonstrations. For example, in 1894 the New York Volkszeitung reported that it was the official organ of more than 300 trade unions, sections of the SAP, Turner societies, workers' singing societies, amateur theaters, socialist schools and labor lyceums, Freidenker societies, women's organizations, clubs, mutual benefit and insurance societies, and lodges.[1] This meant that all these groups published official notices and announcements of their meetings in this paper, implying that it would reach their members and that they supported the existence of this socialist paper. The pattern of communication among socialists and these different kinds of groups holds true for other cities besides New York, also, although this interaction can only be indicated here. A more precise sociological study would be necessary to work out detailed patterns of involvement.[2]

161

In addition to the socialist press, which contributed to solidarity within the working-class community between party members and the unaffiliated, the whole socialist subculture which grew up in these ethnic communities fulfilled a similar function, and it is in this context that the socialist literature discussed in Chapter V should be situated. In many areas of their life outside the workplace and the more narrow contexts of electoral and union activity, these socialists, along with other members of the community, created institutions designed as alternatives to others within the ethnic group and the society at large, to further enlightenment and communal and cooperative social relationships. Chapter III discussed the socialist workers' theaters, workers' singing societies, festivals and opportunities for communal demonstrations and leisure as alternatives to similar activities among non-socialist groups. Similarly, from the earliest days of the socialist movement, there were workers' gymnastic societies (Turners), producers' and consumers' cooperatives, workers' sick and death benefit societies,[3] special organizations or groups for women, workers' educational societies and socialist schools for children and adults. All of these various groups and organizations which aimed at providing opportunities for education and enlightenment, mutual help and support, and communal leisure activities reached out to form a fraternal network within the German-American working class community which included men, women and children and had the effect of protecting and insulating them from capitalist society.[4] For immigrants, in particular, settling in a country with a different language and different customs, such a supportive network provided a cushion against cultural shock and economic difficulty. Thus, the cultural network operating under the influence of the socialists and other progressive groups had both a backwards- and a forwards-looking character, reflecting the general problems of living and writing in a situation of immigration and exile. On the one hand, they reached to familiar forms of group interaction in an effort to preserve solidarity and values in the new social context; they were concerned with transmitting the German language and a sense of identification with German history and culture to their children. But on the other hand, they used the German language to transmit the concepts of socialism and attempt to create working class solidarity in many areas of life within their ethnic group and with the working class of other language groups. Their organizations and societies and the press which they created with so much effort and pride were all destined to fade away with the gradual assimilation of the ethnic group, but they made their contribution while it lasted as a definable community. Thus, what Lee Baxandall says of the radical immigrant press might be applied just as well to this whole cooperative social network:

> The feuilleton material that appeared in such publications as the New York Volkszeitung and its many counterparts across the land was meant to be hegemoniacal. It did more than resist; it was meant to perform the same kind of everyday function -- amusing, inspiring, informing, orienting -- as the counterparts in the capitalist press, but more humanly, more fully. (5)

This, then, is the context in which German-American socialist literature was situated and in which these writers attempted to have a certain effect. To review once more the characteristics of such "operative" literature emphasized by literary historians: it is viewed in an "anti-bürgerlicher Traditionszusammenhang," as constituting an alternative to the concept of literature as a realm of individual esthetic expression with no extra-literary purpose. In contrast, this operative literature was integrally connected to the (socialist) workers' movement, and was written with the intent of carrying out a double function: proletarian organization and enlightenment, and the creation of cultural identity. It was suggested in Chapters III and IV that this concept of operativity should not be accepted as an unqualifiedly positive alternative to the bourgeois tradition, but that it should be approached in a more differentiated manner. By making the methodological distinction between form, content and functional context, rather than simply pointing out the occasions upon which this literature was used in the workers' movement, it has been possible to indicate the contradictory makeup of this early socialist literature. On the level of form, there is little innovation, but rather there is generally an arbitrary reutilization of traditional techniques. In particular, the use of allegory sustains the image of the process of socialism as a natural development in which the role of the human subject is of unclear significance.[6] Also, the use of rhetorical forms of appeal, exhortation and command presupposes a model in which it is the task of the writer to instruct the recipient and create positive models for him to identify with and follow, rather than encouraging him to interpret both the literary work and his own experience. On the level of content, there are some works which deal with concrete aspects of the immigrant worker's experience, but there is a general tendency towards abstraction. The preoccupation with the stages in the development of socialism outlined in Chapter V makes this literature seem more and more like part of a ritual expression removed from reality, particularly if we imagine socialists gathering together after Haymarket, in the last decade of the 19th century, and singing of the certain, imminent coming of socialism. In addition, socialist writers who continually invoked the future cooperative society did not take account of the real opportunities for advancement which immigrants found in American society and the possibility that this might make them less receptive to socialist arguments. However, it was in the context of socialist gatherings and group activity that this literature was able at least in part to fulfill the functions of organization and contributing to creating cultural identity. Here, participants could sense that they possessed their own writers, their own literature, and their own performing groups, and that they were able to sustain these things independently. Here, at party or union meetings, demonstrations, festivals, or in smaller community groups, the abstract calls to unite, to fight for freedom, could be invested by the audience with a particular meaning in the given context. Thus, while it is questionable whether this literature in itself could have had the effect of persuading people not already in sympathy with its socialist premises, it certainly contributed to the formation of cultural (and thus political) identity among those who were already inclined to read the socialist press or attend various types of workers' gatherings. It did this not through a concern with problems and conflicts encountered in everyday life, in subjective experience, but through "the straight sentimental portrait of the historic proletarian mission"[7] with which socialists and their sympathizers could identify. Therefore, rather than simply applying standards from today to evaluate and dismiss this early socialist literature as "non-

Brechtian" or "undialectical," it seems also appropriate to evaluate it in the context of its own time, as a qualifiedly positive alternative available to the German-American working class in the context of German-American literature and culture as a whole.

The rediscovery of the many strains in the radical tradition of the United States will be of little more than academic significance if it is carried out merely in the spirit of antiquarianism, of collecting quaint artifacts from the past. On the other hand, the visions of the 19th century socialists, and their cultural and political forms of organization, cannot serve us as direct models in late capitalist society, in an age of mass media and communications. At one time, however, up until the Second World War in both Germany and the United States, the workers' movement also encompassed a cultural movement, with a broader scope to its efforts which extended into many spheres of life.[8] In the United States, with the growth of the "pure and simple" unionism of the American Federation of Labor, the organized workers' movement became less and less concerned with cooperative cultural ventures, and similarly, trade unions in the Federal Republic of Germany have hardly been concerned with redeveloping and creating new spheres of activity outside economic issues. The earlier workers' movement developed means of communication and opportunities for group interaction. It will remain to be seen how present-day movements for social change will be able to integrate these political, economic and cultural aspects of societal transformation into their strategy and goals.

The importance of the progressive political and cultural heritage of immigrant groups such as the Germans or of "native" American radicalism is perhaps most evident when looked at from the perspective of repression. Our knowledge of this tradition has always been suppressed, and socialist and working-class culture has been denigrated and trivialized as inferior to so-called "high culture." We have seen that socialist publications were banned in Germany during the period of the Anti-Socialist Laws, but they were constantly smuggled in by the political exiles despite official surveillance. Until 1972, Haymarket Square was marked by a statue of a Chicago policeman commanding "peace in the name of the people" rather than by a memorial to those who died in the struggle for the eight-hour day. In the wake of growing conservative trends in the Federal Republic of Germany, a historical documentation entitled 1886, Haymarket was confiscated in Bavaria in 1976, and a court case was necessary before it could be sold in bookstores again.[9] These particular examples reflect a general policy of neglect: the history of radicalism and the labor movement, and its literature and culture, is not taught in schools and seldom even at universities. The struggle which continues over the preservation and dissemination of the radical tradition, over a reinterpretation of the forgotten part of the German-American legacy, is in fact a struggle for the power of a sense of historical development and progress which we can win from the past.

APPENDIX I

PERIODICAL PUBLICATIONS OF THE GERMAN-AMERICAN SOCIALISTS

This appendix includes newspapers and other periodicals published after 1865, and only includes the publications of Adolf Douai, Wilhelm Weitling and Joseph Weydemeyer from the antebellum period. The dates of publication are given, as well as other interesting facts such as circulation and editorship. Party affiliation is indicated where known.

Publications marked with a + are available in archives. Those that are not so marked are only available in an extremely small number of issues, or their location is unknown. Unfortunately, this is the case for the majority of these periodicals.

The main source for this information is Karl Arndt and May Olson, German-American Newspapers and Periodicals, 1732-1955, 2nd ed. , New York: Johnson Reprint, Co. , 1965.

California
> San Francisco
>> California Arbeiter-Zeitung, 1887-1893. Official organ of Deutsche Gewerkschaften und Arbeiter-Vereine
>> Vorwärts der Pacific Küste, 1910?-1919?. Organ of the Socialist Party of San Francisco.

Illinois
> Belleville
>> Tagblatt und Arbeiter-Zeitung, 1884-1912?
> Chicago
>> Der Anarchist, 1888-1894?. Anarchistisch-communistisches Organ, published by the Autonomen Gruppen Amerikas.
>> Der Arbeiterfreund, 1874.
>> + Arbeiter-Sängerbund des Nordwestens. Festzeitung für das 5te Bundes-Sängerfest abgehalten am 24-27 Juni 1910, in Chicago. Nos. 1-3, Dec. 1909-April 1910.
>> + Arbeiter-Sängerbund von Amerika (Bezirk West). Fest-Programm des 10ten Bundes-Sängerfest. 22-24 Juni 1928, Chicago.
>> Arbeiterstimme, 1889, published by the Central Labor Union.
>> + Chicagoer Arbeiter-Zeitung, 1876-1919. Editors: Conrad Conzett, Paul Grottkau, August Spies, Joseph Dietzgen, Max Baginski, Albert Currlin. Sympathetic to the Social-Revolutionaries in Chicago.
>> + Der Deutsche Arbeiter, 1869-1871?. Official organ of the German Central Workingmen's Union.
>> + Die Fackel, 1879-1919. Sunday edition of Arbeiter-Zeitung. Editor early in 1880's: Wilhelm L. Rosenberg. Circulation: 1880: 5000. 1890: 16,000, 1895: 25,000, 1910: 24,000, 1919: 24,000.

Chicago, cont.

        Illinoiser Volkszeitung, 1893-?. Published by SAP.

        Der Klassen-Kampf, 1919-1920. Organ of the Industrial Workers of the World.

    + Neues Leben, 1902-1910. Organ of the Socialist Party of Illinois.

        Die neue Zeit, 1877-1879?

        Chicagoer Sozialist, 1876-1879?

        Stimme des Volks, 1860-?. Edited and published by Joseph Weydemeyer.

        Sturmglocke, n. d. Edited by Max Baginski.

        Volkszeitung, 1877-1879?

    + Vorbote, 1874-1924. Weekly edition of Arbeiter-Zeitung.

Iowa

Davenport

    + Arbeiter-Sängerbund des Nordwestens. Festzeitung für das 4te Bundes-Sängerfest abgehalten am 23-26 Juni, 1907, in Davenport, Iowa. No. 1, June 1906.

Kentucky

Louisville

        Die Neue Zeit, 1877?-1878?. Published by the Louisville section of the WPUSA.

Louisiana

New Orleans

        Der Hammer, 1876.

Michigan

Detroit

    + Der Arme Teufel, 1884-1900. Edited by Robert Reitzel. Contributors included the authors Bruno Wille, John Henry Mackay, and Karl Henckell.

    + Der Herold, 1884-1918. Organ of the Central Labor Union.

Minnesota

New Ulm

    + Der Fortschritt, 1891-1915. Organ der Farmer Alliance und der Arbeiter (Populist).

Missouri

St. Louis

    + Der Anarchist, 1889-1895. Anarchistisch-Communistisches Organ der Gruppe Autonomie. Edited by Claus Timmermann.

    + Arbeiter-Sängerbund des Nordwestens. Festzeitung für das Bundes-Sängerfest abgehalten am 17. bis 20. Juni 1904 in St. Louis, Mo. Nos. 1-7, May 1, 1903 - June 10, 1904. Cooperative Printing House.

    + Arbeiter-Zeitung, 1898-1935?

        Die Neue Zeit, 1865?-?. Edited by Joseph Weydemeyer.

    + Die Parole, 1884-1891?. Affiliated with the IWPA.

St. Louis, cont.
+ St. Louis Tageblatt, 1888-1898. Edited by Adolf Hepner.
+ Volksstimme des Westens, 1877-1880. Organ of SAP, edited by August Otto-Walster.

New Jersey
Elizabeth
Agitator, 1893.
Newark
+ New Jersey Arbeiter-Kalender, 1899-?
New Jersey Arbeiterzeitung, 1884-1890. Edited by M. v. Stern.
Vorwärts, 1877?-1879?

New York
Buffalo
+ Buffaloer Arbeiter-Zeitung, 1885?-1918?. Organ of the Vereinigten Deutschen Gewerkschaften.
New York City
Amerikanische Arbeiterzeitung, 1886. Anarchist, edited by Wilhelm Hasselmann.
+ Der Arbeiter, 1927-1937. Official German organ of the Communist Party of the USA.
+ Arbeiter-Sängerbund der Nordöstlichen Staaten von Amerika, Festzeitung für das 4te Bundes-Sängerfest am 1-4 Juli 1905, Brooklyn. Nos. 1-6, June, 1, 1904 - June 15, 1905.
+ Arbeiter-Stimme, 1874-1878. Organ of the Sozial-demokratischen Arbeiterpartei von Nord-Amerika (1874-76), Organ of the SAP (1876-78) under the title Social-Demokrat. Editors were Gustav Lyser, August Otto-Walster, Alexander Jonas, Adolf Douai.
+ Die Arbeiter-Union, 1868-1870. Organ of the Nationalen Arbeiter-Verbindung. Edited by Adolf Douai.
+ New Yorker Arbeiter-Zeitung, 1864-1865. Influenced by Schulze-Delitzsch.
+ Die Brandfackel, 1893-1895. Anarchist, edited by Claus Timmermann.
+ Deutsches Volksecho, 1937-1939. Organ of the CPUSA. Edited by Stephan Heym.
+ Die Einheitsfront, 1934.
+ Freiheit, 1883-1910. Edited by Johann Most.
+ Gewerkschafts-Zeitung, 1879-1881?
+ Illustrierter deutsch-amerikanischer Volkskalender, 1938?-1939?
+ Neue Arbeiter-Zeitung, 1873-1875. Organ of the First International.
+ Pionier-Kalender, 1882-1933.
+ Die Reform, 1853-1854. Edited by Joseph Weydemeyer.
+ Die Republik der Arbeiter, 1850-1855, edited by Wilhelm Weitling.
+ Die Revolution, 1852. Edited by Joseph Weydemeyer.
Sänger-Zeitung, n. d. Organ of the Arbeiter-Sänger von Amerika.
+ Solidarität, 1906-1939?. Published by the Arbeiter-Kranken- und Sterbekasse.

New York City, cont.

- + Der Sozialist, 1885-1892. Organ of the SAP, edited by Wilhelm L. Rosenberg.
- + Sturmvogel, 1897-1899. Anarchist. Edited by Claus Timmermann.
- + Der Tramp, 1888. Humoristisches Wochenblatt, edited by Wilhelm L. Rosenberg and Georg Biedenkapp.
- + New Yorker Volkszeitung, 1878-1932. Organ of the SAP and then of the SP. Editors included Alexander Jonas, Adolf Douai, Sergius Schewitsch, Hermann Schlüter. Circulation: 1879: 8000. 1890: 19,680. 1910: 17,000. 1932: 23,000.
- + Vorwärts, 1877-1932. Weekly edition of New York Volkszeitung. Circulation: 1880: 5700. 1900: 10,000. 1915: 45,000, 1930: 15,000.
- + Vorwärts, 1892-1894. Organ of the SAP.

Ohio

Cincinnati

Die Arbeiter von Ohio, 1877-?. Organ of the Arbeiter-Partei von Cincinnati.

Freiheitsbanner, n.d. Supported SAP.

Ohio Volkszeitung, 1876?-1878? Organ of the SAP.

- + Cincinnati Tageblatt, 1895-1896, Organ of the Deutscher Gewerkschaftsrat.
- + Cincinnati Zeitung, 1886-1901. Edited by August Otto-Walster, 1886-90.

Cleveland

- + Arbeiter-Sängerbund des Nordwestens, Festzeitung für das 7te Bundes-Sängerfest abgehalten an 1-4 Juli, 1916, in Cleveland, No. 5.
- + Echo, 1911-1920. Organ of the German Branch of the SP of Ohio and Indiana.
- + Socialistische Arbeiter-Zeitung, 1900-1908. Organ of the SAP.
- + Volks-Anwalt, 1889-1898. Organ of the SAP until 1896, then Organ of the Social-Demokratischen Federation von Nordamerika.
- + Clevelander Volksfreund, 1886-1918, Organ of the SAP.

Pennsylvania

Philadelphia

- + Der Hammer, 1882-1887. Organ of the Metall-Arbeiter-Union.
- + Kalender des Philadelphia Tageblatt, 1899?-1904?
- + Philadelphia Tageblatt, 1877-1944?. Organ of the Vereinigten Deutschen Gewerkschaften.

Pittsburgh

Pittsburger Volkszeitung, 1891-1894?

Texas

San Antonio

- + San Antonio Zeitung, 1853-1856. Edited by Adolf Douai.

Wisconsin
  Milwaukee
      + Arbeiter-Sängerbund des Nordwestens, Festzeitung für das 8te Bun-
        des-Sängerfest abgehalten am 30. Juni, 1-3 Juli 1922 in Milwaukee.
        Nos. 1-4, Feb. 1922 - June 1922.
        Milwaukee'r Arbeiter-Zeitung, 1882-1889?. Organ of the Central
        Labor Union.
      + Der Emanzipator, 1877, Organ of the WPUSA.
      + Milwaukeer Leuchtkugeln, 1876. Supplement to Der Socialist.
        Die Rothe Laterne, 1876. Supplement to Der Socialist.
      + Der Socialist, 1875-1878?. Organ of the First International, edited
        by Gustav Lyser.
        Milwaukee Volkszeitung, 1890-1892.
        Vorwärts, 1878-1879.
        Vorwärts, 1887-1898.
      + Die Wahrheit, 1889-1910, Organ of the Sozialdemokratischen Partei
        von Wisconsin.
      + Wisconsin Vorwärts, 1892-1932. Organ of the Sozialdemokratischen
        Partei von Wisconsin, edited by Victor L. Berger.

  Sheboygan
        Arbeiter-Zeitung, 1908?-1909?

APPENDIX II

AMERICAN PUBLICATIONS BANNED IN GERMANY UNDER THE ANTI-SOCIALIST
LAW

Sources:

Atzrott, Otto, Königl. Polizei-Sekretair zu Berlin. Sozialdemokratische Druckschriften und Vereine verboten auf Grund des Reichsgesetzes gegen die gemeingefährlichen Bestrebungen der Sozialdemokratie vom 21. Oktober 1878.
Berlin: Carl Heymanns Verlag, 1886.

Nach zehn Jahren. Material und Glossen zur Geschichte des Sozialistengesetzes.
Bd. II, Die Opfer des Sozialistengesetzes. London: German Cooperative
Publishing Co., 1890.

Teich, Christian. Alphabetisches Verzeichniss aller auf Grund des Reichs-Ge-
setzes vom 21. Oktober 1878 erlassenen Verfügungen gegen die Socialdemokratie bis 30. Juni 1878 nebst dem betr. Reichsgesetz, dem Verzeichniss der
in den einzelnen Bundesstaaten für die Ausführung des Gesetzes zuständigen
Behörden und den von den Landespolizeibehörden dazu ergangenen Ausführungs-
Bestimmungen. Lobenstein: Vlg. von Teichs Buchhandlung, n.d.

I. Periodical Publications (with the date banned)

    Amerika (St. Louis, 1879)
    California Arbeiter-Zeitung (San Francisco, 1879)
    Chicagoer Arbeiter-Zeitung, (Chicago, 1879)
    Die Fackel (Chicago, 1887)
    Der Freidenker (Milwaukee, 1879)
    Freiheit (New York/London, 1879)
    New Yorker Volkszeitung (New York, 1884)
            Sonntagsblatt (New York, 1884)
            Vorwärts, Wochenblatt (New York, 1879)
    Philadelphia Tageblatt (Philadelphia, 1879)
    Proletár (Bohemian, New York, 1885)
    Der Sozialist (New York, 1885)
    Amerikanische Turnzeitung (Milwaukee, 1885)
    Volny Sokol Caropis Katolicky (Bohemian, Chicago, 1886)
    Vorbote (Chicago, 1881)

II. Other Publications (with place of publication and date banned)

    Anarchismus oder Kommunismus (Chicago, 1886). Debate between Paul
            Grottkau of the SAP and Johann Most of the IWPA.
    Arbeiter-Liederbuch. Gedichte und Lieder freisinniger und besonders sozial-
            demokratischer Tendenz (Chicago, 1881).

Bakunin, Michael. Gott und der Staat (Philadelphia: Vlg. der Gruppe II der
	IAA, 1885).
Bibliothek internationale, Heft 1,2,3. (New York: John Müller. 1887).
Douai, Adolf. Kindergarten und Volksschule als socialdemokratische Anstal-
	ten (Leipzig). Written in the U. S.
Franklin, B. Die natürliche Offenbarung über Selbsthülfe (Davenport, 1881).
Fritzsche, Friedrich W. "Für die Freiheit Deutschlands. Die Abgesandten
	der deutschen Sozialdemokratie an die Gesinnungsgenossen in den
	Ver. Staaten" (New York, 1881). Leaflet.
Gerau, Fr. "Was der Sozialismus will, und wie er es will." (New York:
	Published by the SAP, 1885).
Greis, John. Republik oder Monarchie (Chicago, 1884). Originally published
	in 1849.
Heinzen, Karl. Wer und was ist das Volk. (Sandusky, Ohio: Verein zur Ver-
	breitung radikaler Prinzipien, 1878).
Hepner, Adolf. Hepners deutsch-amerikanische Arbeiter-Bibliothek, Heft 1
	(Bebel, August: Die Ziele der Arbeiterbewegung), (New York, 1884).
Internationale Arbeiter-Association. "Proklamation. An die Arbeiter der
	Vereinigten Staaten von Nordamerika." Pittsburg, 16. Okt. 1883.
	Der Internationale Sozialisten-Congress. Internationale Druckerei
	der Freiheit (1884).
Jonas, Alexander. Reporter und Sozialist. (New York: published by the SAP,
	1885).
K. , E. Der Zeitgeist (Chicago: Vlg. von Charles Ahrens, 1878).
Krapotkin, Peter. An die jungen Leute (New York, 1885).
Krasser, Hermann. "Anti-Syllabus." (Chicago).
___	"Ceterum censeo." (Chicago, 1878).
Langner, Carl. "Ein Streifzug auf dem Gebiete der kulturgeschichtlichen
	Entwicklung im Zusammenhang mit der Idee des Sozialismus. Vor-
	trag gehalten vor dem Verein der 'Liberalen Liga.'" (Evansville,
	1885).
Lassalle, Ferdinand. Die Agitation des Allgemeinen Deutschen Arbeiter-
	Vereins (Chicago, 1880).
___	"Arbeiter-Programm. Ueber den besonderen Zusammenhang der ge-
	genwärtigen Geschichtsperiode mit der Idee des Arbeiterstandes."
	(Chicago: Vlg. von Charles Ahrens, 1878).
___	Gesammelte Reden und Schriften (New York, 1883, 1884).
___	Verschiedene kleine Aufsätze (Chicago, 1880).
"Mahnruf! an alle Arbeiter der Vereinigten Staaten Nord-Amerikas. Flugblatt
	des Sozial-Revolutionären Clubs, N.Y." (New York, 1881).
"Manifest des Congresses der Sozialistischen Arbeiter-Partei abgehalten vom
	26. bis 28. Dez. 1883 zu Baltimore, Md." (1884).
Die moderne Gesellschaft (Chicago, 1887).
Most, Johann. Acht Jahre hinter Schloss und Riegel (New York, 1886).
___	August Reinsdorff und die Propaganda der That (New York, 1885).
___	Die Eigenthumsbestie (New York, 1884).
___	Die freie Gesellschaft (New York, 1884).

Most, Johann. Die revolutionäre Kriegswissenschaft (New York, 1885).

___ Sturmvögel. Gedichte (New York, 1888).

___ "Zum Gedächtnis an den tapferen, opfermuthigen, getreuen Genossen Hermann Stellmacher. Die Gruppe N.Y. der IAA an die Proletarier aller Länder. Flugblatt." (New York, 1884).

"Neujahrsgruss. Den Lesern der Chicagoer Arbeiter-Zeitung, Fackel und Vorbote von den Trägern gewidmet" (Chicago, 1884).

Nieuwenhuis, Ferdinand. Kapital und Arbeit (New York, 1888).

"Offener Brief an den deutschen Reichskanzler Bismarck" (New York, 1879).

Otto-Walster, August. "Ein verunglückter Agitator oder die Grund- und Bodenfrage. Lustspiel in 2 Akten." (St. Louis: Druck von der Volksstimme des Westens, 1879).

Rother Katechismus für das deutsche Volk (Boston and New York, 1881).

"Die Section New York der sozialistischen Arbeiterpartei an die Bevölkerung der Ver. Staaten. Flugblatt." (New York, 1881).

Spies, August [?]. Die Nihilisten. Festspiel. (Chicago, 1883).

Stern, Maurice. Proletarier-Lieder (Jersey City, 1885).

Stiebeling, Georg. Lesebuch für das Volk (New York, 1883).

"Der Vetter aus Amerika. Eine Erzählung für Landsleute, erbaulich zu lesen." (1881).

GERMAN IMMIGRATION TO THE UNITED STATES, 1820-1968

1820-1830	7,729
1831-1840	152,454
1841-1850	434,626
1851-1860	951,667
1861-1870	787,468
1871-1880	718,182
1881-1890	1,452,970
1891-1900	505,152
1901-1910	341,498
1911-1920	143,945
1921-1930	412,202
1931-1940	114,058
1941-1950	226,578
1951-1960	477,765
1961-1968	169,791

Source: Webster's Guide to American History. Springfield, Mass.: Merriam-Webster, 1971, p. 714.

APPENDIX IV

BIOGRAPHICAL SKETCHES OF GERMAN-AMERICAN SOCIALIST WRITERS

The following information on German-American socialist writers is taken from the German-American socialist press and the following sources:

Auer, Ignaz. Nach 10 Jahren. Material und Glossen zur Geschichte des Sozialisten-gesetzes. London: German Cooperative Publ. Co., 1889-90.

Geschichte der deutschen Arbeiterbewegung. Biographisches Lexikon. Berlin: Dietz, 1970.

Kamman, William. Socialism in German American Literature. Philadelphia: Americana Germanica Press, 1917.

Kosch, Wilhelm. Deutsches Literatur-Lexikon. Bern: 1956, 2nd ed.

Lexikon sozialistischer deutscher Literatur. (Halle 1963). s. Gravenhage: van Eversdijck, 1973 (Raubdruck).

Schlüter, Hermann. Die Internationale in Amerika. Chicago: Deutsche Sprach-gruppe der Sozialist. Partei der Ver. Staaten, 1918.

Biedenkapp, Georg (1843 Londorf/Hessen - 1924 Frankfurt a. M.). Dr. Phil., 1885 to New York. Anarchist tendencies. Published in the New York press. Together with Wilhelm Rosenberg, started his own satirical publication, Der Tramp (1888). Publications in Germany on scientific and historical topics.

Bücher, Friedrich. Member of the Furniture Workers' Union in Philadelphia in 1875.

Bufe, Franz. A cigarmaker by trade. Born in Saxony, to America in 1884. Active in workers' singing societies.

Conzett, Conrad (1848 Chur/Switzerland - 1897). Trade unionist and member of the First International in Chicago. A typesetter for the Chicago Vorbote. In 1876 a delegate from the Workingmen's Party of Illinois to the Philadelphia Unity Congress which founded the WPUSA. Editor then of the WPUSA's official German paper, the Vorbote. Committed suicide.

Derossi, Carl (1844-1910). Member of the five-man executive committee of the SPD in 1878. Immigrated to New York, was active in the SAP, and contributed poetry to the press and workers' singing societies.

Douai, Adolf (1819/Altenburg - 1888 New York). Descendant of a French refugee family. Studied in Leipzig 1838-41, spent six years as a private tutor in Russia before establishing a Realschule in Altenburg. Arrested for taking part in the 1848 revolution. Immigrated to New Braunfels, Texas, published an abolitionist newspaper (San Antonio Zeitung, 1853-56). Forced to flee by slavery supporters. Lived and taught four years in Boston. After 1866, active as a teacher and journalist in New York. Member of the SAP, editor of the New York Volkszeitung from 1878-88. Although his literary production was concentrated in the 1850's, when he published a utopian socialist novel (Fata Morgana, 1859) and a number of other fictional works, he continued to be active as a journalist. As a party official he testified twice to U.S. Congress committees on the relationship between capital and labor, presenting fundamentals of socialism to the dumbfounded legislators. Another of his consuming interests was educational reform geared towards removing children from religious and bourgeois influence. His pamphlet "Kindergarten und Volksschule als sozialdemokratische Anstalten" (1876) was influential in shaping the system of German socialist schools for children which grew up in the city of New York.

Drescher, Martin (1863 Wittstock in der Mark - 1920 Ottowa). Studied in Breslau, Berlin, Göttingen. Lived an adventurous life as a tramp in the U.S., arriving in 1891, then became more interested in socialism. Worked on various socialist papers, including the Milwaukee Vorwärts. Turned towards anarchism, edited Robert Reitzel's Der arme Teufel in Detroit 1898-1900, then worked on the Chicago Arbeiter-Zeitung. Finally, edited the Chicago magazine Die Glocke and turned away from socialism.

Forker, Max. A speaker and political organizer for the SAP, who traveled throughout the U.S. spreading the doctrines of socialism and organizing new party sections.

Franz, Jakob. Published Sozialdemokratische Lieder und Deklamationen (Zürich, 1875). Active member of the SAP in Brooklyn, contributed to the New York press.

Fritzsche, Friedrich Wilhelm (1825 Leipzig - 1905 Philadelphia). A cigar-maker who became a SPD representative in the Reichstag. Came to the U.S. with Louis Viereck on a speaking tour for the SPD in 1881, and both returned soon afterwards for good. Contributed poems and short stories to the press, wrote for the Philadelphia Tageblatt.

Geissler, Ludwig. Published the radical newspaper Der Hammer in New Orleans in 1876. Participated in the attempt to found a communistic colony, "Liberty Settlement," at Covington, La. Contributed short stories to the press, wrote for the Chicago Fackel.

Glauch, Hermann (1855 Döbeln/Saxony - ?). Lived in Cincinnati in 1872, then in San Francisco. Poems published in the socialist press of these cities.

Grottkau, Paul (1846-1899). To the U.S. in the late 1870's. Editor of the Chicago Arbeiter-Zeitung and Vorbote. Active in the SAP in Chicago and Milwaukee. To San Francisco in 1889, editor of the Kalifornia Arbeiter-Zeitung.

Grunzig, Julius (1861 - ?). Arrested in 1879 in Berlin for distributing copies of the Socialdemokrat and then denied admission to the university there. Became a contributor to the New York Volkszeitung, editor of the Newark New-Jersey Arbeiterzeitung, and published short stories in the Pionier-Kalender.

Hofmann, Emilie (1844 - ?). To the U.S. about 1872. Of proletarian background. Poems published in the press.

Jacoby, Leopold (1840 Lauenberg/Hinterpommern - 1895 Zürich). Studied in Berlin, worked for various newspapers. Dr. Phil. in zoology at Halle, then studied medicine in Marburg. Doctor in the Franco-Prussian War, turn towards socialism in his poetry collection Es werde Licht! (1871). To the U.S. in 1882, lived in Cambridge, Mass. and gave private lessons. Contributor to German-American socialist press. To Milan in 1888, lectured there at the academy on German literature.

Jonas, Alexander (1834-1912). Son of a well-to-do Berlin bookseller. Immigrated in 1869. For several years, active in Freidenker circles and efforts to promote women's rights. Joined the SAP in 1877, editor of Arbeiter-Stimme 1876-78. A founder and editor of the New York Volkszeitung, contributed poetry and prose sketches of proletarian life in New York.

Lyser, Gustav (1841 Dresden - ?). Father (Ludwig Burmeister) took part in the Vormärz. Worked on the socialist paper Volksfreund in Braunschweig. Expelled from the SDAP in 1873. Immigrated in 1874, edited the Social-Demokrat, organ of the North American SDAP until 1875. Expelled from the party in 1875 due to his opposition to trade unionism. In 1876, edited the Milwaukee Sozialist, Rothe Laterne and Milwaukeer Leuchtkugeln. Attended the Unity Congress in Philadelphia in 1876. To Chicago in 1878, co-editor of the socialist papers there and active supporter of the Lehr- und Wehrverein. Returned to Milwaukee in 1880, eventually dropped out of the labor movement.

Otto-Walster, August (1834-1898 Dresden). Took part in the founding of the Eisenach party, the SDAP, in 1869 and worked as a socialist organizer and journalist in Dresden. In 1875, invited by the SDAP in New York to edit their paper, the Social-Demokrat. In 1876, he attended the final conference of the First International in New York as a delegate of the SPD. Relocated to St. Louis, where he edited the SAP paper Volksstimme des Westens (1877-80), and then to Cincinnati, where he also continued his journalistic activity. Late in the 1880's, he dropped out of the socialist movement, turned increasingly towards alcoholism, and returned to Germany in 1890. One of the most frequently printed writers in the German and German-American socialist press. His novel Am Webstuhl der Zeit (1873) was a popular choice for serialization, as were shorter works and monumental poems such as "Das rote Gespenst und die Cäsaren" (1870) on the spirit of revolution through the ages. He was also the most active organizer of socialist workers' theaters in the U.S., founding amateur groups in New York, St. Louis and other cities which included his own original plays in their repertoire. He was in contact with Eleanor Marx and Edward Aveling on their American tour in 1886, and in their book on The Working-Class Movement in America (1888), they praised his literary involvement as follows:

> "Trying to make anybody who has not known Otto-Walster understand what manner of man this rare soul is, needs a George Meredith at least, if not a Heine or a Balzac, or these two last in one. There are two aspects of the poetry of a movement like that of Socialism. The

one is furnished by the genuine proletariat, by their sufferings, their awakening, their feeling after hope, their aspiration, their understanding, their resolve and their victory, and of this song only the earlier verses are as yet sung confusedly. The clear voice of these, and yet more, the full clarion of battle and the paean of triumph are not yet sounded.

But the other aspect of the poetry of the working-class movement is already more definite and distinct in form. It is yielded by the artistic souls that, famishing in the desert of today, are making for the promised land beyond, and mark the way thither by their singing. Of such as these is Walster. Poet, dramatist, novellist, an artist to his soul's core, he descends into the common ways of men so that he may help to lead men from them. He makes the path out of the desert at once plainer and more smooth. (207-8).

Pudewa, Hermann (1847 Schlesien - 1902 Chicago). Son of a weaver. About 1870 to the U.S. An editor of the Chicago Arbeiter-Zeitung.

Reitzel, Robert (1849-1898). One of the most well-known German-American writers, loosely associated with the anarchist movement in Detroit. Published a weekly journal, Der arme Teufel, from 1884-1900, which included contributions from the circle of "Die Jungen" in Germany.

Reuber, Karl. A cabinet-maker living in Pittsburgh, whose poems often appeared in the press. Concentrates on calls for unity and the eight-hour working day. A co-founder of the ADAV of Pittsburgh and member of the German cabinet-makers' union.

Rosenberg, Wilhelm Ludwig (1850 Hamm/Westphalia - 193?). Held his doctorate in philosophy, taught Latin and French in Frankfurt a.M. Began to write for Die neue Welt in 1875, his articles arousing the ire of the censor. To the U.S. in 1880. Co-edited several papers, including the Chicago Arbeiter-Zeitung and the Sozialist of the SAP. While he edited the latter, he was also National Executive Secretary of the SAP, from 1885-90. During this time, many of his poems appeared in the socialist press. After 1890, he spent six years in Cincinnati devoting himself to literary and journalistic work. In 1890, the SAP split over the question of trade unionism, with the New York Volkszeitung supporting it and Rosenberg taking a position against it. The majority of the party agreed with the New York group, and Rosenberg withdrew from the socialist movement. Late in the 1890's, he returned to his teaching profession in Cleveland. Published five volumes of poetry, at least a dozen plays (some for workers' theater), a collection of "sketches" on the life of the poor, helped run a music publishing company in New York. A concern for the emancipation of women is sometimes evident in his works. Sporadic contributions to the socialist press until his death sometime in the 1930's.

Saam, Christian. Contributed poems to the Social-Revolutionary press.

Sahm, Karl (1821 Grumbach/Rheinpreussen - 1883 New York). Studied music in Paris 1843-47. Forty-eighter, immigrated to New York in 1853. Gave music lessons and directed several singing societies. Wrote no less than 300 male choruses, 40 solos, also duets, etc., one comic opera, children's operettas, several longer compositions. Also wrote many of the texts.

Schewitsch, Sergius (1848-1912 Munich). Although he received his university education in St. Petersburg, Schewitsch spent much of his childhood in England and Germany, and became one of the most active socialist speakers, journalists and writers in German-American circles in New York after immigrating in 1877. Having had some contact with the Nihilist movement in Russia, Schewitsch continued to sympathize somewhat with this sort of terrorism, but he was also a member of the SAP and one of the few foreign-born socialists who became a popular political speaker in English. Resigned his prominent position as editor of the New York Volkszeitung to edit The Leader, a journal supporting the candidacy of the United Labor Party of Henry George in the 1886 election. Eleanor Marx and Edward Aveling described him as follows:

> "A cosmopolitan of the cosmopolitans. Russian by birth, this re-
> markable man speaks and writes perfectly German, French, English
> and American. He can conduct a newspaper and address a meeting
> in any one of five tongues. He has a clear understanding of the con-
> ditions of society in the States, of the political situation there, of
> the position of the working-class movement, and this intimate know-
> ledge of the land of his present adoption is accompanied by a know-
> ledge not less intimate of the general European movement and its
> details in different countries. His wife, an actress of considerable
> power, was Helena von Rackovitz, the heroine of the duel that ended
> in the death of Ferdinand Lassalle."
> (The Working-Class Movement in America, p. 198-99).

The veneration of Lassalle among German-American socialists led to constant tribulations for Schewitsch and Rackovitz, for within these circles she was looked upon as the loose woman who had brought about Lassalle's death. The two eventually returned to Russia, to claim an inheritance, then lived in Munich. Both committed suicide in 1912.

Schiller, Josef (Schiller-Seff) (1846 Reichenberg/Liberec - 1897 Germania/Pennsylvania). Son of a weaver, important in socialist circles in Bohemia and Austria as a party official, journalist and poet. Censorship drove him to America in 1896, where he died the next year in poverty. Contributed to the German-American socialist press.

Schmidt, Ernst (1830 Franken - 1900 Chicago). Exiled in Switzerland in 1848. Returned to Germany, became a doctor. To the U.S. in 1856, participated in the abolitionist movement in Chicago. Active supporter of the Social-Revolutionaries, SAP candidate for mayor in 1879. One of the most ardent defenders of the Haymarket martyrs and their families, and a leader in the movement for the pardon of Fielden, Schwab and Neebe.

Schupp, Martin. Contributor to the New York _Volkszeitung_, connected to the circle of anarchists in New York around Johann Most, contributor to his _Freiheit_.

Schwab, Michael (1854 - Chicago 1898). A Haymarket martyr. During the 1870's his poems appeared in the SPD press. Editorial writer for the Chicago _Arbeiter-Zeitung_. Sentenced to life in prison, pardoned by Governor John Altgeld in 1893.

Stern, Maurice Reinhold v. (1860 Reval/Estland - 1938 Ottensheim bei Linz a.d. Donau). Humanistic education, in the Russian army. Railroad official. To Germany in 1881, in America from 1881-85. Worked in New York as a clerk, iron-mill worker, etc. Founded the New Jersey _Arbeiterzeitung_ in Newark. To Zürich in 1885, to Austria in 1903. Published numerous volumes of poetry in Europe.

Winnen, Jakob. Cabinet-maker. To the U.S. in the early 1870's. Active member of the First International in Chicago, co-founder of Chicago _Vorbote_.

Zorn, Julius (c. 1853 Pforzheim/Baden - ?). Brewer. To the U.S. in 1874, worked in various factories until 1899, when he was elected head of the "Brauerei-Arbeiter-Verband." Held this office until 1904, then worked as a bookkeeper in this union's main office in Cincinnati. In 1914 secretary of the _Arbeiter-Sängerbund_ _des_ _Nordwestens_.

FOOTNOTES

I. Introduction

[1]Cf. Georges Haupt, "Why the History of the Working-Class Movement?" in: New German Critique, 14 (Spring 1978), p. 7-28.

[2]Al Gedicks, "The Development of Socialist Political Culture Among Finnish Immigrants," unpublished manuscript, who states that the classic statements of this view are Oscar Handlin's The Uprooted and Marcus Lee Hansen's The Immigrant in American History, p. 2.

[3]Pat Herminghouse, in her article "German-American Studies in a New Vein: Resources and Possibilities," in: Unterrichtspraxis, Vol. IX, No 2 (Fall 1976), p. 3-14, provides a useful critique of previous trends in research in this area, and urges that we re-examine this ethnic group in order to overcome stereotypes.

[4]Cf. John Laslett, Labor and the Left, A Study of Socialist and Radical Influences in the American Labor Movement, 1881-1924 (New York: Basic Books, 1970), particularly the introduction and conclusion.

[5]With respect to the history of German Social Democracy, Kurt Brandis, influenced by Karl Korsch, attempted in his Der Anfang vom Ende der Sozialdemokratie. Die SPD bis zum Fall des Sozialisten-Gesetzes (1927) to relate the history of the organization to its material, political and social bases. In the "Nachwort" to the 1975 Rotbuch edition, a collective of authors explicates the methodological implications of this procedure, and states that "Nur dieser methodische Zugang besitzt noch einen Aktualitätsbezug, nicht mehr der Gegenstand selbst." (109).

[6]Haupt, "Why the History of the Working-Class Movement?" p. 18.

[7]Cf. Hartmut Keil, "Studies of the American Labor Movement in West Germany," in: Labor History, Vol. 18, No. 1 (Winter 1977), p. 122-133. Keil is presently researching the impact of German socialists on the United States labor movement.

[8]These would include historians such as E. P. Thompson, The Making of the English Working Class (London, 1963), and Eric Hobsbawm, Labouring Men: Studies in the History of Labour (London, 1964), among others.

[9]Stanley Aronowitz, False Promises. The Shaping of American Working Class Consciousness (New York: McGraw Hill, 1973), and Herbert Gutman, Work, Culture and Society in Industrializing America (New York: Vintage, 1977).

[10]To name a few of the many studies either completed or currently in progress, these would include Al Gedicks' dissertation on Finnish-American Socialist Culture (University of Wisconsin, 1979), Paul Buhle's work on Jewish immigrant socialists and his article on "Italian-American Radicals and Labor in Rhode Island, 1905-1930," in: Radical History Review 17 (Spring 1978), the special issue of Cultural Correspondence on "The Origins of Left Culture in the U.S.: 1880-1940" (Spring 1978).

[11]Laslett, Labor and the Left, is a model analysis of four unions and the influence of socialism within them.

[12]R. H. Tawney, quoted in Gutman, Work, Culture and Society, p. 55.

[13]Cf. Georges Haupt, Programm und Wirklichkeit. Die internationale Sozialdemokratie vor 1914 (Berlin: Luchterhand, 1970), pp. 122ff., who criticizes the "doktrinäre Optik" which has characterized much of the historical writing on the Second International:
"Die wirkliche Klippe ist jedoch der Apriorismus, dessen 'sich die Marxisten bedienten', ... und der zugegebenermassen nicht nur ihre Apanage ist. Wenn das rein ideologisch bestimmte Studium es ermöglicht, die widersprüchliche Entwicklung zwischen realer Bewegung und Doktrin zu verschweigen, so führt die geschichtliche Betrachtung der Internationale, ohne von den Streitigkeiten der Vergangenheit Abstand zu nehmen, oder der Versuch, sie zu aktualisieren, nur zu einer subjektiven Interpretation und zu anachronistischen Beweisführungen. Die politische Geschichte wird dann eine politisierte, ja eine konformistische Geschichte, eine Anpassung der Vergangenheit an die ideologische Situation der Gegenwart."
And furthermore: "Das Problem ist gerade, den Sozialismus als Bewegung und Ideologie nicht von der kollektiven Aktion des Proletariats, auf die er sich beruft, zu trennen, auch nicht von jenem Teil der Arbeiterbewegung, die sich dem Einfluss der Ideologien entzieht. Man muss der Analyse eine Richtung geben, indem man sie künftig auf die Bewegung gründet und nicht auf die Ideologie, deren Funktion und sozialer Inhalt erst dann verstanden werden können." (125).

[14]Quoted in Gutman, Work, Culture and Society, p. 67.

[15]E. P. Thompson on Herbert Gutman, back cover of Work, Culture and Society.

[16]Haupt, "Why the History of the Working Class Movement?" p. 15, 21.

[17]See the bibliography in Philip Foner, ed., American Labor Songs of the Nineteenth Century (Urbana: Illinois, 1975), p. 327ff.

[18]Although several of the recent articles and books on early German socialist literature mention the continuation of this tradition abroad and particularly in the United States, the lack of primary material in German archives prevents these studies from going into more detail.

[19]The most important organization of Nazi sympathizers was the New-York-based Amerikadeutscher Bund (later known as the Bund Amerikanischer National-Sozialisten.)

[20]Wilhelm Schneider, Die auslandsdeutsche Dichtung unserer Zeit (Berlin: Weidmann, 1936), p. 10.

[21]Ibid., p. 19.

[22]Pat Herminghouse, "German-American Studies," p. 3-14.

[23]There has been more attention devoted to the more "respectable" group of forty-eighters. Cf. Ernst Bruncken, German Political Refugees in the United States

During the Period from 1815-1860 (San Francisco: R. & E. Associates, reprint 1970 of 1904 edition), Eitel Dobert, Deutsche Demokraten in Amerika. Die Achtundvierziger und ihre Schriften (Göttingen: Vandenhoek & Ruprecht, 1958), and the research of Carl Wittke, including his Refugees of Revolution (Philadelphia: Univ. of Pa. Press, 1952) and his biography of Wilhelm Weitling, The Utopian Communist (Baton Rouge: LSU Press, 1950).

[24] John Higham, Strangers in the Land (New York: Atheneum, 1970), p. 196.

[25] Ibid., p. 208.

[26] Ibid., p. 219.

[27] The few exceptions include Pat Herminghouse (see note 3), Carl Wittke (see note 23), and Maria Wagner, who is doing research on the forty-eighter and feminist Mathilde Annecke. These are, however, not typical of the field as a whole.

[28] Along with these conferences on German-Americana, another example of these integrative methodological tendencies is a recently published Festschrift for Karl Arndt, edited by Gerhard Friesen and Walter Schatzberg, The German Contribution to the Building of the Americas (Hanover, N.H.: Clark Univ. Press, 1977), which concentrates on pre-Civil-War America from the perspective of documenting the "respectable" contributions of the Germans.

[29] This discussion is based on Wolfgang Emmerich, Zur Kritik der Volkstumsideologie (Frankfurt: Suhrkamp, 1971).

[30] Adolf Schroeder, "The Survival of German Traditions in Missouri," in: Friesen and Schatzberg, The German Contribution, p. 308.

[31] Emmerich, Zur Kritik, p. 168.

[32] Schroeder, "Survival of German Traditions,", p. 308.

[33] Here it is worthwhile to note the widespread manifestations of alienation from and hostility to the official Bicentennial celebration, which were expressed most dramatically in the "People's Bicentennial" activities centered in Philadelphia. This grass roots movement sought to focus on the revolutionary heritage which was being glossed over officially and in the media.

[34] Cf. Emmerich, Zur Kritik, p. 166.

[35] Ibid., p. 169.

II. A Brief History of Nineteenth Century German-American Socialism

[1] Philip Foner, History of the Labor Movement in the United States (New York: International, 1947), Vol. I, p. 58.

[2]Cf. the title article by Gutman in his Work, Culture and Society, p. 3–79.

[3]Cf. Gutman, and also Andreas Wehowsky, "To Make Ourselves More Flexible Than We Are. Reflections on Norbert Elias," in: New German Critique, 15 (Fall 1978).

[4]Gutman, Work, Culture and Society, p. 4–5, and p. 19ff. for many more examples.

[5]Cf. Alfred Krovoza, "Die Verinnerlichung der Normen abstrakter Arbeit und das Schicksal der Sinnlichkeit," in: Peter Brückner et. al., ed., Das Unvermögen der Realität (Berlin: Wagenbach, 1974), p. 13–37, especially p. 23ff. on the transformation of time structures and perceptions.

[6]Gutman, Work, Culture and Society, p. 22.

[7]Gerd Korman, Industrialization, Immigrants and Americanizers (Madison, Wisc.: State Historical Society, 1967), p. 140.

[8]Cf. Foner, Labor Movement, Vol. I, p. 122.

[9]Ibid., p. 70ff.

[10]Ibid., p. 222. The term "mechanic" means an artisan, a craftsman.

[11]Foner, Labor Movement, Vol. I, p. 226, gives examples of workers who were thus organized.

[12]Cf. Carl Wittke, Refugees of Revolution (Philadelphia: Univ. of Pa. Press, 1952), p. 178.

[13]Quoted in Stanley Feldstein and Lawrence Costello, The Ordeal of Assimilation: A Documentary History of the White Working Class (New York: Anchor, 1974).

[14]This is the definition of nativism given in the standard work on the subject, John Higham's Strangers in the Land. Patterns of American Nativism 1860–1925 (New York: Atheneum, 1970), p. 4.

[15]Foner, Labor Movement, Vol. I, p. 88.

[16]For the complete text of this song, see Edith Fowke and Joe Glazer, Songs of Work and Protest (New York: Dover, 1973), p. 188–9.

[17]Quoted by Hermann Schlüter, who translated this statement into German, in his Die Anfänge der deutschen Arbeiterbewegung in Amerika (Stuttgart: Dietz, 1907), p. 25.

[18]See Wittke, Refugees, for examples of violent attacks on the German minority group in various cities, p. 185ff.

[19]Ibid., p. 178.

[20]These quotes are taken from Wittke, Refugees, p. 182–183.

[21]Thomas R. Whitney, A Defence of the American Policy (New York, 1856), p. 171 and 176, qoted in Wittke, Refugees, p. 184.

[22]Useful sources on the Forty-Eighters in America are Wittke, Refugees, and Eitel W. Dobert, Deutsche Demokraten in Amerika (Göttingen: Vandenhoek & Ruprecht, 1958).

[23]Heinzen, who emigrated to the United States in 1850, continued to attack Marx and the Communists in his journal, Der Pionier.

[24]Cf. the chapter on "The Turners and Socialism" in William F. Kamman, Socialism in German-American Literature (Philadelphia: Americana Germanica Press, 1917). Cf. also "Sozialismus und Turnerei," in: Jahrbücher der Deutsch-Amerikanischen Turnerei, Bd. I, Heft IV (1891), p. 145-154.

[25]See the chapter in Wittke, Refugees, on "The Slavery Issue," for a discussion of the various standpoints within the German ethnic group.

[26]After the war was over, in 1866, Blacks in San Antonio sent Douai a newspaper with the inscription "Diese von Negern geeignete und gesetzte Zeitung wird auf derselben Presse gedruckt, auf welcher Dr. Adolf Douai zuerst in Texas die Neger-Emanzipation verfocht. Sei ihm das der Dank der farbigen Rasse, dass sie seine Bemühungen für ihre Freiheit an Andenken halten." Quoted in Hermann Schlüter, Die Internationale in Amerika (Chicago: Deutsche Sprachgruppe der Sozialistischen Partei der Vereinigten Staaten, 1918), p. 101.

[27]"Sozialismus und Turnerei," in: Jahrbücher der Deutsch-Amerikanischen Turnerei, Bd. I, Heft IV (1891), p. 147.

[28]San Antonio Zeitung, July 5, 1853, p. 1.

[29]Cf. the chapter on "German Fenianism" in Wittke, Refugees.

[30]Christian Esselen in Atlantis, June 1855, N.S. II, pp. 413-418, quoted in Wittke, Refugees, p. 108.

[31]Cf. Wittke, Refugees, p. 217f. on the controversy over the part which Germans played in the outcome of the election of Lincoln.

[32]Useful sources on Communitarian Socialism and utopian communities in the United States are Charles Nordhoff, The Communistic Societies of the United States (New York, 1875), J.H. Noyes, History of American Socialism (Philadelphia 1870), Heinrich Semler, Geschichte des Socialismus und Communismus in Nordamerika (Leipzig, 1880), A. Sartorius von Waltershausen, Der moderne Sozialismus in den Vereinigten Staaten von Amerika (Berlin, 1890).

[33]Cf. Foner, Labor Movement, Vol. I, p. 179, on the cooperatives. See also Peter Brückner/Gabriele Ricke, "Ueber die ästhetische Erziehung des Menschen in der Arbeiterbewegung," in: Brückner et. al., eds., Das Unvermögen der Realität, especially p. 38ff. on the relationship between the organized workers' movement and the older tradition of solidarity among artisans and peasants:
"Die ganze Kultivierung des Proletariats richtete sich auch gegen eine ältere Geschichte der Handwerker- und Bauernsolidarität. Verloren geht im 19. Jhdt. eine in Resten überlieferte jahrhundertealte Kampfestradition. ... Kultivierung: die zerstört hier Elemente der Klassen-Erinnerung. Die Organisationen der

Handwerker, die sich um 1830/40 herum auf 'gegenseitige' Hilfe gründen, und
die Marx in Paris kennenlernte, haben eben jene, z. T. noch vorkapitalistischen
Traditionen von Widerstand und Solidarität im Sinn gehabt. "
This article provides an excellent, essential discussion of cultural politics
within the socialist movement in Germany, culminating in theses on the compensatory character of socialist realism, and posing the question: "Ist es viel-
leicht die faktische Wirkungslosigkeit von Kunst, was sie dem realen Sozialismus so teuer macht?" (p. 64).

[34]Cf. Schlüter, Die Anfänge, p. 80.

[35]Cf. Wittke, Utopian Communist, p. 194, and Foner, Labor Movement, Vol. I,
p. 228f, for a list of the trades thus organized.

[36]Cf. Wittke, Utopian Communist, p. 200.

[37]Quoted in Schlüter, Die Anfänge, p. 86.

[38]Cf. Wittke, Utopian Communist, p. 174.

[39]Quoted in ibid. , p. 195.

[40]Ibid. , p. 205.

[41]Marx to Weydemeyer, Aug. 2, 1851, in: Karl Marx and Frederick Engels.
Letters to Americans, 1848-1895 (New York: International, 1953), p. 25.

[42]Marx to Weydemeyer, Dec. 19, 1851, in: Letters to Americans, p. 30.

[43]Die Revolution, Jan. 6, 1852, p. 1.

[44]Marx to Adolf Cluss, April 1853, in: Letters to Americans, p. 53.

[45]Quoted in Die Reform, Dec. 29, 1853, p. 1.

[46]Ibid.

[47]Cf. Karl Obermann, Joseph Weydemeyer (New York: International, 1947),
p. 55f. This is the most extensive work to date on Weydemeyer.

[48]Quoted in Schlüter, Die Anfänge, p. 144.

[49]Published in Die Reform, July 13, 1853.

[50]Quoted in Schlüter, Die Anfänge, p. 142-3.

[51]Cf. Ibid. , p. 143-4.

[52]Die Reform, Mar. 19, 1853.

[53]Cf. Maria Wagner, Mathilde Franziska Annecke, eine deutsche Dichterin des
Vormärz und amerikanische Feministin in Selbstzeugnissen und Dokumenten
(forthcoming study).

[54]Die Reform, Mar. 14, 1853, p. 3.

[55]Die Reform, June 29, 1853, p. 3.

[56] Die Reform, July 20, 1853, p. 3.

[57] Schlüter, Die Anfänge, p. 138, lists the unions in the Arbeiterbund.

[58] Cf. Ibid., p. 174, 177.

[59] Thus, the Socialist (Socialist Party of the United States) historian Hermann Schlüter, in Die Anfänge, states that clearly Weitling could not gain a foothold in the masses of workers, whose "natürliche Waffen, die Streiks und der Klassenkampf in allen seinen Formen, durchaus andere waren als jene, die Weitling empfahl." (88). Or, speaking of the decline of Weitling's Arbeiterbund, Philip Foner maintains that "most German workers disagreed with Weitling as soon as they began to understand his limited outlook on immediate questions confronting them." (Labor Movement, Vol. I, p. 229).

[60] Karl Marx and Frederick Engels, The Civil War in the U.S. (New York: International, 1974), p. 279-280.

[61] The epithet "Gilded Age" is taken from the title to Mark Twain's novel of that name published in 1873, which deals with the enormous speculation, corruption, wealth and poverty characteristic of that period.

[62] Cf. Foner, Labor Movement, Vol. I, p. 440.

[63] Vernon Lidtke, The Outlawed Party. Social Democracy in Germany, 1878-1890 (Princeton: Princeton Univ. Press, 1966), p. 12-13.

[64] Cf. Samuel Bernstein, The First International in America (New York: Sentry, 1965), p. 17.

[65] Cf. David Herreshoff, The Origins of American Marxism (New York: Monad, 1967), p. 68, on the Communist Club.

[66] "Statuten des Kommunisten-Klubs in New York," quoted in Foner, Labor Movement, Vol. I, p. 233.

[67] On the New York Allgemeiner Deutscher Arbeiterverein, see Schlüter, Die Internationale, p. 80ff.

[68] Engels to Sorge, Sept. 12 and 17, 1874, in: Letters to Americans, p. 114.

[69] The best reports on these anti-war demonstrations are to be found in the German-American paper published by freethinkers in New York, Die Neue Zeit (published from 1869-1872). This makes it clear that there was substantial opposition to the war from Germans in the United States, though most scholars have maintained that the Germans supported the war wholeheartedly.
This paper is also interesting for its supportive attitude towards women's rights, which was one of the main topics in its editorial columns. Mathilde Annecke was a correspondent, as were the New York feminists Auguste Lilienthal and Mathilde Wendt.

[70] Quoted in Bernstein, First International, p. 85.

[71]Cf. Ibid., p. 86. For the reactions to the Commune in the United States, see the chapter on "The Paris Commune in America," in Bernstein, First International, and also Samuel Bernstein, "American Labor and the Paris Commune," in: Science and Society, Spring 1951, p. 144-162.

[72]Quoted in Herreshoff, Origins, p. 92.

[73]Letterbook in the Sorge papers, State Historical Society of Wisconsin, f. 14-16, quoted in Bernstein, First International, p. 55.

[74]These include the Milwaukee Der Socialist (1875-1878), with its Sunday edition, Milwaukeer Leuchtkugeln (1876) and supplement, Die Rothe Laterne (1876), edited by Gustav Lyser and notable for its emphasis on women's rights; the French Le Socialiste; and Woodhull & Claflin's Weekly, where the Communist Manifesto was first published in the United States.

[75]Quoted in Bernstein, First International, p. 237.

[76]Speaking of sectarianism in the United States, Marx wrote to Friedrich Bolte on Nov. 23, 1871 that "the development of socialist sectarianism and that of the real labor movement always stand in inverse ratio to each other. So long as the sects are justified (historically), the working class is not yet ripe for an independent historical movement. As soon as it has attained this maturity all sects are essentially reactionary. For all that, what history exhibits everywhere was repeated in the history of the International. What is antiquated tried to reconstitute and assert itself within the newly acquired form." Letters to Americans, p. 90.

[77]Quoted in Bernstein, First International, p. 114.

[78]Cf. Werner Thönnessen, The Emancipation of Women. The Rise and Decline of the Women's Movement in German Social Democracy 1863-1933 (Bristol: Pluto Press, 1973).

[79]Friedrich Sorge quotes this from the statutes of the section in his Labor Movement in the United States, translated by Brewster and Angela Chamberlin, (Westport, Ct.: Greenwood, 1977), p. 157. This book is a translation of a series of articles Sorge wrote for the German SPD journal Die neue Zeit from 1891-1895.

[80]Quoted in Bernstein, First International, p. 117-8. It is worth mentioning here that the sections of the International in Milwaukee, far removed from the New York scene, were decidedly more sympathetic to women's rights, as can be seen from the Internationalists' paper there, Der Socialist. Section 3 of the International in Milwaukee was the only women's section in the United States. Articles in this paper supported women's suffrage, and took the viewpoint that socialists should not relegate the women's question to second place, that it was important to fight against all oppression.
For example, an article entitled "Sozialismus und Frauenfrage" stated: "Man hat von socialistischer Seite behauptet, dass man -- so zu sagen 'von Partei wegen' -- die Frage erst in zweiter Linie in Angriff nehmen könne, da sie nicht allen Parteimitgliedern genehm und daher ein Hindernis, gleichsam ein Ballast,

für den Erfolg der socialistischen Sache bilde. Die Thatsachen haben diese Voraussetzung Lügen gestraft." (Jan. 29, 1876, p. 2).
The most important representatives of this standpoint were Gustav Lyser, editor of the Socialist, and Emilie Lyser, head of the women's section. Mathilde Annecke may have also contributed to this paper.

[81]Marx to Friedrich Bolte, Nov. 23, 1871, in: Letters to Americans, p. 89.

[82]Cf. Bernstein, First International, p. 129.

[83]Engels to Sorge, Sept. 12 and 17, 1874, in: Letters to Americans, p. 114.

[84]Quoted in Schlüter, Die Internationale, p. 361-2.

[85]Information about these small parties can be found in Bernstein, First International, and Schlüter, Die Internationale.

[86]Cf. Bernstein, First International, p. 249.

[87]Ibid., p. 284. See also Philip Foner, ed., The Formation of the Workingmen's Party of the United States. Proceedings of the Union Congress Held at Philadelphia, July 19-22, 1876 (New York: AIMS No. 18, 1976).

[88]Bernstein, First International, p. 290.

[89]See Herbert Gutman, "Class, Status, and the Gilded Age Radical: A Reconsideration," in his Work, Culture and Society. This article on J. P. McDonnell provides an excellent model for the study of radicalism in the late 19th century.

[90]The major studies of this strike are David Burbank, City of Little Bread. The St. Louis General Strike of 1877 (St. Louis: n. pub., 1957), Robert Bruce, 1877: Year of Violence (New York: Bobbs-Merrill, 1959), and Philip Foner, The Great Labor Uprising of 1877 (New York: Monad, 1977). See also the bibliographies given in these studies.

[91]Foner, Labor Movement, Vol. I, p. 439.

[92]Ibid., p. 442, which also gives more statistics on the effects of the depression.

[93]Quoted in Foner, 1877, p. 7.

[94]Bruce, 1877, p. 254.

[95]Quoted in Foner, 1877, p. 175.

[96]For a positive presentation of the role of the militia in an anti-labor novel of the time dealing with the strike, see John Hay, The Breadwinners (New York: Harper, 1883), Hay's depiction of socialists is also typical:
"A few tonguey vagrants and convicts from the city and from neighboring towns, who had come to the surface from nobody knew where, were beginning to exercise a wholly unexpected authority. They were going from place to place, haranguing the workmen, preaching what they called socialism, but what was merely riot and plunder." (215).

[97]Quoted in Foner, 1877, p. 187.

[98] Cf. Higham, Strangers, p. 30.

[99] Allan Pinkerton, Strikers, Communists, Tramps and Detectives (New York: Dillingham, 1878), p. 67,87.

[100] Quoted in Bruce, 1877, p. 225.

[101] Quoted in Foner, Labor Movement, Vol. I, p. 470.

[102] Quoted in Higham, Strangers, p. 31.

[103] Quoted in Foner, 1877, p. 157, 154, and 210.

[104] Pinkerton, Strikers, p. 80.

[105] Cf. Higham, Strangers, p. 31f.

[106] Cf. Foner, 1877, p. 224, which lists the votes received by the WPUSA.

[107] Herreshoff, Origins, p. 114.

[108] The reports in the New York Volkszeitung are the best sources on candidates, strategies, and election results.

[109] Cf. Foner, Labor Movement, Vol. I, p. 487, and Daniel Bell, Marxian Socialism in the U.S. (Princeton: Princeton Univ. Press, 1967), p. 24f. on cooperation between the SAP and the Greenbacks.

[110] These are the terms used by Adolf Douai to criticize purists who refused to cooperate with the Greenbacks, in his article "Bericht über den Fortgang der sozialistischen Bewegung," in: Jahrbuch für Sozialwissenschaft und Sozialpolitik, 2 (1881), p. 172.

[111] Cf. "The Influence of Edward Kellogg upon American Radicalism, 1865-1896," by Chester M. Destler, in his American Radicalism, 1865-1901 (Chicago: Quadrangle, 1966). See also Foner, Labor Movement, Vol. I, p. 420ff. on Kellogg and the National Labor Union.

[112] Quoted by Herreshoff, Origins, p. 101.

[113] Ibid., p. 119. See p. 116ff. on the SLP and Populism.

[114] Hartmut Keil, "The New Unions: German and American Workers in New York City, 1870-1885," unpublished manuscript. The following discussion of German-American unionism is based primarily on this paper by Keil. Cf. also Laslett, Labor and the Left, on the influence of socialists within unions.

[115] Keil, "The New Unions."

[116] Foner, Labor Movement, Vol. II, p. 33.

[117] Abraham Cahan, The Education of Abraham Cahan (Philadelphia: Jewish Publication Society, 1969), p. 317. An interesting book which offers insight into New York working class and socialist life among Jewish immigrants is a compilation of letters from residents of the Lower East Side to the Jewish Daily Forward, with answers written mainly by Cahan, in the style of a socialist "Dear Abby," A Bintel Brief (New York: Ballantine, 1971).

[118]Cf. Ira Kipnis, The American Socialist Movement, 1897-1912 (New York: Columbia, 1952), p. 29.

[119]Socialist Labor Party Papers, Wisconsin State Historical Society. Platform, Constitution and Proceedings of the Party Convention in Baltimore, Dec. 26-28, 1883, p. 2 of Proceedings.

[120]Socialist Labor Party Papers, Wisconsin State Historical Society. "Gesamt-tätigkeitsbericht des National-Exekutiv-Committees der SAP vom 1. Januar 1884 bis 1. Oktober 1885," p. 4.
Two contemporary sources gave personal accounts of the importance the SAP press had for them. After immigrating from Russia, Abraham Cahan wrote: "New York had a German-language socialist daily newspaper called the New Yorker Volkszeitung. For us it was a real treasure. In Russia such a publica-tion was a secret and dangerous enterprise, circulated underground and issued irregularly. But here it was issued regularly every day and openly circulated! This newspaper was the reason some of us learned German even before we learned English. It played a major role in our intellectual development. Every day we could read in its pages challenging Marxist interpretations of the news." (The Education of Abraham Cahan, p. 227).
Also, a German socialist worker who traveled to the U.S. in 1910 wrote of his impressions as follows: "Die New Yorker Volkszeitung ist ein prächtiges Denk-mal der Gesinnungstreue und des Opfermutes deutscher sozialistischer Prole-tarier im Ausland. Erst eine spätere Zeit wird ganz zu würdigen verstehen, was sie für den Sozialismus, für die politische Ehrlichkeit und die deutsche Geisteskultur in Amerika geleistet hat. Ich halte sie für eines der besten so-zialistischen Blätter." Fritz Kummer, Eines Arbeiters Weltreise (Jena: Thü-ringer Verlagsanstalt, 1913), p. 75.

[121]Quoted in Philip Foner, "Protests in the USA Against Bismarck's Anti-Social-ist Law," in: International Review of Social History, 21 (1976), p. 30-51. Here, p. 32.

[122]Ibid.

[123]See ibid. and the reports in the New York Volkszeitung on these meetings of January, 1879.

[124]These are reported on in the New York Volkszeitung, Dec. 20, 1880, p. 4.

[125]New York Volkszeitung, Jan. 20, 1881, p. 4, and July 10, 1881, p. 4.

[126]See the report of the National Executive Committee of the SAP at its 1885 con-vention, in: Socialist Labor Party Papers, Wisconsin State Historical Society. See also Nach zehn Jahren. Material und Glossen zur Geschichte des Soziali-sten-Gesetzes, Teil II: Die Opfer des Sozialistengesetzes (London: German Cooperative Publishing Co., 1890), p. 55-6. The preface to this useful collec-tion of material states:
"Wenn aber die Gewalthaber glaubten, die Ausgewiesenen und Vertriebenen dadurch unschädlich gemacht zu haben, dass sie dieselben nötigen jenseits des Ozeans sich ein neues Heim zu suchen, so ist die Schergenrechnung auch in

diesem Falle wieder zu Schanden geworden. Unsere braven Genossen, denen polizeiliche Brutalität und blinde Verfolgungswut den Aufenthalt im Vaterland unmöglich machte, haben deswegen dasselbe noch nicht vergessen, und wenn sie auch an den Kämpfen unserer Partei in Deutschland nicht mehr aktiv teilnehmen konnten, so haben sie doch in pekuniärer Hinsicht die Kämpfer auf das Kräftigste unterstützt. ...

Aber nicht nur pekuniäre Opfer haben diese Genossen für die Bewegung in Deutschland gebracht, sie wirken auch unermüdlich dafür, den Kreis unserer Anhänger unter dem deutschen Elemente Amerikas zu erweitern. Und wenn in Amerika das Verständnis für die Vorgänge in Deutschland immer klarer wird, und die Zahl derjenigen Deutsch-Amerikaner, welche des naiven Glaubens waren, dass nach den Kriegen von 1866 und 1870/71 sich 'Alles so herrlich erfüllt' habe, immer kleiner wird, so haben unsere Ausgewiesenen und Vertriebenen ihr redlich Teil zu diesem Umschwunge beigetragen."

[127]Detailed reports on their speeches and activities are given in the spring of 1881 in the New York Volkszeitung.

[128]New York Volkszeitung, Feb. 6, 1881, p. 4.

[129]On June 15, 1881, von Madai wrote: "Unter den Amerikanern selbst sind zwar sozialistische Anschauungen nur wenig verbreitet, es sind aber eine grosse Menge Deutscher dort, welche aus der Heimath derartige Ideen mit hinübergebracht haben, und, wenn sie dieselben in Amerika auch nicht verwerten können, dennoch jede Gelegenheit benutzen, ihnen in der Heimath durch moralische und pekuniäre Unterstützung Geltung zu verschaffen."
Quoted in Reinhard Höhn, ed., Die vaterlandslosen Gesellen. Der Sozialismus im Licht der Geheimberichte der preussischen Polizei, 1878-1914, Bd. I (1878-1890) (Cologne: Westdeutscher Vlg. 1964), p. 93.

[130]The itinerary of their trip is printed in the SAP paper Der Sozialist, Sept. 25, 1886, p. 8.

[131]"Zusammenfassender Bericht des Polizeipräsidiums über die Agitationsreise Wilhelm Liebknechts durch die USA," quoted in Gerhard Becker, "Die Agitationsreise Wilhelm Liebknechts durch die USA 1886," in: Zeitschrift für Geschichtswissenschaft, 15 (1967), p. 842-862.

[132]"Bericht Nr. 421 des deutschen Geschäftsträgers in Washington vom 21. September 1886 an den Reichskanzler Fürst von Bismarck über die Reise Wilh. Liebknechts in Amerika," quoted in Karl Obermann, "Die Amerikareise Wilhelm Liebknechts im Jahre 1886," in: Zeitschrift für Geschichtswissenschaft, 14 (1966), p. 614.

[133]See also Wilhelm Liebknecht, Ein Blick in die neue Welt. Reisebeschreibung (Stuttgart: Dietz, 1887). Here Liebknecht does not discuss the political situation in the United States, but concentrates on his impressions of the people and the landscape he encountered.

[134]Obermann, "Die Amerikareise," p. 613.

[135]New York Volkszeitung, Oct. 25, 1878, p. 2.

[136]Quoted in Höhn, Die vaterlandslosen Gesellen, p. 328.

[137]Quoted in ibid. , p. 248. It appears that the police used the threat of anarchism and terrorism to justify continued repression of the socialists, also. For example, the largest portion of the 1885 police report on socialism in the United States is concerned with Most and the group of anarchists around Freiheit, who are viewed as a threat to Europe. Police President von Madai wrote: "Das ganze Dichten und Trachten dieser Leute ist auf den gewaltsamen Umsturz in ihrer Heimath gerichtet. ... Allem Anschein nach werden auch die jetzigen Dissidenten mit der Most'schen Gruppe sich wieder vereinigen, so dass die von dieser verbrecherischen und fanatischen Gesellschaft drohenden Gefahren wieder genau so gross sind, wie vorher." (Höhn, p. 262-3).

[138]See the Appendix listing these publications at the end of this book.

[139]See Henry David, The History of the Haymarket Affair (New York: Farrar & Rinehart, 1936), on the Lehr- und Wehrvereine.

[140]Vorbote, Sept. 7, 1878, p. 8.

[141]New York Volkszeitung, Mar. 8, 1878, p. 2.

[142]Cf. David, Haymarket, p. 83ff. on the influence of Most in the United States. See also the biography by Rudolf Rocker, Johann Most (Berlin: Vlg. "Der Syndikalist," 1924).

[143]David, Haymarket, p. 82ff. gives a detailed discussion of the Pittsburgh Congress.

[144]Ibid. , p. 150.

[145]Ibid. , p. 113. Other official publications were the Bohemian papers Boudoucnost (Chicago) and Proletar (New York), and the German Parole (St. Louis).

[146]The fact that there is no full-length, comprehensive study of the Knights of Labor is a striking instance of the neglect by historians of radical movements for social change. However, some dissertations are currently in progress on this, the largest group of organized workers in 19th century America.

[147]Foner, Labor Movement, Vol. II, p. 103.

[148]Pardon message of Governor John Altgeld, quoted in David, Haymarket, p. 495.

[149]Quoted in ibid. , p. 38-9.

[150]Ibid. , p. 216.

[151]Ibid.

[152]Ibid. , p. 217.

[153]Quoted in Higham, Strangers, p. 54.

[154]Ibid. , p. 53.

[155]Quoted in Higham, Strangers, p. 50.

[156]Quoted in William Preston, Aliens and Dissenters. Federal Suppression of Radicals, 1903-1933 (New York: Harper, 1963), p. 32.

[157]Ibid., p. 33.

[158]Ibid., p. 233.

[159]Joseph Dietzgen, member of the SAP and editor of its New York paper, Der Sozialist, in 1885, was one important exception to the socialists' general criticism of the Social-Revolutionaries. After the Chicago Arbeiter-Zeitung had been shut down by police, he agreed to become its editor and resume its publication early in May. Arguing that the Social-Revolutionaries in Chicago should be supported, he came into conflict with the SAP leadership in New York. Dietzgen died in 1888.

[160]Quoted in David, Haymarket, p. 211.

[161]Ibid., p. 537ff. discusses this anti-labor legislation.

[162]Quoted in Foner, Labor Movement, Vol. II, p. 118.

[163]Ibid., p. 129f.

[164]Engels to Sorge, Mar. 16, 1887, in: Letters to Americans, p. 164.

[165]See Herreshoff, Origins, p. 111, on the Henry George movement as an example of late agrarianism.

[166]Joseph Dietzgen was known in Germany for his philosophical writings. Max Baginski had accompanied Gerhardt Hauptmann in 1891 to the district of the Silesian weavers.

[167]Der Pionier, 1891, p. 54.

[168]Engels to Sorge, Feb. 8, 1890, in: Letters to Americans, p. 224-5.

[169]In: Der Pionier, 1888, p. 38-9.

[170]Henry Kuhn and Olive Johnson, The Socialist Labor Party During Four Decades, 1890-1930 (New York: N.Y. Labor News Co., 1931), p. 11.

[171]Daniel De Leon, quoted by Herreshoff, Origins, p. 132.

[172]Cf. ibid., p. 127.

[173]Socialist Labor Party Papers, State Historical Society of Wisconsin, Report of the National Executive Committee at the 9th Party Convention, July 4-10, 1896, p. 20.

[174]Bell, Marxian Socialism, p. 45.

[175]Cf. David Shannon, The Socialist Party of America (Chicago: Quadrangle, 1967), p. 43ff. on the language federations.

[176]Cf. William Z. Foster, History of the Communist Party of the United States (New York: International, 1952), p. 260ff. Page 262 gives a list of the left-wing press in the United States (not all these papers are affiliated with the CPUSA).

[177]Vivian Gornick, The Romance of American Communism (New York: Basic Books, 1977) has compiled a revealing series of interviews with people who were members of the Communist Party from the twenties to the present, who discuss how the Party affected all aspects of their lives.

[178]Cf. Oskar Negt and Alexander Kluge, Oeffentlichkeit und Erfahrung (Frankfurt: Suhrkamp, 1972), on the ideology of the Lager, p. 341ff. and 391ff: "Aber was auf der Basis ein Bedürfnis nach wechselseitigem Schutz, Zusammenhalt, Solidarität ist, erstarrt auf der abstrakten Organisationsebene von Oeffentlichkeit, Partei und ganzen Ländern in ein Schema, das, auf die Basis zurückwirkend, solidarische Verbindungen zerstört, die Individuen und Gruppen voneinander abgrenzt und erst auf mechanische Weise erneut verbindet."(343). And furthermore: "Die Grenzziehung zwischen politisch bewussten und bewusstlosen Massen liegt dem Lagerdenken zugrunde. Diese Grenzziehung ist aber ein fundamentales Kennzeichen von idealistisches Denken. Dieses Denken nimmt an, dass durch Appelle und gute Gründe, durch moralisches oder wissenschaftliches Bewusstsein, ein dauerhaftes Verhalten der Arbeiter erzeugt werden könnte." (391).

[179]Quoted in R. L. Moore, European Socialists and the American Promised Land (New York: Oxford, 1970), p. 71.

[180]In: Letters to Americans, p. 285-7.

[181]See Moore, European Socialists, for a summary of how European socialists viewed the United States. See also John Laslett and Seymour Lipset, eds., Failure of a Dream? Essays in the History of U.S. Socialism (New York: Doubleday, 1974), for an excellent collection of articles and critical responses on American socialism.

[182]Engels to Sorge, Dec. 2, 1893: in: Letters to Americans, p. 258.

[183]Frederick J. Turner, "The Significance of the Frontier in American History," in: Annual Report of the American Historical Association for the Year 1893, p. 199-227.

[184]Engels to Sorge, Jan. 6, 1892, in: Letters to Americans, p. 239.

[185]This is the impression Liebknecht gives in his Ein Blick in die neue Welt.

[186]Quoted in Moore, European Socialists, p. 115.

[187]It was Werner Sombart who asserted that "On the reefs of roast beef and apple pie socialistic Utopias of every sort are sent to their doom." Quoted in Bell, Marxian Socialism, p. 4.

[188]U.S. Congress. Senate. Committee on Education and Labor. Report of the Committee of the Senate on Relations between Labor and Capital (Washington,

1883-. Four volumes published). Douai's testimony appears in Vol. II, p. 702-743. In addition to describing the platform and goals of the SAP, a large part of his testimony concerns the subservience of education to the vested interests of church and state, with suggestions for the reform of U.S. schools.

[189]Quoted from Henry Nash Smith, ed., Popular Culture and Industrialism, 1865-1890 (New York: Anchor, 1967), p. 313-4.

[190]Ibid., p. 312.

[191]Cf. Engels to Sorge, Dec. 2, 1893: "The Constitution, based as in England upon party government, ... causes every vote for any candidate not put up by one of the two governing parties to appear to be lost. And the American, like the Englishman, wants to influence his state; he does not throw his vote away." Letters to Americans, p. 258.

[192]Adolf Douai, "Die Auswanderung als Mittel zur Lösung der sozialen Aufgabe," in: Jahrbuch für Sozialwissenschaft und Sozialpolitik, 2 (1881), p. 105.

[193]Lidtke, Outlawed Party, p. 4.

[194]Engels to Sorge, Dec. 31, 1892: in: Letters to Americans, p. 243.

[195]Philip Rappaport. "Ueber die Arbeiterbewegung in Amerika," in: Die neue Zeit, VII (1889), p. 66.

[196]Adolf Hepner, "Die Aussichten des Sozialismus in Amerika," in: Die neue Zeit, Vol. XII, Part I, (1893-94), p. 646.

[197]Cf. James Stevenson, Daniel DeLeon (Dissertation: University of Wisconsin, 1977), p. 10.

[198]Cf. ibid., p. 53.

[199]These three factors are developed in ibid.

[200]Cf. ibid., p. 53.

[201]Oskar Negt, "Don't Go By Numbers, Organize According to Interests," in: New German Critique, 1 (Winter 1974), p. 49.

[202]Cf. Werner Sombart, Warum gibt es in den Vereinigten Staaten keinen Sozialismus? (Tübingen: Mohr, 1906).

[203]Bell, Marxian Socialism, p. 5.

[204]Cf. Stevenson, Daniel DeLeon, p. 13.

[205]See my entries on several of these organizations, including the Arbeiterbildungsvereine, Arbeitergesangvereine, Arbeiter Kranken- und Sterbekasse, and the Sozialistischer Turnerbund, in: Don Tolzmann, ed., Encyclopedia of German-American Voluntary Organizations (Westport, Ct.: Greenwood Press, forthcoming in 1982).
At times, socialist papers or individuals urged party members to concentrate on political and union agitation, rather than to involve themselves in these other

groups. For example, the 1883 convention of the SAP called the Brooklyn Labor Lyceum a "grossartiges Unternehmen" but feared that it would exercise an "ungünstiger Einfluss" on the Brooklyn Section because it would divert members from "party work." And at the 1885 convention, a resolution on "Private Kooperativ-Unternehmungen" was passed which read: "Beschlossen: dass die SAP Produktiv- oder Konsum-Genossenschaften, Arbeiterhallen, Sozialistische Schulen als unpraktische, die Arbeiterbewegung schwächende Gründungen betrachtet und ihre Mitglieder und die Arbeiter im Allgemeinen von derartigen Unternehmungen abräth." In 1887, the party revised its position, stating at its convention that party members should try to get control over such organizations since they seemed well established. (Source: SAP papers, Wisconsin Historical Society, Convention Proceedings of 1883, 1885 and 1887).

[206]Cf. Negt, Oeffentlichkeit, p. 341ff.

[207]Negt, "Don't Go By Numbers," p. 49.

III. German-American Socialist Literature: the Political and Functional Context

[1]See the discussion of these differing concepts of literature in Chapter IV below.

[2]Jürgen Kocka, "Arbeiterkultur als Forschungsthema," in: Geschichte und Gesellschaft, 5 (1979), Heft 1, p. 5-12. This special issue is devoted to "Arbeiterkultur im 19. Jahrhundert."

[3]Linus Spuler, "Von deutschamerikanischer Dichtung," in: German-American Studies, 1 (1969), Heft 1, p. 9.

[4]Frank Trommler, "Vom Vormärz zum Bürgerkrieg. Die Achtundvierziger und ihre Lyrik," in: Sigrid Bauschinger et. al., eds., Amerika in der deutschen Literatur (Stuttgart: Reclam, 1975), p. 93.

[5]Ibid., p. 94.

[6]Chicago Arbeiter-Zeitung, Feb. 8, 1888, p. 2.

[7]Wilhelm L. Rosenberg, "Das Heimweh im Deutsch-Amerikanischen Liede," in: Festzeitung für das 4te Bundes-Sängerfest des Arbeiter-Sängerbundes des Nordwestens der Ver. Staaten (Davenport, Iowa), June 1906, No. 1, p. 5.

[8]Ibid., p. 5.

[9]Ibid., p. 5 and 7.

[10]Friedrich Wilhelm Fritzsche, Blut-Rosen. Sozial-politische Gedichte (Baltimore: Kern, 1890), p. 7.

[11]Wilhelm L. Rosenberg, An der Weltenwende (Cleveland: Vlg. der Windsor Ave. Pub. Co., 1910), p. 5. This book is a collection of Rosenberg's poetry which was published earlier in the socialist press.

[12]Cf. Jost Hermand, Von deutscher Republik (Frankfurt: Insel, 1968).

[13]Cf. Reinhold Grimm and Jost Hermand, eds., Exil und innere Emigration (Frankfurt: Athenäum, 1972), especially Jost Hermand, "Schreiben in der Fremde. Gedanken zur deutschen Exilliteratur seit 1789," p. 7-30.

[14]In Germany, the workers' dramatic clubs, singing societies, and Bildungsvereine served also as covers for political discussions and organizing during the period of the Anti-Socialist Laws.

[15]August Bebel, letter of Sept. 21, 1909, to the editors of the New York Solidarität, in: Solidarität, Oct. 1909, No. 7, p. 4-5.

[16]August Otto-Walster and Leopold Jacoby were the most prominent writers who returned to Germany.

[17]The agit-prop troupe associated with the Communist Party in New York City, the Proletbühne, wrote and performed its own plays. See Dan Friedman, The Proletbühne (Dissertation, University of Wisconsin, 1978).

[18]Later programs to encourage workers to write also focused on reports dealing with their situation at the workplace. Cf. the Arbeiterkorrespondentenbewegung in the Soviet Union and the Weimar Republic, and the Bitterfelder Weg in the GDR.

[19]Cf. Bernd Witte, Deutsche Arbeiterliteratur, p. 5ff. Cf. also the discussion in Chapter IV below.

[20]Cf. Cäcilia Friedrich, ed., Minna Kautsky. Auswahl aus ihrem Werk (Berlin: Akademie, 1965).

[21]Cf. Cäcilia Friedrich, ed., Aus dem Schaffen früher sozialistischer Schriftstellerinnen (Berlin: Akademie, 1966).

[22]Cf. Mary Jo Buhle's forthcoming book on feminism and socialism in the United States, to be published by the University of Illinois press, which includes a detailed chapter on women in the German-American socialist movement, including Augusta Lilienthal and Johanna Greie, important lecturers and writers.

[23]This is similar to the SPD in Germany, which also did not articulate a cultural policy but relied for the most part on bourgeois standards and traditions. Cf. Fülberth, Proletarische Partei.

[24]Cf. the categories developed by Witte, Deutsche Arbeiterliteratur, introduction.

[25]Cf. Peter v. Rüden, Sozialdemokratisches Arbeitertheater 1848 bis 1914 (Frankfurt: Athenäum, 1973), Chapter I, on the history and use by socialists of Festspiele and lebende Bilder.

[26]More socialist writers wrote novels in Germany, and these were usually published in serialized form in the SPD press. German-American socialist papers sometimes serialized novels by Otto-Walster, Minna Kautsky and others.

[27]Schewitsch in the New York Volkszeitung, Aug. 21, 1881, p. 4.

[28]In addition to such drawings, which represent the typical graphic art associated with the socialist movement, the German-American artist Robert Koehler painted what is said to be the first painting to depict a modern industrial confrontation between striking workers and their capitalist employer. Entitled "The Strike" (1886), this painting was inspired by the events of the strike of 1877. See Lee Baxandall's article on this painting and a reproduction of it in 1199 News, (Nov. 1972).
In addition, another painting by Koehler, "The Socialist," shows a man delivering a speech with great conviction, while spread out before him is a newspaper called Der Sozialist, undoubtedly a German-American paper.

[29]The best source for original musical scores is the archives of the "Sozialistische Liedertafel" and "Arbeiter-Männerchor" of New York, kept in the Lincoln Center Library in New York City.

[30]Wilhelm L. Rosenberg, "Eine practische Aufgabe für die proletarischen Sänger," in: Festzeitung des Arbeiter-Sängerbundes des Nordwestens, St. Louis, No. 6 (May 1, 1904), p. 18.

[31]Ibid.

[32]The New York SAP paper Der Sozialist lists publications by Rosenberg and Kirchner over the years, and some of the scores are in the musical archives referred to in note 29 above.

[33]For Sahm's biography, see Der deutsche Pionier, 15 (1883), p. 348-9.

[34]New York Volkszeitung, June 8, 1885, p. 1.

[35]These general tendencies should not be taken as absolute, however, since counterexamples can be found in the Socialist Party through the 1920's and in the German sections of the Communist Party. Nevertheless, more recent groups of immigrants assumed a much more militant stance than did the Germans.

[36]Other socialist calendars referred to in the press include the Kalender des Philadelphia Tageblatt, the New Jersey Arbeiter-Kalender, and the Volkskalender of the "Arbeiter Kranken- und Sterbekasse." In addition, the socialist press also recommended to its readers the Freidenker-Almanach and the Amerikanischer Turnerkalender.

[37]New York Volkszeitung, Feb. 21, 1881, p. 4.

[38]Pionier, 1931, p. 97.

[39]For Lyser's biography and a translation of one of his plays, see Heinz Ickstadt and Hartmut Keil, "A Forgotten Piece of Working-Class Literature: Gustav Lyser's Satire of the Hewitt Hearing of 1878," in: Labor History, Vol. 20, No. 1 (Winter 1979), p. 127-140.

[40] One exception is Johann Most's _Freiheit_, with its small, fanatical group of supporters.

[41] See, for example, the catalog of the Labor News Company listed in _Der Sozialist_, April 9, 1887, and the New York "Volkszeitungs-Bibliothek" listed on the back cover of _Der Pionier_ in the 1890's.

[42] Cf. _Arbeiter-Liederbuch_ (Chicago: G. A. Lönnecker, 1873) which was banned by the Anti-Socialist Laws, _Liederbuch für freie deutsche Schulen und Familien_ (New York: Vlg. Labor Lyceum, 1905), Hermann Schlüter, ed., _Sozialistisches Arbeiter-Liederbuch_ (Chicago: Hrsg. von der Deutschen Sprachgruppe der Sozialistischen Partei der V.S., n.d.). Of course, collections of songs and poetry were available from Germany, also.

[43] _Der Sozialist_, April 9, 1887, lists the German publications available through the Labor News Company.

[44] For reports on the _Arbeiter-Bühne_, see New York _Volkszeitung_, Jan. 28, Feb. 25, Mar. 25, Apr. 15, Apr. 22, May 6, 1877.

[45] The best source on the local activities of party sections around the country is _Der Socialist_, the official organ of the SAP.

[46] This was the "Dramatischer Verein 'Fortschritt,'" in Newark. New York _Volkszeitung_, Aug. 7, 1895, p. 4.

[47] _Der Sozialist_, April 2, 1892, p. 3.

[48] See, for example, the statements in _Volksstimme des Westens_, Jan. 3, 1878, p. 4, and _Der Sozialist_, Feb. 23, 1889, p. 3.

[49] _Der Sozialist_, Jan. 12, 1889, p. 1.

[50] To give an idea of what was available, in 1887 the SAP's Labor News Company listed the following dramatic works in its catalog: Schweitzer, _Ein Schlingel_. Kegel, _Pressprozesse_ and _Ein Opfer_. C. Max (pseudonym for Conrad Derossi), _Die Anarchisten_. Karl Heyner, _Der Deserteur_. Otto-Walster, _Rienzi_. Lassalle, _Franz von Sickingen_. Rosenberg, _Vor der Wahlschlacht_. Karl Heinzen, _Lustspiele_. (_Der Sozialist_, Apr. 9, 1887, p. 7).

[51] Cf. New York _Volkszeitung_, Mar. 3 and Apr. 21, 1889, on performances of Pattberg's _Der Reiche und der Bettelmann_ and _Müller Mehlstaub und Bettler Hungermann_ by children at the school of the Brooklyn Labor Lyceum.

[52] For Most's biography, see Rudolf Rocker, _Johann Most_ (Berlin: Vlg. "Der Syndicalist," 1924).

[53] New York _Volkszeitung_, Oct. 29, 1894, p. 1. Cf. also the discussions of how the German government and police perceived the connections between international anarchism and naturalism in Manfred Brauneck, _Literatur und Oeffentlichkeit im ausgehenden 19. Jahrhundert_ (Stuttgart: Metzler, 1974). The oppositional group of "die Jungen" around the "Freie Volksbühne" maintained connections to anarchist circles in Germany and abroad. For example, Bruno Wille was a

regular contributor to Robert Reitzel's Der arme Teufel, an anarchist paper published in Detroit. Max Baginski, who had accompanied Hauptmann on his trip to the Silesian weavers' district in 1891, became the editor of the Chicago Arbeiter-Zeitung. Also, "die Jungen" had close contacts with Johann Most in New York, according to Brauneck. With reference to performances of Die Weber, Brauneck (91f.) points out that one of the most influential critics of the time, Heinrich Bulthaupt, emphasized the connections between international anarchism and naturalism, especially Die Weber, in his Theater und Gesellschaft. His arguments were used in the Reichstag in the Umsturzdebatte, when the SPD was to be discredited by associating it with anarchism. Accordingly, the German press and police kept up with performances of Die Weber abroad. The German press reported in detail on Most's theater in New York and Chicago in 1894, and the report in the Berlin police files reads: "Durch Theaterstücke, wie die Weber behaupten die anarchistischen Seiten, ihrer Sache mehr zu nützen, wie durch Volksversammlungen." (Brauneck, p. 92 and 247). Ironically, Most's New York "Freie Bühne" performed an adaptation of Bulthaupt's drama Die Arbeiter (1877). Rewritten by two Chicago anarchists, and featuring Most himself as the worker hero, the new version, now entitled Strike, totally reversed the conciliatory tones of the original to call for class struggle and violent revolution. See: Freiheit, June 1, 8, 15, 22, 1901, for a serialization of the play and reports on the performance.

[54]I am indebted to Hartmut Keil for this information.

[55]Four years later, the eight men arrested after the Haymarket incident were to find themselves on trial for conspiracy. In their speeches before court, they indicted the unjust social system which had led them to become Social-Revolutionaries.

[56]Die Nihilisten, (Chicago, 1882), p. 19.

[57]Fackel, Mar. 12, 1882, p. 8.

[58]Ibid.

[59]Chicago Arbeiter-Zeitung, Mar. 20, 1882, p. 4.

[60]Fackel, Mar. 12, 1882, p. 8.

[61]St. Louis Parole, Mar. 1885, p. 1.

[62]An example of a socialist workers' theater which performed almost solely those plays for workers' theater which were published in Germany was the group in Milwaukee. The "Heinrich Bartel Collection" at the Milwaukee County Historical Society contains listings of its repertoire.

[63]Cf. Dan Friedman, The Proletbühne (Dissertation: University of Wisconsin, 1978).

[64]For a brief history of the German workers' singing societies, see Inge Lammel, Das Arbeiterlied (Leipzig: Reclam, 1970). See also Inge Lammel, Bibliographie der deutschen Arbeiterliederbücher 1833-1945 (Leipzig: Deutscher Vlg. für Musik, 1971).

[65]Der Arbeiter, Apr. 15, 1928 and Aug. 4 and 31, 1929.

[66]Festzeitung des Arbeiter-Sängerbundes des Nordwestens, (Davenport, Iowa), No. 1 (June 1906), p. 9.

[67]Ibid., p. 13.

[68]Printed in the Festzeitung des Arbeiter-Sängerbundes des Nordwestens. (St. Louis), No. 3 (Oct. 1, 1903), p. 4.

[69]Cf. the reports in the New York Volkszeitung, Feb. 18 and June 28, 1883.

[70]New York Volkszeitung, Sept. 18, 1883, p. 4.

[71]Cf. the reports in the New York Volkszeitung, Aug. 10, 1891, p. 1, and Sept. 22, 1891, p. 2.

[72]Festzeitung des Arbeiter-Sängerbundes des Nordwestens, (St. Louis), No. 1 (May 1903). p. 6.

[73]See note 29 above.

[74]Cf. Sergius Schewitsch, "Die Blüthen des Sonntagsgesetzes," New York Volkszeitung, Apr. 28, 1878, p. 4, which describes the kind of illicit cheap entertainment available behind closed doors on a Sunday in New York, and argues for the abolishment of such "blue laws."

[75]Festzeitung des Arbeiter-Sängerbundes des Nordwestens, (Chicago), No. 1 (Dec. 1909), p. 11.

[76]Cf. Peter Brückner/Gabriele Ricke, "Ueber die ästhetische Erziehung des Menschen in der Arbeiterbewegung," in: Brückner et. al., Das Unvermögen der Realität (Berlin: Wagenbach, 1974), p. 37-69.

[77]Festzeitung des Arbeiter-Sängerbundes des Nordwestens, (St. Louis), No. 1 (May 1, 1903), p. 5, article by Philip Rappaport on "Kampf und Sang."

[78]L. Kranzfelder, "Die Mission der Arbeiter-Gesangvereine," in: Festzeitung des Arbeiter-Sängerbundes des Nordwestens, (Chicago), No. 1 (Dec. 1909), p. 9.

[79]Cf. Brückner/Ricke, "Ästhetische Erziehung," p. 63.

[80]Cf. Festzeitung des Arbeiter-Sängerbundes des Nordwestens, (St. Louis), No. 3 (Oct. 1, 1903), p. 15.

[81]Ibid., No. 2 (July 18, 1903), p. 5.

[82]Ibid., p. 6.

[83]Chicago Arbeiter-Zeitung, July 3, 1901, p. 1.

[84]Chicago Arbeiter-Zeitung, July 2, 1901, p. 1.

[85]Festzeitung des Arbeiter-Sängerbundes des Nordwestens, (Chicago), No. 2 (Feb. 1910), p. 5, article by Jacob Winnen, "Musik und die Aufgabe der Arbeiter-Gesangvereine."

[86]For a typical statement on the effect of socialism on art, see the editorial on "Kultur und Sozialismus" in the Chicago Arbeiter-Zeitung, Feb. 6, 1888, p. 2.

[87]The arguments in Brückner/Ricke, "Aesthetische Erziehung," are important for the following discussion.

[88]Ibid., p. 38-9.

[89]Ibid., p. 39.

[90]Ibid., p. 63.

[91]In general, this literature is abstract and is more concerned with telling readers what to do: Unite! Be a man! than with developing experimental models of conflicts. It would be important to ask whether this sort of literature was common to socialist writers in other ethnic groups in the United States and to specify just what the differences are.

[92]Cf. Fülberth, Proletarische Partei.

[93]For an analysis of non-working class festivals, see Reinhold Grimm and Jost Hermand, eds., Deutsche Feiern (Wiesbaden: Athenaion, 1977). For a recent analysis of the May Day phenomenon, see Gottfried Korff, "Volkskultur und Arbeiterkultur. Ueberlegungen am Beispiel der sozialistischen Maifesttradition," in: Geschichte und Gesellschaft, 5 (1979), No. 1, p. 83-103.

[94]See the reports in the New York Volkszeitung before and after Mar. 20, 1883.

[95]Cf. Korff, "Volkskultur."

[96]New York Neue Arbeiter-Zeitung, Aug. 30, 1873, p. 1.

[97]Milwaukee Vorwärts, Mar. 19, 1898, p. 1.

[98]Korff, "Volkskultur," p. 94.

[99]New York Volkszeitung, June 30, 1878, p. 4.

IV. Excursus on German Workers' Literature: A 'Forschungsbericht'

[1]Bernd Witte, Deutsche Arbeiterliteratur von den Anfängen bis 1914 (Stuttgart: Reclam, 1977), p. 5. The following discussion on the reasons for the neglect of workers' literature is based in part on Witte's introduction to this book.

[2]For surveys of this "Arbeiterdichtung" see: Christian Rülcker, Ideologie der Arbeiterdichtung, 1914-1933 (Stuttgart: Metzler, 1970), and Günter Heintz, ed., Deutsche Arbeiterdichtung 1910-1933 (Stuttgart: Reclam, 1974).

[3]Cf. Witte, Deutsche Arbeiterliteratur, p. 7f. For the prevalence of bourgeois concepts of art within the SPD, see Georg Fülberth, Proletarische Partei, bürgerliche Literatur (Neuwied: Luchterhand, 1972).

[4]Franz Mehring, "Kunst und Proletariat," quoted in Oesterreichische Gesellschaft für Kulturpolitik, ed. , Arbeiterdichtung (Wuppertal: Hammer, 1973), p. 239-40.

[5]For a more detailed discussion of this debate see Gerald Stieg/Bernd Witte, Abriss einer Geschichte der deutschen Arbeiterliteratur (Stuttgart: Klett, 1973), p. 7ff. Also, see the collection of definitions and statements in OEGK, ed. , Arbeiterdichtung.

[6]Julius Bab, Arbeiterdichtung, 2nd ed. (Berlin, 1929), p. 3ff, quoted in OEGK, ed. , Arbeiterdichtung, p. 195.

[7]Quoted in Stieg/Witte, Abriss, p. 9. This is similar to Mehring's evaluation of early socialist literature.

[8]Quoted in Stieg/Witte, Abriss, p. 9-10.

[9]Ibid. , p. 10.

[10]Quoted in OEGK, ed. , Arbeiterdichtung, p. 208.

[11]Fritz Martini in Paul Merker/Wolfgang Stammler, Reallexikon der deutschen Literaturgeschichte (Berlin, 1958), 2nd ed. , Vol. I, p. 97f. , quoted in OEGK, ed. , Arbeiterdichtung, p. 209.

[12]Jürgen Rühle, Literatur und Revolution (Cologne, 1962), 2nd ed. , p. 187f. , quoted in ibid. , p. 211.

[13]Gero von Wilpert, Sachwörterbuch der Literatur (Stuttgart, 1964), 4th ed. , p. 37, quoted in ibid. , p. 212.

[14]Quoted in Stieg/Witte, Abriss, p. 10, from Deutsche Literaturgeschichte von den Anfängen bis zur Gegenwart (Stuttgart: Kröner, 1965), 13th ed. , p. 544.

[15]Manfred Häckel, ed. , Leopold Jacoby (Berlin: Akademie, 1971), p. liii.

[16]Lexikon sozialistischer deutscher Literatur (LSDL) (s'Gravenhage: van Eversdijck Raubdruck, 1973), p. 18. The introduction is by Silvia Schlenstedt.

[17]Häckel, Jacoby, p. xlii.

[18]LSDL, p. 19.

[19]Ibid.

[20]Ibid. , p. 18.

[21]Ibid. , p. 18-20.

[22]Fritz Hüser, "Arbeiterdichtung? Neue Industriedichtung?" in: Beiträge und Studien zur Arbeiterdichtung und Sozialen Literatur des 19. und 20. Jahrhunderts Folge I (Dortmund, 1967), quoted in ÖGK, ed. , Arbeiterdichtung, p. 213.

[23]Ibid. , p. 214.

[24]See Jost Hermand, "Bundesrepublik Deutschland," in: Walter Hinderer, ed. , Geschichte der politischen Lyrik in Deutschland (Stuttgart: Reclam, 1978), p. 315-337.

[25]Michael Pehlke, "Ein Exempel proletarischer Dramatik. Bemerkungen zu Friedrich Bosses Streikdrama 'Im Kampf,'" in: Literaturwissenschaft und Sozialwissenschaften (Stuttgart: Metzler, 1971), p. 400-434.

[26]An example of the latter is given by Hermand, in "Bundesrepublik Deutschland," p. 324, where he quotes Hans Magnus Enzensberger as stating that "Kampfgesänge und Marschlieder, Plakatverse und Hymnen, Propaganda-Choräle und versifizierte Manifeste," like all "Agitations-Formen" have nothing to do with "Poesie." (Einzelheiten II, Frankfurt 1962).

[27]Gerald Stieg, "Themen zur Arbeiterlyrik in Deutschland 1863-1933," in: OEGK, ed., Arbeiterdichtung, p. 36.

[28]Witte, Deutsche Arbeiterliteratur, p. 9-10.

[29]Stieg/Witte, Abriss, p. 12-13.

[30]Martin Ludwig, Arbeiterliteratur in Deutschland (Stuttgart: Metzler, 1976), p. 3.

[31]This is in contrast to Friedrich Knilli, who takes a fundamentally uncritical approach to this literature in his article "Kitsch im Klassenkampf?" in: OEGK, ed., Arbeiterdichtung, p. 76-92.

[32]Stieg/Witte, Abriss, p. 12.

[33]Ibid., p. 12-13.

[34]Ibid., p. 13.

[35]Ibid., p. 12.

[36]Witte, Deutsche Arbeiterliteratur, p. 14.

[37]Ibid.

[38]Cf. also Stieg/Witte, Abriss, p. 26ff. on allegory.

[39]Witte, Deutsche Arbeiterliteratur, p. 14-15.

[40]Ibid., p. 17.

[41]This is explicitly stated in the preface to Stieg/Witte, Abriss.

[42]Witte, Deutsche Arbeiterliteratur, p. 13.

[43]Ibid., p. 9.

[44]Ibid., p. 12.

[45]Stieg/Witte, Abriss, p. 36.

[46]Witte, Deutsche Arbeiterliteratur, p. 10.

[47]Ibid., p. 12.

V. German-American Socialist Literature: The Works

[1]For a collection of primary material arranged according to the topics discussed in this chapter, see volume II of Carol Poore, German-American Socialist Literature in the Late Nineteenth Century (Dissertation, University of Wisconsin, 1979).

[2]Chicago Vorbote, July 1, 1876, p. 5.

[3]Philip Foner, ed., American Labor Songs of the Nineteenth Century (Urbana: Univ. of Illinois Press, 1977), p. 287-88.

[4]Emil Friedrich, "Wilhelm Liebknecht," in: New York Sozialist, Sept. 18, 1886, p. 4.

[5]Gustav Lyser, "Requiescant in Pace!" in: Chicago Vorbote, Aug. 11, 1877, p. 1.

[6]Wilhelm Rosenberg, "Hazleton," in his An der Weltenwende, Gedichte (Cleveland: Vlg. der Windsor Ave. Publ. Co., 1910), p. 62f.

[7]For more information on Gustav Lyser, see Heinz Ickstadt and Hartmut Keil, "A Forgotten Piece of Working-Class Literature: Gustav Lyser's Satire of the Hewitt Hearing of 1878," in: Labor History, Vol. 20, No. 1 (Winter 1979), p. 127-140.

[8]Lyser's play was originally printed in the Chicago Vorbote, Aug. 17 and 24, 1878.

[9]Cf. Ickstadt/Keil, "A Forgotten Piece ...," p. 132. For the actual testimony of socialists, including Adolf Douai, before the Hewitt committee, see U.S. Congress, Investigation by a Select Committee of the House of Representatives Relative to the Causes of the General Depression in Labor and Business (Washington, D.C., 1879), p. 17-42.

[10]Thus, as discussed in Chapter II, the tramp was often blamed for society's ills. For example, Allan Pinkerton, in his Strikers, Communists, Tramps and Detectives (1878) saw tramps as one of the causes of the 1877 strike and riots. Socialists, on the other hand, pointed out that unemployment had caused the large numbers of tramps and that they would be only too happy to work. Cf. August Otto-Walster's short story, "Deutsche Tramps in Amerika," in: Wolfgang Friedrich, ed, August Otto-Walster, Leben und Werk (Berlin: Akademie, 1966), p. 198-225.

[11]New York Volkszeitung, Aug. 21, 1881, p. 4.

[12]Martin Schupp in Freiheit, Jan. 9, 1904, p. 2.

[13]Wilhelm Rosenberg, "Der Weltenherrscher," in: An der Weltenwende, p. 15.

[14]Reported in the Chicago Vorbote, July 1, 1876, p. 5.

[15]Sergius Schewitsch, "Cash!" in: Chicago Fackel, April 11, 1880, p. 3.

[16] Johann Most's song "Wer schafft das Gold zu Tage" expressed this positive evaluation of productive labor in contrast to the lazy rich, and was one of the most popular songs of German Social Democracy.

[17] Carl Derossi, "Erwach' o Volk, erwache!" in: New York Sozialist, April 13, 1889, p. 3.

[18] One example of such a pyramidal construction of society appeared in the satirical publication Der Tramp, edited by Georg Biedenkapp and Wilhelm Rosenberg, Jg. 1, No. 1, Probenummer, p. 5.

[19] New York Volkszeitung, Sept. 18, 1879 and following dates.

[20] Cf. Hartmut Keil and Heinz Ickstadt, "Elemente einer deutschen Arbeiterkultur in Chicago zwischen 1880 und 1890," in: Geschichte und Gesellschaft, 5 (1979), Heft 1, p. 120: "Literatur als Ausdruck subjektiver Erfahrung fehlt ... so gut wie ganz."

[21] Also, the prose written by socialists had throughly traditional ways of treating these "private" areas, particularly women and love relationships. One important example is August Otto-Walster's novel Am Webstuhl der Zeit (1873), one of the most popular and often-reprinted novels by a socialist writer. The love relationships and marriages are portrayed quite conventionally, as in the popular literature of the time.

[22] A partial list of poetry collections by German-American socialists which include "non-political" poetry is: Georg Biedenkapp, Brennende Lieder und Strophen (1900); Georg Biedenkapp, Sankta Libertas (1893); Emilie Hofmann, Veilchen und Rothe Nelken (1905); Wilhelm Rosenberg, Liebesglück und Liebesleid (1916); Martin Schupp, Lerchensang und Schwerterklang (1902). In addition, many other German-American socialist writers published single poems dealing with "private" themes. Robert Reitzel, one of the most well-known German-American writers, was associated with anarchist circles in Detroit but wrote primarily lyric poetry along with political essays. See his Des armen Teufel gesammelte Schriften (Detroit: Reitzel Klub, 1913).

[23] I am indebted to Mary Jo Buhle for information on the attitude of German-American socialists towards women's emancipation.

[24] Cf. the discussion in Chapter II on socialists and women's issues.

[25] Carl Derossi, "Der Sozialisten Siegeszug," in: Sozialistische Liedertafel archives, Lincoln Center Music Library, New York. Manuscript.

[26] For the term "starke Genossen" and a discussion of the sex roles in the Rote Eine-Mark-Romane of the Weimar Republic, see Michael Rohrwasser, Saubere Mädel, starke Genossen (Frankfurt: Roter Stern, 1975). See also Wolfgang Emmerich's review of this book: "The Red One-Mark-Novel and the 'Heritage of our Time,'" in: New German Critique, 10 (Winter 1977), p. 179-191. It seems that the positive characteristics attributed to the workers in the socialist literature of the pre-World-War-One period are reutilized and developed in these proletarian novels.

[27]Cf. Mary Jo Buhle, "German-American Socialism and the Woman Question," unpublished manuscript.

[28]Werner Thönnessen, The Emancipation of Women (Bristol: Pluto, 1973).

[29]Gustav Lyser, "Hurrah!" in: New York Arbeiter-Stimme, Dec. 13, 1874, p. 3.

[30]Cf. the discussion in Chapter II on the disciplining of the working class as capitalism developed, and the various forms of resistance to this.

[31]Cf. Keil/Ickstadt, "Elemente einer deutschen Arbeiterkultur in Chicago," p. 114-115, who trace the existence of comparable moral norms in the Knights of Labor:
"Der Normenkatalog der Knights of Labor --- Fleiss, Ehrlichkeit, Enthaltsamkeit, Familienbewusstsein, Häuslichkeit, Respekt für die Frau -- indiziert sowohl die Verwurzelung der amerikanischen (d. h. der angelsächsischen) Arbeiterschaft im kulturellen System des amerikanischen Viktorianismus, stützte aber zugleich den Widerstand (kennzeichnet freilich auch dessen Grenzen), den sie ihrer drohenden Proletarisierung entgegensetzte.
Vergleichbar ist die Affinität der deutschen Sozialisten zu den ethischen Wertvorstellungen des deutschen Kleinbürgertums. In zahlreichen Kurzgeschichten erscheint der Arbeiter gegenüber einer moralisch korrumpierten Bourgeoisie als der legitime Erbe bürgerlicher Tugenden. Deutsche Arbeiterkultur unterschied sich jedoch von den puritanischen Auffassungen etwa der Knights of Labor durch grössere Entspanntheit im Bereich sinnlicher Erfahrung."

[32]Wilhelm Rosenberg, "Wie lange noch?" in: An der Weltenwende, p. 95ff.

[33]Conrad Conzett, "An die Arbeiter," in: Chicago Vorbote, June 24, 1876, p. 2.

[34]Hermann Pudewa, "Auf zur That! Mahnruf an die Nichtverbändler," in: New York Arbeiter-Stimme, July 23, 1876, p. 4.

[35]Gustav Lyser, "Neujahr 1875!" in: New York Arbeiter-Stimme, Jan. 3, 1875, p. 3.

[36]Wilhelm Rosenberg, "Was wird aus dir?" in: An der Weltenwende, p. 17.

[37]Cf. Herbert Gutman, "Protestantism and the American Labor Movement," in his Work, Culture and Society, especially p. 88ff. on millenialism within the American labor movement and the frequency of these apocalyptic images of revolution among English-speaking workers.

[38]Alexander Jonas, "Die Göttin der Freiheit. Eine Vision," in: New York Volkszeitung, July 13, 1884, p. 4.

[39]In the sense of providing time for leisure, education and cultural pursuits, the demand for the eight-hour day was also a cultural demand, and not only a bread-and-butter issue, though this was of course crucial.

[40]Carl Derossi, "Der Arbeit Jubelfest," in: Sozialistische Liedertafel archives, Lincoln Center Music Library, New York. Manuscript.

[41]Carl Sahm, "Banner-Lied," in: Sozialistische Liedertafel Archives, Lincoln Center Music Library, New York. Manuscript.

[42]Anon., Die Nihilisten (Chicago: Socialistic Publishing Society, 1882).

[43]The Festzeitungen of the Arbeiter-Sängerbund des Nordwestens featured such a strong worker and happy family on their covers.

[44]For the concept of "concrete utopia," see Jost Hermand, "The Necessity of Utopian Thinking," in: Soundings, Vol. 58, No. 1, (Spring 1975), p. 97-111.

[45]Carl Derossi. "Der Sozialisten Siegeszug," in: Sozialistische Liedertafel Archives, Lincoln Center Music Library, New York. Manuscript.

[46]Martin Schupp, "Neue Welt und neue Sterne," in his Lerchensang und Schwerterklang (New York: Selbstverlag, 1902), p. 134.

[47]Jakob Franz, "Der Menschheits-Frühling," in: New York Volkszeitung, Mar. 7, 1886, p. 7.

[48]In addition to Douai's testimony before Congress cited in Chapter II, the following passage from Alexander Jonas' Reporter und Sozialist (1884) may serve as a typical statement on the natural evolution of history:
"Niemals noch ist eine Revolution gemacht worden, sondern die gänzliche Umwälzung eines bestimmten Zustandes der Gesellschaft und sein Ueberführen in einen andern, prinzipiell verschiedenen -- und das ist, was ich unter Revolution verstehe -- geschah immer gemäss der natürlichen Entwicklung der Dinge, welche der Einzelne weder aufhalten, noch wesentlich befördern kann. Darin liegt ja gerade die unerschütterliche Sicherheit, mit welcher wir den Sieg unserer Ideen erwarten, dass diese Ideen nicht in der Luft schweben, sondern dem Boden der Wirklichkeit entnommen sind und dass ihre Zielpunkte zusammenfallen mit dem Resultate, welche die materielle Entwicklung der Gegenwart nothwendiger Weise zeitigen muss." (43).

[49]Redaction des Social-Demokrat, "1876," in: New York Social-Demokrat, Jan. 2, 1876, p. 1.

[50]See note 45.

[51]Stieg/Witte, Abriss, p. 30.

[52]Korff, "Volkskultur."

[53]See note 49.

[54]In the article mentioned in footnote 37 above on "Protestantism and the American Labor Movement," Herbert Gutman has detailed the appropriation of Christian concepts of equality, justice and redemption by the broad groups of "business" unionists, Knights of Labor, and socialist and anarchist radicals (109). Of particular interest here are his documentations of the supposedly atheist German-American socialists. For example, he quotes Haymarket martyr August Spies, who linked his beliefs to Thomas Münzer in his speech before court, saying that the Gospel "did not merely promise blessings in heaven, but that it also com-

manded equality and brotherhood among men on earth." (p. 90). In addition, New York Volkszeitung editor Adolf Douai, one of the most consistent advocates of enlightenment and opponents of religious fanaticism, also wrote in 1887: "Our age needs religious enthusiasm for the sake of common brotherhood, because infidelity is rampant and hypocrisy prevails in all churches -- an infidelity of a peculiar kind, being a disbelief in the destiny of men to be brothers and sisters, in their common quality and rights." (p. 110).

[55]Cf. Florian Vassen, "Handarbeit und Griechentum," unpublished manuscript, who states with reference to this early socialist poetry: "es wurden auf der Erscheinungsebene Auswüchse herausgegriffen und dem Spott des Arbeiterpublikums überlassen. Kaum einmal rückte jedoch das Wesen der damaligen Gesellschaftsordnung in den Mittelpunkt." (p. 13).

[56]Writing about poems which remain on the surface of things and issue exhortations and commands, Bertolt Brecht stated: "Flach, leer, platt werden Gedichte, wenn sie ihrem Stoff seine Widersprüche nehmen, wenn die Dinge, von denen sie handeln, nicht in ihrer lebendigen, das heisst allseitigen, nicht zu Ende gekommenen und nicht zu Ende zu formulierenden Form auftraten. Geht es um Politik, so entsteht dann die schlechte Tendenzdichtung. Man bekommt 'tendenziöse Darstellungen,' das heisst Darstellungen, welche allerhand auslassen, die Realität vergewaltigen, Illusionen erzeugen sollen. Man bekommt mechanische Parolen, Phrasen, unpraktikable Anweisungen." (WA 19, p. 394).

[57]On the function of socialist festivals, see Korff, "Volkskultur," p. 5, and Keil/ Ickstadt, "Elemente einer deutschen Arbeiterkultur in Chicago," p. 117.

VI. Conclusion

[1]New York Volkszeitung, June 2, 1894, p. 1.

[2]For a study of the St. Louis German socialist community in the period 1890-1910, see Ray Eberle's Master's Thesis on this topic (Southern Illinois University, 1978). This study was unavailable to me.

[3]The "Arbeiter-Kranken- und Sterbekasse was a national organization founded by exiles in New York and modeled along the lines of a similar organization affiliated with the SPD in Hamburg. It published a paper, Solidarität (1906-1954). In 1937 it had more than 49,000 members and had paid out more than 21 million dollars in benefits. Also, it established homes for old people and recreational farms.

[4]Cf. the following statement on Finnish socialist halls on the Mesabi Mining Range in Northern Minnesota in the first years of the 20th century: "At the clubs they read their literature, discussed their problems, heard lectures, put on plays, sang, danced, flirted, romanced, were married, celebrated the birth of children, conducted strike meetings, held classes for themselves and their children, had parties, became ill, died and began the procession to the

cemetery. At the halls, the miner was able, for a while, to forget his back-breaking toil and his problems of loneliness in what seemed to him a hostile world. He met his own people, reminisced about the homeland, spoke of aspirations and vented his hostility against a system which he thought prematurely robbed him of his manhood." Matti Kaups, quoted in Al Gedicks, "The Development of Socialist Political Culture Among Finnish Immigrants," unpublished manuscript, p. 22.

[5]Lee Baxandall, preface to The Origins of Left Culture in the U.S. 1880-1940, special issue of Cultural Correspondence/Green Mountain Irregulars, Spring 1978, p. 2.

[6]The fact that the criticism of capitalism in this literature tends to remain on a moral level of criticism could have its source in part in the remembrance or experience of personal confrontations with capitalists and employers in an earlier industrial period, before the oppressive forces in society became more anonymous.

[7]Paul Buhle, "The Pinking of American TV," in: Liberation, Vol. 20, No. 4 (June 1977), p. 5.

[8]Thus, all ethnic and language groups took part in union and socialist movements in the U.S. and all developed corresponding cultural and literary activities. A study of these various groups, carried out cooperatively, would be both timely and pertinent. Also, the "native" Americans should not be forgotten in this context. A whole body of workers' songs and literature was written in English which has hardly been studied at all.

[9]Spiegel, Oct. 31, 1977, p. 44.

I. HISTORY

1. General Bibliographies

Egbert, Donald, and Stow Persons, eds. Socialism and American Life, 2 vols. Princeton: Princeton Univ. Press, 1952.

Seidmann, Joel. Communism in the United States, A Bibliography. Ithaca: Cornell, 1969.

2. Special Collections

Ham, F. Gerald, comp. Labor Manuscripts in the State Historical Society of Wisconsin. Madison: State Historical Society, 1967.

Ham, F. Gerald, ed. Records of the Socialist Labor Party of America, Guide to a Microfilm Edition. Madison: State Historical Society, 1970.

International Workingmen's Association. Papers on Microfilm. Madison: Wisconsin State Historical Society, 2 reels.

Socialist Labor Party Papers. Madison: Wisconsin State Historical Society.

Wisconsin State Historical Society. Labor Papers on Microfilm, A Combined List. Madison: State Historical Society, 1960.

3. The German Social Democratic Party (SPD)

Atzrott, Otto. Sozialdemokratische Druckschriften und Vereine verboten auf Grund des Reichsgesetzes gegen die gemeingefährlichen Bestrebungen der Sozialdemokratie vom 21. Oktober 1878. Berlin: Carl Heymanns Vlg., 1886.

Auer, Ignaz. Nach 10 Jahren. Material und Glossen zur Geschichte des Sozialistengesetzes. London: German Cooperative Publishing Co., 1889-90.

Bebel, August. Die Frau und der Sozialismus. Reprint. Berlin: Dietz, 1974.

Bernstein, Eduard. Die Geschichte der Berliner Arbeiterbewegung. 2 vols. Berlin: Buchhandlung Vorwärts, 1907.

Brandis, Kurt. Der Anfang vom Ende der Sozialdemokratie. Reprint. Berlin: Rotbuch, 1975.

Fricke, Dieter. Die deutsche Arbeiterbewegung, 1869-1890. Leipzig: Vlg. Enzyklopädie, 1964.

Geschichte der deutschen Arbeiterbewegung. Biographisches Lexikon. Berlin: Dietz, 1970.

Haupt, Georges. Programm und Wirklichkeit. Die internationale Sozialdemokratie vor 1914. Berlin: Luchterhand, 1970.

Haupt, Georges, "Why the History of the Working-Class Movement?" in: New German Critique, 14 (Spring 1978), p. 7-28.

Höhn, Reinhard. Die vaterlandslosen Gesellen. Die Sozialdemokratie im Licht der Geheimberichte der preussischen Polizei, 1878-1890. Cologne: Westdeutscher Vlg., 1964.

Kleine Geschichte der SPD. 2 vols. Bonn-Bad Godesberg: Vlg. Neue Gesellschaft, 1974.

Lidtke, Vernon L. The Outlawed Party. Social Democracy in Germany 1878-1890. Princeton: Princeton Univ. Press, 1966.

Liebknecht, Wilhelm. Briefwechsel mit deutschen Sozialdemokraten, Vol. I, 1862-1878. Assen: Van Gorcum, 1973.

Liebknecht, Wilhelm. Wissen ist Macht - Macht ist Wissen, und andere bildungspolitisch-pädagogische Aeusserungen. Berlin: Volk und Wissen, 1968.

Teich, Christian. "Alphabetisches Verzeichniss aller auf Grund des Reich-Gesetzes vom 21. Oktober 1878 erlassenen Verfügungen gegen die Socialdemokratie bis 30. Juni 1879 nebst dem betr. Reichsgesetz, dem Verzeichniss der in den einzelnen Bundesstaaten für die Ausführung des Gesetzes zuständigen Behörden und den von den Landespolizeibehörden dazu ergangenen Ausführungs-Bestimmungen." Lobenstein: Vlg. von Christian Teich's Buchhandlung, n.d.

Thönnessen, Werner. The Emancipation of Women, Bristol: Pluto, 1973.

4. United States Labor History

Adelman, William J. Haymarket Revisted. Chicago: Illinois Labor History Society, 1976.

Aronowitz, Stanley. False Promises. The Shaping of American Working Class Consciousness. New York: McGraw Hill, 1973.

Ashbaugh, Carolyn. Lucy Parsons. American Revolutionary. Chicago: Kerr, 1976.

Aveling, Eleanor Marx, and Edward Aveling. The Working-Class Movement in America. London: Sonnenschein, 1888.

Becker, Gerhard. "Die Agitationsreise Wilhelm Liebknechts durch die USA 1886: Ergänzendes zu einer Dokumentation von Karl Obermann." in: Zeitschrift für Geschichtswissenschaft, 15 (1967), p. 842-862.

Bell, Daniel. Marxian Socialism in the United States. Princeton: Princeton Univ. Press, 1967.

Bernstein, Samuel. "American Labor and the Paris Commune." in: Science and Society, Spring 1951.

Bernstein, Samuel. The First International in America. New York: Sentry, 1965.

Bruce, Robert V. 1877: Year of Violence. New York: Bobbs-Merrill, 1959.

Buhle, Mary Jo. Feminism and Socialism in the United States, 1820-1920. Dissertation: Univ. of Wisconsin, 1974.

Buhle, Mary Jo. "German-American Socialists and the Woman Question." Unpublished manuscript.

Burbank, David T. City of Little Bread. The St. Louis General Strike of 1877. St. Louis: David T. Burbank, 1957.

Burbank, David T. "The First International in St. Louis." in: Bulletin of the Missouri Historical Society, 43 (Jan. 1962), p. 163-172.

Currey, J. Seymour. Chicago: Its History and its Builders. Vol. 2. Chicago: S. J. Clarke, 1912.

David, Henry. The History of the Haymarket Affair. New York: Farrar and Rinehart, 1936.

Destler, Chester. American Radicalism: 1865-1901. New London, Conn.: Connecticut College Press, 1946.

Douai, Adolf. "Die Auswanderung als Mittel zur Lösung der sozialen Aufgabe." in: Jahrbuch für Sozialwissenschaft und Sozialpolitik, 2 (1881), p. 99-108.

Douai, Adolf. "Bericht über den Fortgang der sozialistischen Bewegung in Amerika." in: Jahrbuch für Sozialwissenschaft und Sozialpolitik, I. Jg., 1. Hälfte (1879), p. 186-190; I. Jg., 2. Hälfte (1880), p. 236-243; II. Jg., (1881), p. 170-173.

Ely, Richard T. The Labor Movement in America. Rev. ed. New York: Crowell, 1890.

Feldstein, Stanley, and Lawrence Costello. The Ordeal of Assimilation: A Documentary History of the White Working Class. New York: Anchor, 1974.

Fine, Nathan. Labor and Farmer Parties in the United States, 1828-1928. New York: Russell and Russell, 1961 reprint of 1928 ed.

Foner, Philip, ed. The Formation of the Workingmen's Party of the United States. New York: American Institute for Marxist Studies Occasional Paper No. 18, 1976.

Foner, Philip, ed. The Great Labor Uprising of 1877. New York: Monad, 1977.

Foner, Philip. History of the Labor Movement in the United States. 4 vols. New York: International, 1947-.

Foner, Philip. "Protests in the USA against Bismarck's Anti-Socialist Law." in: International Review of Social History, 21 (1976), p. 30-51.

Foner, Philip. When Karl Marx Died. Comments in 1883. New York: International, 1973.

Foner, Philip, and Brewster Chamberlin, eds. Friedrich A. Sorge's Labor Movement in the U.S. A History of the American Working Class from Colonial Times to 1890. Westport, Conn.: Greenwood Press, 1977.

Foster, William Z. History of the Communist Party of the United States. New York: International, 1952.

Fried, Albert. Socialism in America. A Documentary History. New York: Doubleday, 1970.

Grob, Gerald N. Workers and Utopia. A Study of Ideological Conflict in the American Labor Movement, 1865-1900. Evanston, Ill.: Northwestern Univ. Press, 1961.

Gutman, Herbert. Work, Culture and Society in Industrializing America. New York: Vintage, 1977.

Hass, Eric. The SLP and the Internationals. New York: N.Y. Labor News Co., 1949.

Herreshoff, David. The Origins of American Marxism. New York: Monad, 1973.

Higham, John. Strangers in the Land. Patterns of American Nativism, 1860-1925. New York: Atheneum, 1970 reprint of 1955 ed.

Hillquit, Morris. History of Socialism in the U.S. 5th ed. New York: Russell and Russell, 1965.

Investigation by a Select Committee of the House of Representatives Relative to the Causes of the General Depression in Labor and Business. 45th Congress, 3rd session, 1879.

Johnson, Oakley C. Marxism in United States History before the Russian Revolution, 1876-1917. New York: Humanities, 1974.

Keil, Hartmut. "The New Unions: German and American Workers in New York City 1870-1885." Unpublished manuscript.

Keil, Hartmut. "Studies of the American Labor Movement in West Germany." in: Labor History, Vol. 18, No. 1 (Winter 1977), p. 122-33.

Kipnis, Ira. The American Socialist Movement, 1897-1912. New York: Columbia Univ. Press, 1952.

Korman, Gerd. Industrialization, Immigrants and Americanizers. Madison: State Historical Society of Wisconsin, 1967.

Kuhn, Henry, and Olive M. Johnson. The Socialist Labor Party During Four Decades, 1890-1930. New York: New York Labor News Co., 1931.

Laslett, John, and S.M. Lipset, eds. Failure of a Dream? Essays in the History of U.S. Socialism. Garden City, N.Y.: Anchor, 1974.

Laslett, John. Labor and the Left. New York: Basic Books, 1970.

Marx, Karl, and Friedrich Engels. Letters to Americans, 1848-1895. New York: International, 1953.

Miller, Sally M. The Radical Immigrant. New York: Twayne, 1974.

Moore, R. L., ed. The Emergence of an American Left. New York: Wiley, 1973.

Moore, R. L. European Socialists and the American Promised Land. New York: Oxford Univ. Press, 1970.

Obermann, Karl. "Die Amerikareise Wilhelm Liebknechts im Jahre 1886." in: Zeitschrift für Geschichtswissenschaft, 14 (1966), p. 611-617.

Obermann, Karl. Joseph Weydemeyer. New York: International, 1947.

Pinkerton, Allan. Strikers, Communists, Tramps and Detectives. New York: Dillingham, 1878.

Preston, William. Aliens and Dissenters: Federal Suppression of Radicals, 1903-1933. Cambridge: Harvard Univ. Press, 1963.

Quint, Howard. The Forging of American Socialism. Columbia, S.C.: Univ. of South Carolina Press, 1953.

Riis, Jacob A. How the Other Half Lives. New York: Hill & Wang, 1957 reprint of 1890 ed.

Rosenblum, Gerald. Immigrant Workers: Their Impact on American Labor Radicalism. New York: Basic Books, 1973.

Schaack, Michael J. Anarchy and Anarchists. Chicago: Schulte, 1889.

Schlüter, Hermann. Die Anfänge der deutschen Arbeiterbewegung in Amerika. Stuttgart: Dietz, 1907.

Schlüter, Hermann. Die Internationale in Amerika. Chicago: Deutsche Sprachgruppe der Sozialistischen Partei, 1918.

Shannon, David A. The Socialist Party of America: A History. New York: Macmillan, 1955.

Smith, Henry, ed. Popular Culture and Industrialism, 1865-1890. New York: Anchor, 1967.

Sombart, Werner. Why Is There No Socialism In The United States? White Plains, N.Y.: IASP, 1976.

Sorge, Friedrich A., comp. Briefe und Auszüge aus Briefen von Joh. Phil. Becker, Jos. Dietzgen, Friedrich Engels, Karl Marx u.a. an F.A. Sorge und Andere. Stuttgart: Dietz, 1906.

Stevenson, James. Daniel DeLeon. Dissertation, Univ. of Wisconsin, 1977.

U.S. Congress. Senate. Committee on Education and Labor. Report of the Committee of the Senate on Relations Between Labor and Capital. Washington, 1883-. 4 vols. published.

Ware, Norman J. The Labor Movement in the U.S. , 1860-1895. n.p.: Appleton, 1929.

5. Memoirs and Autobiographies

Ameringer, Oscar. If You Don't Weaken. New York: Holt, 1940.

Cahan, Abraham. The Education of Abraham Cahan. Philadelphia: Jewish Publication Society, 1969.

Foner, Philip, ed. The Autobiographies of the Haymarket Martyrs. New York: Humanities, 1969.

Gompers, Samuel. Seventy Years of Life and Labor. New York: Dutton, 1957.

Hillquit, Morris. Loose Leaves from a Busy Life. New York: Rand, 1934.

Kummer, Fritz. Eines Arbeiters Weltreise. Stuttgart: Schlicke, 1913.

Liebknecht, Wilhelm. Ein Blick in die neue Welt. Reisebeschreibung. Stuttgart: Dietz, 1887.

Lilienthal, Meta. Dear Remembered World. New York: Richard Smith, 1947.

Peukert, Josef. Erinnerungen eines Proletariers aus der revolutionären Arbeiterbewegung. Berlin: Vlg. des Soz. Bundes, 1913.

Spies, August. Reminiscenzen. Chicago: Christine Spies, 1888.

6. Germans in the United States

Bers, Günter. Wilhelm Hasselmann, 1844-1916. Cologne: n. pub. , 1973.

Billigmeier, Robert. Americans from Germany. Belmont, Cal.: Wadsworth, 1974.

Bosse, Georg. Das deutsche Element in den Vereinigten Staaten. New York: Steiger, 1908.

Bruncken, Ernst. German Political Refugees in the U.S. During the Period from 1815-1860. San Francisco: R & E Associates, 1970 reprint of 1904 ed.

Cronau, Rudolf. Drei Jahrhunderte deutsches Lebens in Amerika. 2nd ed. Berlin: Dietrich Reiner, 1924.

"Denkschrift zum 25-jährigen Jubiläum der Gründung des Brooklyn Labor Lyceum, 1882-1907. " New York: Cooperative Press, 1907.

Dobert, Eitel W. Deutsche Demokraten in Amerika. Die Achtundvierziger und ihre Schriften. Göttingen: Vandenhoek & Ruprecht, 1958.

Ernst, Robert. Immigrant Life in New York City, 1825-1863. New York: n. pub. , 1949.

Faust, Albert. The German Element in the U.S. 2 vols. New York: Houghton-Mifflin, 1909.

Friesen, Gerhard, and Walter Schatzberg, eds. The German Contribution to the Building of the Americas. Hanover N.H.: Clark Univ. Press, 1977.

Handlin, Oscar. The Uprooted. New York: Grosset & Dunlap, 1951.

Hawgood, John. The Tragedy of the German-Americans. New York: Putnam, 1940.

Heinrici, Max, ed. Das Buch der Deutschen in Amerika. Philadelphia: Walther, 1909.

Holzmann, Hanni. The German Forty-Eighters and the Socialists in Milwaukee: A Social Psychological Study of Assimilation. Master's Thesis: Univ. of Wisconsin, 1948.

Huch, C. F. "Geschichte der freien Sonntagsschule des Arbeiterbundes bis zum Jahre 1884." in: Mitteilungen des Deutschen Pionier-Vereins von Philadelphia, 14 (1910), p. 28-40.

Huebener, Theodore. The Germans in America. New York: Chilton, 1962.

Labor Lyceum Association, Philadelphia. "Constitution and Bylaws." Philadelphia: LLA, 1901.

Labor Lyceum Association, Philadelphia. "Souvenir zum 25. Jubiläum, 10 & 11 Okt. 1914." Philadelphia: LLA, 1914.

Lehr- und Wehrverein. "Constitution and Bylaws." Chicago: Soc.-dem. Printing Assoc., n.d.

Rippley, La Vern J. The German-Americans. Boston: Twayne, 1976.

Rocker, Rudolf. Johann Most. Berlin: Vlg. "Der Syndikalist," 1924.

"Tactics of the Lehr- und Wehrverein of Chicago." Chicago: Soc.- dem. Printing Assoc., 1879.

Wittke, Carl F. Refugees of Revolution. Philadelphia: Univ. of Pa. Press, 1952.

Wittke, Carl F. The Utopian Communist, A Biography of Wilhelm Weitling. Baton Rouge: LSU Press, 1950.

Zucker, A. E. ed. The Forty-Eighters. New York: Columbia Univ. Press, 1950.

II. LITERATURE AND CULTURE

1. General Bibliographies

Arndt, Karl J.R., and May Olson. German-American Newspapers and Periodicals, 1732-1955. 2nd ed. Heidelberg: Quelle & Meyer, 1965.

Lammel, Inge. Bibliographie der deutschen Arbeiterliederbücher, 1833-1945. Leipzig: Dt. Vlg. für Musik, 1971.

Pochmann, Henry, and Arthur Schultz. Bibliography of German Culture in America to 1940. Madison: Univ. of Wisc. Press, 1953.

Tolzman, Don H. German-Americana. A Bibliography. Metuchen, N.J.: Scarecrow, 1975.

Ward, Robert E. Dictionary of German-American Creative Writers, Vol. 1, Bibliographical Handbook. Cleveland: German-American Publishing Co., 1978.

2. Special Collections

Heinrich Bartel Manuscript Collection. Milwaukee County Historical Society.

Sozialistische Liedertafel, New York, and Arbeiter-Männerchor, New York. Musical Archives. Lincoln Center Branch of the New York Public Library.

3. German-American Socialist Literature: Primary Sources

(Note: The following list includes only separately published works. For examples of literature published by German-American socialists in their press, the reader is referred to Volume II of my dissertation, see note 1, p. 206).

Individual Works

Anon. (probably Paul Grottkau and Wilhelm Rosenberg, though attributed to August Spies). Die Nihilisten. Chicago: Socialist Publishing Society, 1882.

Arbeiter-Liederbuch. Gedichte und Lieder freisinniger und besonders sozial-demokratischer Tendenz. Chicago: G.A. Lönnecker, 1873.

Biedenkapp, Georg. Brennende Lieder und Strophen. New York: Im Selbstverlag, 1900.

Biedenkapp, Georg. Sankta libertas, Gedichte. New York: Im Selbstverlag, 1893.

Binder, Heinrich. Liederklänge aus vier Jahrzehnten. New York: Stechert, 1895.

Bufe, Franz. Licht und Schatten. Diverse Gedichte. Moline, Ill.: Selbstvlg., 1906.

Castelhun, Friedrich. Gedichte. Milwaukee: Freidenker, 1st ed. 1883, 3rd ed. 1901.

Douai, Adolf. Fata Morgana. St. Louis: Westermann & Co., 1859.

Douai, Adolf. "Kindergarten und Volksschule als sozialdemokratische Anstalten."
Leipzig: Vlg. der Genossenschaftsbuchdruckerei, 1876.

Douai, Adolf. Land und Leute in der Union. Berlin: Janke, 1864.

Dreisel, Hermann. Gesammelte Schriften. Milwaukee: Freidenker, 1905.

Drescher, Martin. Gedichte. Chicago: n. pub., 1909.

Fern, Edna (pseud. for Fernande Richter). Gesammelte Schriften. 4 vols. Zürich
and Leipzig, n. pub., 1899-1901.

Fritzsche, Friedrich W. Blut-Rosen. Sozialpolitische Gedichte. Baltimore:
Kern, 1890.

Geissler, Ludwig A. "Allegorisches Weihnachtsfestspiel." in: Volksstimme des
Westens, Jan. 18, 1880, p. 3.

Geissler, Ludwig A. Looking Beyond. New Orleans: L. Graham, 1891.

Germanus (pseud. for Martin Schupp). Lerchensang und Schwerterklang. New
York: Selbstvlg., 1902.

Glauch, Hermann. Gedichte. Oakland, Cal.: Druck des "Oakland Journal," 1897.

Hempel, Max. Gedichte. St. Louis: Cooperative Printing House, 1909.

Henniger, Alex. "Arbeit und Fortschritt. Ein Gedicht über soziale Reform."
San Francisco: Lafontaine, 1870.

Hoehn, G. A. New America. St. Louis: Socialist Newspaper Union, 1896.

Hofmann, Emilie. Veilchen und Rothe Nelken. Indianapolis: Aetna Printing Co.,
1905.

Hutzler, Sara. Jung-Amerika. Bilder aus dem New-Yorker Leben. Breslau:
Schottländer, 1884.

Jacoby, Leopold. Erinnerungen und Gedichte. Berlin: Aufbau, 1959.

Jonas, Alexander. Reporter und Sozialist. New York: National-Exekutiv-Comite
der SAP, 1884.

Magnus (pseud.). "Zu den Waffen! Posse in 4 Aufzügen." New York: n. pub., 1893.

Max (pseud.). "Die Anarchisten. Tragikomödie in 2 Aufzügen." New York: John
Oehler, 1885.

Most, Johann. "Souvenir an den Prinz Heinrich von Preussen." New York: n. pub.,
n. d.

Most, Johann, comp. Sturmvögel. Revolutionäre Lieder und Gedichte. Heft 1 & 2.
New York: n. pub., 1888.

Otto-Walster, August. "Ein verunglückter Agitator oder Die Grund- und Bodenfrage.
Lustspiel." St. Louis: Druck der Volksstimme des Westens, 1877.

Peter, Karl. Gesammelte Schriften. Milwaukee: Freidenker, 1887.

Rappaport, Philip. Looking Forward. Chicago: Kerr, 1906.

Reitzel, Robert. Des armen Teufel gesammelte Schriften. Detroit: n. pub.,
1913. 3 vols.

Reuber, Karl. Gedanken über die neue Zeit. Pittsburgh: Urben, 1872.

Reuber, Karl. Hymns of Labor. Pittsburgh: Barrows & Osbourne, 1871.

Rosenberg, Wilhelm L. An der Weltenwende. Gedichte. Cleveland: Vlg. der
Windsor Ave. Pub. Co., 1910.

Rosenberg, Wilhelm L. Aus dem Reiche des Tantalus. Alfresco-Skizzen. Zürich:
J. Schabelitz, 1888.

Rosenberg, Wilhelm L. Crumbleton. Soziales Drama. Cleveland: German-American Printing Co., 1898.

Rosenberg, Wilhelm L. "Die Geisterschlacht. Zum Gedächtnis der Aufhebung des
Sozialisten-Gesetzes in Deutschland." Cincinnati: Rosenberg & Schiele, n. d.

Rosenberg, Wilhelm L. Krieg dem Kriege. Gedichte. Cleveland: Windsor Ave.
Pub. Co., 1915.

Rosenberg, Wilhelm L. Liebesglück und Liebesleid. Lyrische Gedichte. Cleveland: Windsor Ave. Pub. Co., 1916.

Rosenberg, Wilhelm L. "Die Macht des Aberglaubens. Lustspiel." Cleveland:
Windsor Ave. Pub. Co., n. d.

Rosenberg, Wilhelm L. "Der Spion. Drama." Cleveland: Windsor Ave. Pub. Co.,
n. d.

Rosenberg, Wilhelm L. "Vor der Wahlschlacht, Lustspiel." New York: John
Oehler, 1887.

Rosenberg, Wilhelm L. Weltverrat und Weltgericht. Cleveland: Windsor Ave.
Publ. Co., c. 1921.

S., A. (probably August Spies). "Wat Tyler. Drama." in: Fackel, Apr. 24, 1887.

Sattler, Otto. Krieg. Gedichte der Zeit. New York: Rochow, 1914.

Sattler, Otto. New York und die Welt. Gedichte. New York: Modern Library, 1913.

Sattler, Otto. Stille und Sturm. New York: Reltana, 1910.

Saur, Rudolph. Gedichte. Washington: Selbstvlg., 1898.

Schlag, Hugo. "Thomas Münzer. Geschichtliches Trauerspiel in 4 Akten." New
York: Samisch & Goldmann, 1883.

Schlüter, Hermann, ed. Sozialistisches Arbeiter-Liederbuch. Chicago: Deutsche
Sprachgruppe der Sozialistischen Partei der V.S., n. d.

Segall, Julius. Gedichte. Milwaukee, 1920.

Stern, Maurice Reinhold v. Proletarier-Lieder. Jersey City: n. pub., 1885.

Stern, Maurice Reinhold v. Stimmen im Sturm. Zürich: J. Schabelitz, 1888.

Vereinigte Freie deutsche Schulen von New York und Umgegend, ed. Liederbuch für "Freie Deutsche Schulen" und Familien. New York: Vlg. Labor Lyceum, 1905.

Anthologies containing works by German-American socialist writers

Beisswanger, Konrad, ed. Stimmen der Freiheit. Nürnberg: Beisswanger, 1st. ed. 1900, 4th ed. 1914.

Friedrich, Wolfgang, ed. Im Klassenkampf. Deutsche revolutionäre Lieder und Gedichte aus der zweiten Hälfte des 19. Jhdts. Halle: Vlg. Sprache und Literatur, 1962.

Häckel, Manfred, ed. Gedichte über Marx und Engels. Berlin: Akademie, 1963.

Kaiser, Bruno, ed. Die Pariser Kommune im deutschen Gedicht. Berlin: Dietz, 1958.

Vorwärts! Eine Sammlung von Gedichten für das arbeitende Volk. Zürich: Vlg. der Volksbuchhandlung, 1886.

4. German-American (Socialist) Literature: Secondary Sources

Faust, Albert B. "Non-English Writings - German." in: Cambridge History of American Literature, IV. New York: Putnam, 1921, p. 572-90.

Friedman, Daniel. The Proletbühne. Dissertation: Univ. of Wisconsin, 1978.

Herminghouse, Pat. "German-American Studies in a New Vein: Resources and Possibilities." in: Unterrichtspraxis, Vol. IX, No. 2 (Fall 1976), p. 3-14.

Ickstadt, Heinz, and Hartmut Keil, "A Forgotten Piece of Working-Class Literature: Gustav Lyser's Satire of the Hewitt Hearing of 1878." in: Labor History, Vol. 20, No. 1 (Winter 1979), p. 127-140.

Kamman, William F. Socialism in German American Literature. Philadelphia: Americana Germanica Press, 1917.

Knoche, Carl. The German Immigrant Press in Milwaukee. Dissertation: Ohio State Univ., 1969.

Learned, M.D. The German-American Turner Lyric. Baltimore: Schneidereith, 1897.

Trommler, Frank. "Vom Vormärz zum Bürgerkrieg. Die Achtundvierziger und ihre Lyrik." in: Sigrid Bauschinger, et. al., eds. Amerika in der deutschen Literatur. Stuttgart: Reclam, 1975, p. 93-108.

Wagner, Maria. Mathilde Franziska Annecke, eine deutsche Dichterin des Vormärz und amerikanische Feministin in Selbstzeugnissen und Dokumenten.
Frankfurt: Fischer, 1979.

5. SPD Literature Before 1914: Secondary Sources

"Arbeiterkultur im 19. Jahrhundert." Theme for issue of Geschichte und Gesellschaft, Heft 1, 5 (1979).

Arnold, Heinz, ed. Handbuch zur deutschen Arbeiterliteratur. 2 vols. Munich:
Edition Text und Kritik, 1977.

Brückner, Peter, and Gabriele Ricke. "Ueber die ästhetische Erziehung des
Menschen in der Arbeiterbewegung." in: Brückner et. al., eds. Das Unvermögen der Realität. Berlin: Wagenbach, 1974, p. 37-68.

Friedrich, Wolfgang. Die sozialistische deutsche Literatur in der Zeit des Auf-
schwungs der Arbeiterbewegung während der 60er Jahre des 19. Jhs. bis
zum Erlass des Sozialistengesetzes. Halle: Habilitationsschrift, 1965.

Fülberth, Georg. Proletarische Partei und bürgerliche Literatur. Neuwied:
Luchterhand, 1972.

Geschichte der deutschen Literatur vom Ausgang des 19. Jhs. bis 1917. Vol. 9.
Berlin: Volk und Wissen, 1974.

Knilli, Friedrich, and Ursula Münchow. Frühes sozialistisches Arbeitertheater,
1847-1918. Munich: Hanser, 1970.

Knilli, Friedrich. "Der wahre Jakob -- ein proletarischer Superman? Ueber die
Bildsprache der revolutionären Sozialdemokratie." in: Akzente, 17 (1970),
p. 353-369.

Lammel, Inge. Das Arbeiterlied. Leipzig: Reclam, 1970.

Lethen, Helmut, and Helga Gallas. "Arbeiterdichtung - Proletarische Literatur.
Eine historische Skizze." in: Alternative, Jg. 9, Heft 51 (Dec. 1966), p. 156ff.

Lexikon Sozialistischer Deutscher Literatur. (Halle 1963). S'Gravenhage: van
Eversdijck, 1973, (Raubdruck).

Ludwig, Martin. Arbeiterliteratur in Deutschland. Stuttgart: Metzler, 1976.

Münchow, Ursula. "Die ersten Anfänge der sozialistischen Dramatik in Deutschland." in: Weimarer Beiträge, Heft 4 (1963), p. 729-750.

Münchow, Ursula. "Naturalismus und Proletariat." in: Weimarer Beiträge, Heft
4 (1964), p. 599-617.

Oesterreichische Gesellschaft für Kulturpolitik, ed. Arbeiterdichtung. Wuppertal:
Hammer, 1973.

Pehlke, Michael. "Ein Exempel proletarischer Dramatik. Bemerkungen zu Friedrich Bosses Streikdrama 'Im Kampf.'" in: Literaturwissenschaft und Sozialwissenschaften. Stuttgart: Metzler, 1971, p. 400-434.

Rüden, Peter v. Sozialdemokratisches Arbeitertheater, 1848-1914. Frankfurt: Athenäum, 1973.

Schröder, Gustav. Das sozialistische deutsche Bühnenstück von den sechziger Jahren des 19. Jhs. bis zum Zusammenbruch der zweiten sozialistischen Internationale. Potsdam: Habilitationsschrift, 1965.

Stieg, Gerald, and Bernd Witte. Abriss einer Geschichte der deutschen Arbeiterliteratur. Stuttgart: Klett, 1973.

Trommler, Frank. Sozialistische Literatur in Deutschland. Stuttgart: Kröner, 1976.

Vassen, Florian. "'Handarbeit und Griechentum.' Das Verhältnis von intellektuellem Bildungsbegriff und proletarischer Literatur in der deutschen Sozialdemokratie des 19. Jhs." Unpublished manuscript.

Völkering, Klaus. "Max Kegel: Auf, Sozialisten, schliesst die Reihen!" in: Weimarer Beiträge, H. 1, 20 (1974), p. 161-170.

Völkering, Klaus. "Zur frühen sozialistischen Literatur." in: Weimarer Beiträge, 17 (1971), Heft 10, p. 139-164.

Witte, Bernd. Deutsche Arbeiterliteratur von den Anfängen bis 1914. Stuttgart: Reclam, 1977.

Zentralinstitut für Literaturgeschichte der Akademie der Wissenschaften der DDR (Ursula Münchow, ed.). Textausgaben zur frühen sozialistischen Literatur in Deutschland. Berlin: Akademie, 1964f.